D0321922

Weaving a Tapestry of Resistance

Critical Studies in Education and Culture Series

Coming Out in College: The Struggle for a Queer Identity
  Robert A. Rhoads

Education and the Postmodern Condition
  Michael Peters, editor

Critical Multiculturalism: Uncommon Voices in a Common Struggle
  Barry Kanpol and Peter McLaren, editors

Beyond Liberation and Excellence: Reconstructing the Public
Discourse on Education
  David E. Purpel and Svi Shapiro

School in a "Total Institution": Critical Perspectives on Prison
Education
  Howard S. Davidson, editor

Simulation, Spectacle, and the Ironies of Education Reform
  Guy Senese with Ralph Page

Repositioning Feminism and Education: Perspectives on Educating
for Social Change
  *Janice Jipson, Petra Munro, Susan Victor, Karen Froude Jones, and
  Gretchen Freed-Rowland*

Culture, Politics, and Irish School Dropouts: Constructing Political
Identities
  G. Honor Fagan

Anti-Racism, Feminism, and Critical Approaches to Education
  Roxana Ng, Pat Staton, and Joyce Scane

Beyond Comfort Zones in Multiculturalism: Confronting the Politics
of Privilege
  Sandra Jackson and José Solís, editors

Culture and Difference: Critical Perspectives on the Bicultural
Experience in the United States
  Antonia Darder

Poststructuralism, Politics and Education
  Michael Peters

Weaving a Tapestry of Resistance

The Places, Power, and Poetry of a Sustainable Society

Sharon E. Sutton

Critical Studies in Education and Culture Series
Edited by Henry A. Giroux and Paulo Freire

BERGIN & GARVEY
Westport, Connecticut • London

973612

Library of Congress Cataloging-in-Publication Data

Sutton, Sharon E.
   Weaving a tapestry of resistance : the places, power, and poetry
of a   sustainable society / Sharon E. Sutton.
       p.   cm. — (Critical studies in education and culture series.
   ISSN 1064-8615)
   Includes bibliographical references and index.
   ISBN 0-89789-277-1 (HC : alk. paper).—ISBN 0-89789-278-X (PB :
alk. paper)
   1. School environment—United States—Case studies. 2. Man—
Influence of environment—United States—Case studies.
3. Environmental education—Activity programs—United States—Case
studies. 4. Community and school—United States—Case studies.
5. Students—United States—Attitudes—Case studies.   I. Title.
II. Series.
   LC210.5.S88   1996
     370.19′34′0973—dc20   95-44320

British Library Cataloguing in Publication Data is available.

Library of Congress Catalog Card Number: 95-44320
ISBN: 0-89789-277-1
       0-89789-278-X (pbk.)
ISSN: 1064-8615

First published in 1996

Bergin & Garvey, 88 Post Road West, Westport, CT 06881
An imprint of Greenwood Publishing Group, Inc.

Printed in the United States of America

The paper used in this book complies with the
Permanent Paper Standard issued by the National
Information Standards Organization (Z39.48-1984).

10 9 8 7 6 5 4 3 2 1

To my dad, who taught me how to beat the odds
while delighting in each day of the struggle

Contents

Series Foreword by Henry A. Giroux   ix

Preface   xiii

Introduction   1

Cast of Characters   29

Staging   33

1. Environmental Texts of Poverty and Privilege   37

2. Up Against the Odds   45

3. The Chosen Ones   63

4. Learning Compliance, Learning Leadership   87

5. Addressing Poverty as Insiders and Outsiders   121

6. Through the Window of a Child's Mind   155

Conclusions: Weaving a Tapestry of Resistance   197

Bibliography   223

Index   229

Series Foreword

Sharon E. Sutton's addition to the *Critical Studies in Education and Culture* makes a novel contribution to the debate over the meaning and purpose of education that has occupied the center of political and social life in the United States over the last decade. Dominated largely by an aggressive and ongoing attempt by various sectors of the Right, including "fundamentalists," nationalists, and political conservatives, the debate over educational policy has been organized around a set of values and practices that take as their paradigmatic model the laws and ideology of the marketplace and the imperatives of a newly emerging cultural traditionalism. In the first instance, schooling is being redefined through a corporate ideology that stressed the primacy of choice over community, competition over cooperation, and excellence over equity. At stake here is the imperative to organize public schooling around the related practices of competition, reprivatization, standardization, and individualism.

In the second instance, the New Right has waged a cultural war against schools as part of a wider attempt to contest the emergence of new public cultures and social movements that have begun to demand that schools take seriously the imperatives of living in a multiracial and multicultural democracy. The contours of this cultural offensive are evident in the call by the Right for standardized testing, the rejection of multiculturalism, and the development of curricula around what is euphemistically called a "common culture." In this perspective, the notion of a common culture serves as a referent to denounce any attempt by subordinate groups to challenge the narrow ideological and political parameters by which such a culture both defines and expresses itself. It is not too surprising that the theoretical and political distance between defining schools around a common culture and denouncing cultural difference as the enemy of democratic life is reactively short indeed.

This debate is important not simply because it makes visible the role that schools play as sites of political and cultural contestation, but because it is within this debate that the notion of the United States as an open and democratic society is being questioned and redefined. Moreover, this debate provides a challenge to progressive educators both in and outside of the United States to address a number of conditions central to a postmodern world. First, public schools cannot be seen as either objective or neutral. As institutions actively involved in constructing political subjects and presupposing a vision of the future, they must be dealt with in terms that are simultaneously historical, critical, and transformative. Second, the relationship between knowledge and power in schools places undue emphasis on disciplinary structures and on individual achievement as the primary unit of value. Critical educators need a language that emphasizes how social identities are constructed within unequal relations of power in the schools and how schooling can be organized through interdisciplinary approaches to learning and cultural differences that address the dialectical and multifaceted experiences of everyday life. Third, the existing cultural transformation of American society into a multiracial and multicultural society structured in multiple relations of domination demands that we address how schooling can become sites for cultural democracy rather than channeling colonies producing new forms of nativism and racism. Finally, critical educators need a new language that takes seriously the relationship between democracy and the establishment of those teaching and learning conditions that enable forms of self- and social determination in students and teachers. This suggests not only new forms of self-definition for human agency, it also points to redistributing power within the school and between the school and the larger society.

Weaving a Tapestry of Resistance is both a critique and a positive response to these concerns and the debates from which they emerge. Through the language of interdisciplinary critique, social analysis, and self-reflection, Sutton seeks to deconstruct the physical environment as a visual text, which makes all too evident the unequal power relations in schools and in the larger society. By focusing on the palpable differences in resources that inevitably parallel race and class differences, she challenges the view of schools as objective, neutral institutions engaged in the transmission of an unproblematic cultural heritage. This volume, which is part of a new discourse that challenges narrow disciplinary boundaries and theoretical paradigms, illuminates how schools function as cultural sites actively engaged in the production not only of knowledge but of social identities. Central to Sutton's vision is an educational process that actively produces, negotiates, and rewrites culture by being centered in democratic governance and the tangible, esthetic energy of a particular locality.

Sutton's work links emergent educational discourses on gender, race, class, and ethnicity with concerns for ecology and conservation. She attempts to rethink the relationship between language and the experience of one's physical surroundings and between pedagogy and the capacity to be socially responsible agents within those surroundings. By emphasizing the centrality of place, power, and culture, Sutton contributes to our understanding of how socially critical knowledge, democratic values, and interpersonal practices can provide a basis for teachers, students, and other cultural workers to redefine their roles as engaged public intellectuals. In this respect, it is part of a larger project for deepening the prospects of democratic schooling in a multiracial and multicultural society and opens up new discursive and public spaces for critical interventions into schools and other pedagogical sites.

The *Critical Studies in Education and Culture* series is concerned with making public schooling a central expression of democratic culture by challenging and transforming those configurations of power that characterize the existing system of education and other public cultures. *Weaving a Tapestry of Resistance* has been included in the series because it moves beyond the boundaries of traditional and existing critical discourses to broaden understanding of how not only schools but also the physical surroundings in which they exist can be sites of either containment or possibility.

Henry A. Giroux

Preface

The physical environment can be understood as a system of three-dimensional, hieroglyphic symbols—a text that conveys information about the social, political, economic, and cultural relations of a society. Places not only sustain individuals in a tangible way by providing shelter for varied private and public activities, they tacitly communicate a way of life. Large gabled homes set back on lushly landscaped lawns symbolically encode an existence quite unlike that presumed to occur in the sleek apartments of New York City's Trump Tower, a rural farmhouse surrounded by fields of wheat, or an inner-city neighborhood with its check-cashing outlets, burned-out buildings, and broken-down cars. Since children are keenly observant of spatial details, what do such disparate places tell them about themselves and their place in society? In what way do the material conditions of poverty or wealth shape children's worldviews, values, and ways of being? Do poor and affluent children's observations of place encourage social roles that exaggerate the differences in their life chances? Is it possible that young people's transactions with their surroundings help to perpetuate environmentally destructive behaviors?

For most children the home, school building, and neighborhood constitute the primary backdrop for their universe of experiences and, as such, constitute widely varying texts that reflect their socioeconomic status. The pages of a text of poverty are ominous and deteriorating, mostly devoted to violence, drugs, and despair; they lack beauty, personal control, or any sense of protectedness—sacredness. Is it possible that the stories of such a text may be teaching poor youth that they are of no value and deserve their lot? Is it feasible that the place-related narratives of impoverishment deter some children's ability to conceive themselves as successful or in charge of their futures? In contrast the pages of a text of wealth are spacious, pristine, and inviolate; they are full of well-tended homes and neighborhoods, distinctively set apart from ordinary life. Is it possible that the stories of this text are instructing well-to-do youth that they are superior and entitled to all they have—to more than others? Is it feasible that the place-related narratives of affluence obstruct other children's capacity to be empathic or altruistic?

Since the hieroglyphic symbols of the physical environment so plainly symbolize socioeconomic status, will young people be less impacted by the extremes of poverty and wealth if they are engaged in learning about those symbols? Can youth reframe the lessons of hopelessness or entitlement contained in their surroundings by being active participants in reshaping those surroundings? The ecological balance of all the Earth's systems—natural, social, political, economic, cultural—are changing so rapidly that familiar patterns of behavior are becoming increasingly inadequate. Can children learn new ways of being by learning to care for the physical environment? Can they begin to conceive a more just, harmonious Earth by collaborating with others to make improvements in their local communities? These are some of the questions that motivated me to write this book.

It is aimed primarily at practitioners and scholars whose work deals with youth including educators, psychologists, social workers, sociologists, and policymakers as well as physical planners, designers, and environmentalists. However, since the book is written in a nontechnical style, it should also appeal to a much wider audience of parents, community activists, and other concerned citizens. I hope to depict the tacit learning that occurs in relation to the school and neighborhood environment, and to probe how that learning might be directed toward social and environmental activism. I begin with the assumption that the development of poor and well-to-do children alike can be compromised or enhanced by the quality of their physical environment. I use an anecdotal approach to illustrate how two groups of children are exposed to differing sets of values through their experiences in socioeconomically dissimilar schools and neighborhoods. Based on these anecdotes, I lay out the parameters for an approach to helping children realize their power to responsibly influence their social universe through activities that are focused on the physical environment.

WHERE THIS STORY BEGINS

Social exchanges among family members, friends, and neighbors; experiences of events during a school day; exploration of the unknown;

sensory engagement with the landscape—all are affected by the characteristics of a particular place and, in turn, impact the social, cognitive, emotional, and physical development of children. The Urban Network, a national outreach program that enables youth to learn about and positively influence the physical environment of their school and neighborhood,[1] is an attempt to enhance children's development through place-related activities. This program is the outcome of a thirteen-year period of experimentation in the classroom with children and teachers, its guiding principles seeded in 1975 when this author worked on construction projects in several elementary schools and community arts organizations. The most long-term of these involvements was an architect-in-residence program at an elementary school in New York City that primarily served low-income minority children. Over a four-year period, fourth-, fifth-, and sixth-grade students were engaged in building large three-dimensional structures in their schoolyard. Children who participated in an empirical study during the third year of the program demonstrated improved social skills as a consequence of their involvement with the design and construction process, and their efforts won the enthusiastic support of local residents.[2] In 1987, these hands-on efforts with children were expanded as I began elaborating instructional materials that could offer teachers the know-how to implement their own architectural projects. In a curriculum piloted internationally at several schools in Mexico and the United States, I broadened my beginning efforts by using videotapes to form an exchange, or a network, among participants. This network was formalized in 1988 and has since directly accommodated almost 200 schools and community organizations around the country. In addition to these discreet implementations, the program reaches thousands of K-12 educators through various professional meetings, workshops, focus groups, and a biannual journal.

Based at the University of Michigan's College of Architecture and Urban Planning, the Urban Network is one of many design education initiatives that encourage culturally based experiential learning. Some of these programs were created by design professionals or by professional organizations, and encompass a career-option focus. Others grew out of classroom teachers' realization that their school building or neighborhood contained a wealth of instructional opportunities and could be used as a fascinating point of departure for interdisciplinary teaching. One teacher's manual explained the versatility of using built space as a backdrop for learning in the following manner:

> Architecture has the beauty of many things. It is an art form, a science, a
> form of self-expression that can be political, cultural, historical, or envi-

> ronmental. Indeed it is so multi-faceted that most imaginative teachers can
> find within architecture a suitable place in which to pursue their particular
> spheres of interest. The cultural anthropologist, for example, can discuss
> and compare types of shelters; the engineer can focus on bridges and
> tunnels; the historian can investigate patterns of local community devel-
> opment; the artist can design architectural embellishments; the mathema-
> tician can investigate structural parameters; the language arts teacher can
> explore a sea of urban literature. In fact if a flow chart were designed with
> architecture at its center, there would be infinite paths to explore through
> a variety of disciplines [Board of Education of the City of New York, 1979,
> p. iv].

In addition to its roots in design education, the Urban Network is akin in its methodology to science-based programs focusing on the natural environment. These curricula are more widely implemented than the arts-based ones and often are buttressed by state-mandated require-ments for the subject matter. Whereas design educators typically focus on creativity and the appreciation of esthetics and culture, many envi-ronmental educators—those dealing with nature—emphasize citizen-ship and the capacity for advocacy. Proponents of the latter approach hope to "increase pupils' awareness of the moral and political decisions shaping their environment and give them the knowledge, attitudes, and skills that will help them to form their own judgments and to participate in environmental politics" (Huckle, 1983, p. 105).

The Urban Network, which has been utilized primarily by social studies and language arts teachers as well as by youth service workers in low-income communities, joins both these streams of thinking. A year-long series of hands-on activities enables children to learn design concepts, use those concepts in exploring other disciplines, and increase their capacity as activists in their local communities. Incorporating input from a national team of consultants, "the Urban Network is a flexible curriculum designed to teach the concepts of architecture, plan-ning, and design to schoolchildren nationwide by involving parents, neighborhood residents, and volunteer professionals" (Thomas, 1991, p. 13). A primary goal is to "enable children to elaborate on their intuitive understanding of the physical environment as a map of soci-ety—one that reflects its beauty as well as its injustices—and to under-stand their own power to participate in its re-creation" (Sutton, 1992, p. 37). Youth might go out into the community, redesigning schoolyards, landscaping vacant lots, proposing legislation at City Hall, or picketing to save a historic structure. In other cases their activities might occur within the classroom, debating community development plans or mounting a letter-writing campaign to call attention to some environ-mental issue. In still other instances, participants might operate within the realm of the imagination, writing poetry or making drawings of places as they would like them to be.

A formative evaluation of the Urban Network yielded the data for this book. Although its purpose was to improve the program, the evaluation led to broader insights about the participants' environmental lives because it took me and my graduate research assistants into a mixture of private, religious, and enriched public schools as well as many inner-city ones in varying states of dilapidation. We visited schools on delightfully busy city streets; in quiet, parklike suburbs; in small, migrant farm communities; amid the vacant lots of urban ghettos; one even occupied the windowless basement of a synagogue. Some buildings were quite large but so underutilized as to appear deserted; others were so overcrowded that the first lunch shift began at 9:30 A.M. Some had exit doors chained closed to protect their charges from malicious intruders; others were wide open to the outside. We observed classrooms with a handful of children spread out at newly lacquered tables, experimenting with an array of colorful supplies and electronic equipment. We visited others with a constantly shifting enrollment of thirty-five to forty children crowded into mismatched furnishings, squinting at ancient books in the harsh rays of sunlight that streamed through unshaded, unwashed windows.

While this evaluation was in progress, problems related to environmental degradation began to attract increasing public interest, especially around the time of the 1992 Earth Summit in Rio de Janeiro. Environmental conservation, which had been included in a minor way in the Urban Network curriculum, became the major focus of activities at a number of schools. As I mulled over the site observations and recalled children's passionate discussions of how they wanted to "save the planet," the reality of their starkly contrasting lives of poverty and wealth began to hit home. Certainly these diverse groups each had a unique relationship to the environmental crisis and each would have to make very different sacrifices to address it. They all were affected by the materialism that was driving excessive consumption, but they were in varying relationships to the mania for growth—some benefiting from their superior ranking on the economic ladder, others marginalized by not being able to access the goods and services that are associated with a proper middle-class life. How would they be able to arrive at a singular solution? How would they be able to sort out their varied perspectives and derive a common understanding of such conflicts as jobs versus deforestation, people versus nature, material wealth versus social justice?

I began to wonder how a multiracial, multicultural democracy could function when its members were growing up with such diverging worldviews. Since poor and affluent children seem to have only a media impression of one another's reality, I began to conceive the difficulty of articulating a truly inclusive common good. Was it possible that design and environmental education programs such as the Urban Network could help? Could children learn to ameliorate the negative aspects of their surroundings by becoming active managers of their immediate community?

In 1963 when Robert Coles (1977) was interviewing children who pioneered desegregation in New Orleans, a young black girl pointed out to him the effect rich persons have on the poor. Her insights and those of other lower-income persons led him to realize that a study of impoverished children should also encompass those "others" who affect that group by virtue of their superior socioeconomic status (pp. x–xiv). Reading this account, I began to think about poverty and privilege as interlocking issues. I became especially concerned about how the extremes of poverty and wealth will play out in the environmental drama that is unfolding. Through a rigorous reflection on my Urban Network experiences, which included structured dialogue with other activist scholars and practitioners, I attempted to investigate children's class-based conceptions of themselves and explore how they might realize a more egalitarian relationship with one another through a shared concern for the physical environment.

HOW THE STORY IS TOLD

This book offers the reader an artist's rendering of the experience of visiting schools in dissimilar socioeconomic settings along with children's own reactions to those settings. Although the incidents described are based on systematic observations of Urban Network participants, the main body of the text is written as a narrative—as fiction—to give the reader a firsthand, tactile experience of the physical environment. By composing portraits, I am able to describe these settings in detail while still protecting the identity of the real schools that participated in the evaluation. Thus, the reader can construct a clear mental image of the neighborhoods, imagine being a child attending the schools, and feel what it is like to learn in the classrooms that are depicted. Such an immediate experience of the material world seems vital to conveying the importance of place in shaping children's lives. The narrative format also enables me to bring the voices of the children onto the pages of this book so they can tell some of their own story. To provide an interpretive framework for the events that occur, I intermingle theoretical commentary with the storyline and, on occasion, use an event as a launching pad for discussing broader issues of social and doubt on my part, and extended the writing of the book by nearly three years. Despite my unorthodox methodology, I hope I have been able to call attention to how, through the educational process and its physical setting, children can learn to either reproduce or resist the status quo.

HOW WE COLLECTED AND ANALYZED THE DATA

Except for Chapter Six, the events in the book are based on site observations conducted over a three-year period at sixteen elementary schools in nine states and one school in Mexico City. School visits varied in length from a two-day stay to repeated visits taking place over a year; year-long involvements ranged from four to seven all-day visits with telephone conversations occurring between visits. School visits encompassed meetings with administrators, workshops and planning sessions with teachers, class and community projects with children, as well as countless informal exchanges. The visits were made by myself or a graduate research assistant, and the majority took the form of a consultation. As our introductory letter to host schools explained: "The purpose of our visit is to help you implement the Urban Network curriculum and to collect the observational data that can help to improve the success of this program in your school and nationwide."

Although the number of site visits varied as did the amount of time that various schools spent on Urban Network activities, my research assistants and I used a standard log format for recording observations after each visit, filling in as much information as was available. Other data were obtained from open-ended interviews, questionnaires, pre- and post-tests, completed projects, photographs, and archival materials. Areas of documentation included the following:

- *Social milieu of the school and neighborhood.* We documented the number and demographic makeup of teachers, staff, and students; class size and teacher-to-student ratio; availability of teaching or community resources; mission statement or school plan; school organization and rules; management styles and interpersonal relationships; and demographics for the surrounding area as reported in the 1990 U.S. Census.
- *Physical milieu of the school and neighborhood.* This comprised building size, structure, and condition; occupancy rate; layout and visual appearance of classrooms, communal spaces, and playground; utilization of corridors; photographs of the school and neighborhood; and housing data for the surrounding area as reported in the 1990 U.S. Census.
- *Parameters of the Urban Network implementation.* We recorded the number of classes and grade levels participating; types of classes

environmental justice. By combining narrative descriptions
lar settings with children's commentaries on these places an
reflections on the structural inequities that shape such situatio
to engage you in formulating your own interpretive frame
debating the positions I take. Trying to understand a complex
enon through multiple perspectives—provided by the ob
data, the literature, and my own rigorous self-reflection—is i
to the inclusive, wholistic ways of thinking and being that und
publication.

Using observations of thirteen poorer schools and four more
ones, I constructed two schools, one in an inner city and ano
well-to-do suburb, both schools depicting moderate rather
treme examples of elementary education. Although I observed
numbers of poor and affluent schools, I have been careful to enc
the same features in both portraits, including leadership style
personal relationships, pedagogy, and the physical context of the
and neighborhood. I do *not* intend to suggest that either o
portraits is representative of a subset of poor or affluent schools.
I have constructed two case studies to illuminate the disassocia
poverty and privilege that characterizes our culture while, at th
time, calling attention to deficits in the education of both group

The first five chapters contain quotations by children, usu
parenthesis, provided to support my analysis. Sometimes the
verbatim statements by children that were taken from a vari
written materials collected during the Urban Network site visits ir
ing pre- and post-tests, essays written during classroom activities
letters. Others were made orally and recorded by me or my res
assistants as accurately as possible after class. The children's es
drawings, and conversations that constitute Chapter Six were no
lected during the site visits, but in a separate study of young peo
perceptions of their neighborhoods conducted to provide data for
specific chapter. Some of these children are introduced earlier in
book as characters in the storyline so that there is a fit between
children whose work is presented and the settings themselves. T
essays and conversations are quoted verbatim except that the con
was altered in minor ways to correspond with the situation presen
in the composite schools, for instance, names of places and friends w
changed to fit the storyline. The events and characters in the narrat
have been devised to prevent recognition of the real circumstances, a
any identifying words and images were removed from the childre
work.

Taking these liberties with the data—especially as an outsider to t
field of education—resulted in no small amount of struggle and se

and subject areas used; time devoted to the program; schedule of activities; availability of financial or teaching-release support; improvement in the social and technical skills covered in the program; and the types of activities and projects completed.

- *Description of the site visits.* We kept track of the utilization of preplanning and follow-up activities; description of class activities; teacher's role versus evaluator's role; children's participation; reactions from teachers and children; and actual work or photographic documentation of projects and work process.

Each evaluator prepared a final report on a particular school. At the end of the three-year period, another research assistant (who was not involved in any of the site visits) helped to put the reports into a consistent format even though some were much more detailed than others due to the varying lengths of site visits and program implementations. This person and I then focused on the last item—description of the site visits—to identify particular events that seemed to inform our primary concern of what children learn through their observations of the physical environment. We noted events that offered evidence of children's and teachers' attitudes about their surroundings, classroom management techniques that encouraged or prevented children's control of space, teaching styles that supported or blocked children's environmental activism, and administrative policies that nurtured or inhibited teachers' leadership in carrying out the program.

These site visit descriptions were written up as factually as possible without editorial comment; then we reviewed them for common themes and conducted literature reviews to elaborate a socially critical perspective on each theme. Subsequently, aspects of the social and physical milieus of the thirteen poorer schools were woven together to create a single composite, and the same was done with the four more affluent ones. The most substantive site descriptions were selected as scenarios through which these composite schools would be portrayed.

As the book concept began to evolve, I felt the need to learn more about how children view their neighborhoods, both as a tangible reality and as a stage for imaginative play. Another one-week study was designed to engage children in communicating ideas about their neighborhoods through drawings, essays, and videotaped conversations. This study began with a two-hour session in which four different groups of ten to twelve children were interviewed. The children, who lived in inner-city urban and affluent suburban neighborhoods, were shown photographs of neighborhoods in diverse socioeconomic and geographic locations and asked what they thought it might be like to live in these neighborhoods. Following this group interview, the children were introduced to the concept of an architect's journal, which typically contains both writing and drawing, and were given specially designed 11" x 17" artist's drawing pads, which contained an assignment for each of seven days. The first assignment was carried out as a group activity in school with the rest of the journal being completed at home. Journals contained a note suggesting that, since there were no right or wrong answers, children might discuss the assignments with family members or friends. The following week, the groups reconvened for a second two-hour session. This time they worked in teams of three or four children to determine how to present their completed journals on videotape. Some teams read their entries and displayed their drawings on camera, others chose to interview each other, still others developed skits or talk shows.

To analyze the written material, two research assistants, neither of whom had worked on the site evaluations, each reviewed half of the journals, making individual cards for the key ideas appearing in each story. They traded journals and repeated the process, then all three of us negotiated agreement on the key ideas expressed in the writings. Neither the group interviews nor the videotapes were analyzed systematically; however, excerpts from the videotapes were shown to a class of fourteen graduate students attending an education seminar at the University of Michigan. The discussion that ensued, which provoked some fairly intense disagreements, was instrumental in helping me and my research assistants to combine the key ideas from our preliminary analysis of the writings into the larger concepts that appear in Chapter Six.

WHAT WERE MY BIASES

Throughout the writing of this book, I have struggled to avoid distorting the data to serve my own agenda as a lifelong advocate for the rights of disadvantaged children, especially given the flexibility of the narrative format. My principal means of assuring a credible interpretation of the data included finding similar conclusions in other studies, discussing my interpretations with other colleagues and with my research assistants, and having drafts of the manuscript reviewed by persons who represented different intellectual areas and held different political views. Nevertheless, it is important for me to also reveal my biases, which unquestionably affected the very framing of the book and the insights put forth, so that readers can use this information to assess the "goodness" of my work.

I am an African American woman who grew up in Cincinnati, the "gateway" to the South, during the era of Jim Crow. Even though I have been discriminated against throughout my educational career, I was also given an opportunity to beat the odds against my lower-class status when I was admitted (by examination) to a unique *public* college preparatory school called Walnut Hills. For six years during the time that the bloody integration of southern schools was in the national news, I attended classes alongside the children of some of Cincinnati's most prestigious families. Most of my classmates were accepted at one or more of the finest colleges and universities in the country, some were awarded Merit Scholarships, and I used my high school musical training to win a full scholarship to attend the Manhattan School of Music in New York City. Thus my childhood was filled with contradictions. I grew up in the skin of a low-income black female while, at the same time, accessing privileges that were not typically available to persons like me. I was simultaneously "up against the odds" and one of "the chosen ones." Living in two worlds made me keenly aware of how steadfastly life chances are linked to class, race, and gender.

The duality of my life continued into adulthood as I worked my way into two white male–dominated professions—classical music, then architecture—and ultimately attained my own position of privilege as a tenured faculty member at a premier research university. With one foot in my birth status and the other in my earned one, I have attempted to achieve an equally empathic understanding of poverty and privilege. However, my birth status has proven to have a far more tenacious hold on my understanding of human nature, making it much more difficult for me to examine privilege in an unbiased manner. This problem was exacerbated by the fact that the pathologies of poverty are highly researched in comparison to a paucity of research on the aberrations of privilege. Given the combined imbalance of personal experience and scholarship, I primarily relied on input from colleagues to test the "goodness" of my arguments.

WHO HELPED

The development of the Urban Network program, its evaluation, and the study that was conducted for Chapter Six were funded by multiple grants from 'the National Endowment for the Arts, the W.K. Kellogg Foundation, and the University of Michigan. The success of the program was greatly enhanced when it was recognized in 1991 by an American Planning Association Education Award and through the continuing support of key design educators around the country including Rolaine Copeland, Dorothy Dunn, Ginny Graves, Ramona K. Mullahey, and Anne Taylor among others. Research assistance was furnished by numerous graduate students and recent Ph.D. recipients in architecture, urban planning, and education. Carole A. Bowker, Lauren Isenberg-Zinn, and Wilfred Oakafor conducted year-long evaluations. Andrea Debruin Parecki played a primary role in collecting the children's work that is presented in Chapter Six. Parecki as well as Moshira El-Rafey, Yve A. Susskind, and Amy Laverty participated in data analysis. Parecki and Susskind both provided important feedback on the formulation of the educational approach described in the Epilogue. Carlos Martín, himself the son of a migrant farm worker, offered insights into the characteristics of migrant farm life as depicted in Chapter Five.

Elinor Bowles has had a definitive impact on the ideas presented here. As editor of my first book, *Learning through the Built Environment*, she helped me to articulate the motivational qualities of children's building activities. Later she provided guidance in the creation of the Urban Network curriculum, enabling me to communicate my approach to teaching children about architecture to a broader audience of educators. As the conceptual editor of this book, she has been an invaluable sounding board and guardian of the need for an evenhanded approach to the subject matter. Professor and novelist Magda Bogin assisted me over a five-year period, from the earliest formulation of the book's concept to the final refinement of its content, always pushing me to be more radical in my thinking. I was also fortunate to have Professors Ken Medlin, Leanne Rivlin, and Helen Weingarten as well as Parecki, who painstakingly reviewed drafts and helped improve the rigor of my arguments. Finally, my deep appreciation to my literary agent, Marie Dutton Brown, who provides both wisdom and compassion in navigating the publishing process.

Beginning in 1986, a W.K. Kellogg National Fellowship not only provided financial support for developing the Urban Network, but was a life-changing experience that broadened my outlook on social and environmental issues. At the first of seven seminars for my group of forty fellows, then fellowship director Dr. Larraine Matusak quoted the musical comedy character Auntie Mame, "I'll open doors for you—doors you never knew existed," Matusak intoned, capturing in that one line the experiences that would occur over the next three years. During our tenure as Kellogg fellows, we were urged to reach beyond the boundaries of our disciplines, keep an open mind, indulge ourselves intellectually, and have the courage to pay the price of leadership. For me, these "opened doors" resulted in a commitment to clarify the person-environment theories that are so shrouded with jargon within the disciplines of architecture and psychology. By learning to communicate with the general public about the effect of one's surroundings on the quality of life, I hoped to raise awareness of how built space can either reinforce social injustices or serve as a means of liberation. The reader can judge my success in reaching this goal.

Many other people and organizations, far too numerous to list, have also contributed to the socially critical perspective that is presented here. Among those who stand out in recent memory are colleagues at the University of Michigan's Program on Conflict Management Alternatives (PCMA). Operating as one of several university-based centers funded nationally by the William and Flora Hewlett Foundation to examine conflict, PCMA pursues a distinctive research agenda that is rooted in social justice theory. As one of its core faculty members, this racially diverse, multidisciplinary group of women and men has given me a safe space in which to articulate the sometimes slippery ideas that are presented here. In particular, many of the concepts presented in this book on the pathologies of privilege were formulated with colleagues in PCMA. Less formalized, but also nurturing of intellectual risk-taking, was a gathering known as the Feminist Practice Work Group at the university's Women's Studies Program. During a two-year series of meetings—when it was often difficult to hold on to the subject of our thoughts—I gained the courage, as Derrick Bell (1992) might say, to acknowledge the fundamental improbability of achieving social justice even as I enjoy my own struggle to unravel its environmental component. Finally, many of the ideas on environmental sustainability have been nourished through my work with Robert Berkebile, Susan Maxman, Marvin E. Rosenman, Don Watson, and a national network of architects who are committed to promoting more conserving design methodologies.

However, none of this work would have been possible without the commitment of thousands of children and adults, in schools and nonprofit organizations, who lent their energy and talent to improving their schools and communities. My deepest gratitude goes to all the principals who rearranged schedules, all the teachers and community workers who made time in their overbooked lives, all the parents who raised money and hauled supplies, all the volunteer professionals who made things work within a local culture, and especially all the children who contributed their boundless imagination and creativity.

NOTES

1. The Urban Network program comprises a curriculum and other publications that offer methods of implementing design education in the classroom, teacher development through workshops and site visits, and research that includes program evaluations and studies of the role of the physical environment in informal learning. The program also sponsors a variety of special events such as conferences and competitions.

2. See Sutton (1985) for details on this program and its evaluation.

Introduction

> [Socialization is] a set of processes . . . by which we are taught to understand the world and the patterns of behavior that will enable us to fit into the places assigned to us within the dominant culture. . . . The overall goal of the process of socialization is the shaping of consciousness, the internalization of dominant norms, which then become so "natural" that they are largely unquestioned as they govern our behavior and attitudes [Rivlin and Wolfe, 1985, pp. 3–4].

The socialization of children occurs through a variety of agencies including families, teachers, religious institutions, and peers as well as television. Undoubtedly, educators play a powerful role in this process, providing students with "institutionally legitimated language" to describe and interpret different aspects of their experience within the context of a particular belief system (Bowers, 1993, p. 6). Outside of the family, teachers are the primary purveyors of a society's values, influencing children's self-image and assigning their status and rank in relation to peers.

In recent years, a number of educational critics concerned with school reform have generated the concept of a *hidden curriculum* to describe those socialization processes that specifically reinforce the status quo. A hidden curriculum encompasses the "unstated values, attitudes, and norms which stem tacitly from the social relations of the school and classroom as well as the content of the course" (Dutton, 1991, p. 167). These critics propose that the way lessons are structured, the daily routines of teachers and students, and the rules of conduct in a school are as influential in shaping children's knowledge as the formal curriculum, both reflecting and reinforcing social inequities. Through a hidden curriculum, children come to accept a social reality that sustains the interests of more powerful groups at the expense of less powerful ones.[1] "School culture is really a battle ground on which meanings are defined, knowledge is legitimated, and futures are sometimes created and destroyed. It is a place of ideological and cultural struggle favored primarily to benefit the wealthy, males, and whites" (Giroux, 1984, p. 133). I begin with this premise of a hidden curriculum, focusing particularly on how values, attitudes, and norms are conveyed through physical space, not only in school but in the everyday lives of socioeconomically diverse children.

Children's relationship to their immediate surroundings is practically always defined by the heritage of race and social class. Their surroundings contain vital physical and social structures that can either sustain and support life or threaten and diminish it. They also provide direct sensory feedback about who a child is and how that child is expected to behave. Just as domestic space teaches children about their roles within the family (who sits where, who eats with whom, who does which chores), public space teaches children their roles in society. Since young children have minimally refined language and belief systems, it seems logical that a primary source of their knowledge comes through direct experience of their physical and social milieu, the former limiting or promoting certain types of activities and exchanges that, in turn, influence what is learned and from whom. These direct observations are elaborated by the language and attitudes assimilated from significant others to form children's views of who they are, and who they can become.

The knowledge gained through engagement with the real world has been discussed by many educators at different times throughout the history of public education. Beginning with Dewey and the progressive education movement of the late 1800s and encompassing Montessori in the early 1900s, there was a notion that children learned best through their senses and that their capacities could be heightened by expanding the range of their hands-on experiences. The ideas of these early theorists, though eclipsed by more mechanistic scientists such as Skinner and Darwin, were revived and expanded by Piaget; later they were adopted by the British educators of the 1960s as well as by art educators who valued sensory learning as a means of nurturing an individual's expressiveness. Because it is so highly motivational, experiential learning is prized as a vehicle through which children can acquire abstract knowledge while developing as creative thinkers who grow through their own practical investigations and attempts at problem solving.

Although teaching methods that incorporate real-world learning have persisted over time, such pedagogy primarily utilizes controlled tactile experimentation with the objects and materials within a classroom, school, or in nature. The indelible knowledge that children gain about themselves in their most ever-present laboratory—the physical space of the home, school, and neighborhood—has not been widely considered as a component of learning. Yet, just as language constitutes a system of spoken and written symbols that gives meaning to reality, a child's immediate surroundings comprise a universe of life-size, three-dimensional, and class-embedded symbols. Any serious investigation of this environmental text would expose those cultural beliefs that maintain the status quo including such social constructions as private property and property rights, which consistently benefit the most powerful (Parenti, 1978, pp. 184–188). Perhaps because this topic is so revealing of social injustice and environmental degradation, engaging children in place-related learning remains an unexplored tool through which to encourage independent thinkers who can challenge the status quo.

In this book, I speculate that what children learn through their senses by observing the physical milieu of a school and neighborhood with all their social and economic overlays is potentially a powerful tool of social change. It seems possible that place-related learning might free young persons from their limited literacy skills as well as from the values, attitudes, and norms that are lodged in culturally bound language and belief systems. It seems feasible that direct, hands-on learning relative to physical space—so concrete a representation of the social order—might enable children to imagine alternative social and environmental relationships.

STAKING OUT A THEORETICAL TERRAIN

The overarching goal of this book is to derive a method of place-related, socially responsive learning that addresses deficits in the education of both poor and affluent children. I use the Urban Network evaluation data as well as a wide range of child development, socially critical, and ecology literature to

- show how poor and affluent children learn through observations of divergent physical settings;
- offer evidence of both groups being socialized to accept social inequities and environmental degradation through explicit and hidden curricula; and

•provide a model of place-related learning that can enable children to envision social change.

My theoretical analysis attempts to bridge three intellectual networks. One group of scholars that I draw on considers the role of the environment in child development; another focuses on the parameters of social change in a multiracial, multicultural society; and the third is concerned with the conservation and equitable distribution of natural resources. The first area of investigation dates back to the beginning of the century when, in reaction to Darwinian theories of survival, psychologists began to explore the relative importance of environment versus heredity in determining children's capacities. However, what the term *environment* meant and what role it played have changed over time. For instance, in the 1940s and 1950s, "when a theoretically grounded view of the role of environmental influences became prominent in child psychology . . . these influences were considered primarily in interpersonal and sociocultural terms" (Wohlwill and Heft, 1987, p. 282). More recently, varied professional groups (psychologists, social workers, educators, planners, and designers) have focused on the situational context of behavior, considering how specific spatial configurations can encourage or inhibit the learning that derives from social exchanges. Environmental psychologists currently emphasize the physical or inanimate features of a given situation, conceptualizing a child's surroundings as both a *text* and a *context* for instruction. To give a few examples, there is a literature dealing with the informal learning that is facilitated by exploration of the urban or rural landscape, a growing body of knowledge on the impact of school building design on learning, and some study of the benefits of learning through environmental activism.

Although this latter work provides some grounding for the ideas presented here, much of it lacks the socially critical perspective that would enable me to address my second area of concern, namely, how social change can occur. For this component, I draw from critical theorists and educators, feminists, and activist scholars whose focus is on such issues as justice and equality, equal access and representation, and the just allocation of social and material goods. In particular, my work is informed by those critical educators who examine the asymmetrical power relationships in society that are reproduced in schools. Whereas this literature is useful in helping me overlay a social critique onto the interpersonal exchanges that are described in this book, the social change literature also has limitations since most of it is singularly lacking in a physical dimension. Yet, many social inequities are place-related, for example, a racial group being restricted as to where they can sit on a bus, live, or attend school; a gender group being denied the right to own property or enter a private club; or an ethnic group being forced to redraw their national boundaries. As Feldman and Stall (1994) noted in their study of low-income housing in Chicago:

> The [places] in which, and often over which, power struggles are manifest, are largely overlooked. Although grassroots activism is implicitly place-bound, the physical setting of grassroots activism is presumed to be a background to the political struggle [p. 192].

To add a spatial dimension to social justice theory, I draw from an emerging area of literature concerning the utilization of physical resources. Scholars in this area (ecologists, ecofeminists, philosophers, ethicists, theologians) explore the cultural values that lead to environmentally destructive ways of life. There is growing consensus within this international community of environmental advocates that the values underpinning the modern industrial era (including competitiveness, individualistic pursuit of material wealth and social status, unlimited consumption, domination of people and nature) are threatening the viability of life on the planet. Although they focus on many of the same issues as traditional social activists, these writers broaden the anthropocentric emphasis on equitable relations among people to include those natural systems upon which all humans depend. In their view the current crisis in natural resources constitutes a compelling reason to reconceive existing social systems and institutions. My task is to join these three steams of thinking—to explore how the physical environment influences learning while reinforcing children's experience of the asymmetrical power relations of schools, both data sets combining to instruct them in the domination of people and nature.

To begin this task, I must define several terms, including *environment*, which has two different meanings in this book. Occasionally the word is used in its narrower sense to indicate natural resources; this definition applies when I discuss such issues as the *environmental crisis* (signifying a crisis in the disposition of natural resources globally) or *sustainability* (to be defined shortly). However, the term is used primarily in its broader sense to indicate the total esthetic impression of a space, which derives from a dynamic interplay between its objective features and the symbolic meaning those features have for various individuals and groups. Objective features include physical structures, people, activities, and a range of other sensory inputs. For example, the landscape of a poor inner-city neighborhood might comprise deteriorating homes, colorful gardens adjoining lots that are overgrown with weeds, narrow streets filled with traffic and noise, the smell of outdoor cooking, the sound of conversation among neighbors as well as the presence of gangs and drug dealers. How those features are perceived—their meaning—results from the viewer's past experiences; perceptions are also influenced by those sociocultural values and norms that set up a certain predisposition to what is observed. Thus, a stranger walking down the street of a poor urban neighborhood might feel a sense of vulnerability that is unrelated to anything actually noticed but that, in turn, influences how that person reacts to specific details. To give another example, a homeowner might feel much more satisfied than a tenant with the same housing because of the security and stability that owning property signifies in our culture. Or consider the different meanings that a given place has for someone who is a citizen versus a person who is a foreigner. When used in this broader sense, the term *environment* is interchangeable with *surroundings* or *setting*.

Although I describe a variety of social relationships in the two schools, my focus is on the physical context that enables or constrains activities and, at the same time, conveys information about individuals and their expectations of one another. "For example, a [circular] arrangement of furniture within a classroom space not only fosters communication in a very functional sense, but it also speaks nonverbally and symbolically on behalf of the teacher to encourage greater social interaction" (Banning, 1990, p. 2). The term *environmental observation* refers to the direct sensory feedback children get from the physical environment of their school and neighborhood, which instructs them about their roles in society.

The socially and environmentally responsible behavior I promote requires the introduction of another term, *sustainability*, which has emerged in recent years among advocates for a more conserving, integrated approach to economic, social, and environmental concerns in local, national, and global communities. According to participants in the 1992 Earth Summit, human activity is sustainable if it meets the needs of the present without compromising the ability of future generations to meet their own needs. "'Sustainable,' by definition, means not only indefinitely prolonged, but nourishing, as the Earth is nourishing to life and as a healthy natural environment is nourishing for the self-actualizing of persons and communities" (Engel, 1990, p. 10). In this book, the term is used similarly with an emphasis on how children of different socioeconomic backgrounds can learn to see their lives as being linked with and through nature.

Earlier I introduced the term, hidden curriculum, indicating my special interest in the spatial characteristics of children's immediate surroundings that exaggerate their socioeconomic differences both within and outside the school. I refer to these sociospatial dimensions of learning as a *hidden curriculum of separateness*. *Power structures*, which refer to the modalities through which authority is exercised, typically are hierarchical ones in which persons of superior status have authority over those of lower status. Though different people assume varying ranks and roles in each of the schools, the interpersonal relationships described in this book are clearly hierarchical in nature. One destructive aspect of such structures is the *patriarchal contract*, a term used by Block (1987) to denote the willing relationship between powerful persons who exert top-down authority and powerless persons who do not have to be responsible for their actions. The external reward system upon which all education is based—including grading, ranking, and credentialing—exemplifies the patriarchal contract, which appears in various guises throughout this book. I use the phrase *socially and environmentally destructive roles and behaviors* to indicate those responses that derive from authoritarian power, namely domination, competitiveness, and materialism. In the conclusions, I focus on *sustainable relationships* that include participatory, democratic governance practices; cooperation within multigenerational groups; and inclusiveness as well as conserving lifestyles that embrace cultural activity.

Finally, I use the term *community caretaking*, which is a variation of a concept developed by Leavitt and Saegert (1990). After studying the mechanisms residents used to stabilize abandoned apartment buildings in Harlem, Leavitt and Saegert proposed that policymakers should view buildings as *community households* that extend the life of individual households. In this way, the naturally occurring survival activities that go on in low-income communities would be formalized, which would give them access to funding (pp. 172–174). My use of the term *community caretaking*, which reflects the informal phenomenon Leavitt and Saegert proposed to institutionalize, describes the processes that take place when domestic skills are applied outside the home as neighbors join forces to address problems and improve the living conditions in their neighborhood.

Based on the terms just defined, I offer the following six propositions (illustrated in Figure 1) as a screen for understanding the events described in this book:

- •Observations of the physical environment—which reflects the materialistic, competitive values of the modern industrial era—instruct children about their roles in society.
- •These environmental observations are reinforced at school through a hidden curriculum of separateness.
- •The hierarchical power structures within schools, which reflect inequities of the larger society, result in a patriarchal contract between teachers and students that maintains the status quo.

- These three elements—environmental observations, a hidden curriculum of separateness, and hierarchical power structures—work in concert to encourage socially and environmentally destructive roles and behavior.
- Such roles and behavior exaggerate differences in material wealth and make it unlikely that children will learn to imagine a more equitable society.
- Place-related learning, which can help children to see their connection with and through nature, might promote more sustainable relationships.

REDEFINING EDUCATION—
A MATTER OF SURVIVAL

An overview of the exponential growth of the Earth's human population in relation to the comparatively static nature of education over the last 165 years can illustrate how inadequate old educational paradigms are for preparing children to live in a global society. Consider that in 1830—the year when common schools first began to appear in this country—the global population consisted of only about one billion persons. The establishment of these schools sparked a now-familiar debate among the white male industrialists and professionals who set their direction concerning parents' role in children's upbringing versus the school's responsibility to promote citizenship, Protestantism, and good work habits. At the heart of these debates was the issue of who should control education and toward what social purpose, with race being accepted as a valid reason for denying, or even prohibiting, access to education.

By 1910, just eighty years later, the global population had doubled to two billion persons, and public schooling had become a major U.S. institution. Although almost half the nation still lived in rural areas, many of the large urban schools that still exist today were being constructed—massive plants with uniform classrooms where children were tracked into appropriate race, sex, and class roles. During that era, "American education had acquired its fundamental structural characteristics, and they have not altered since. Public education was universal, tax supported, free, compulsory, bureaucratically arranged, class-based, and racist" (Rivlin and Wolfe, 1985, pp. 116–129).

As the Earth's population increased to three billion and major corporate interests began to dominate the economy, the class-based, racist nature of the educational system became more apparent. At this time, growing numbers of black children from the South were attending northern schools, and their failures were framed not in

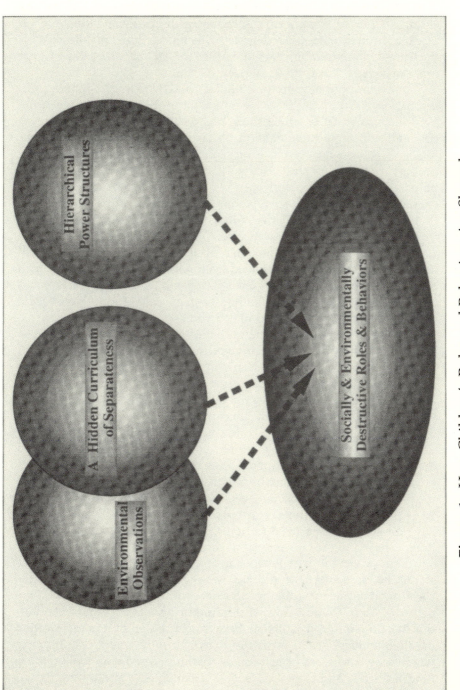

Figure 1: How Children's Roles and Behaviors Are Shaped

terms of specific educational practices but as an outcome of the children's family lives. At the same time, the postwar industrial job market required increasing degrees of technical skills, making education (now measured through a battery of standardized tests) ever more necessary for a life of dignity.

As the world population continued to escalate to four billion in 1975, the nation was looking back on a moment of liberalism between the 1960s and early 1970s when there had been an attempt to transform education through desegregation, child-centered approaches to learning, and the design and use of school settings. However, a major economic depression and soaring inflation in the mid-1970s sparked a mood of conservatism, returning the school system to the structural characteristics that had been formulated at the beginning of the century. In 1987, there were about five billion people on the Earth who were competing in a global economy. Over 40 percent of poor persons in the United States were concentrated in central cities, as were more than half of all African Americans. Yet, an educational system prevailed in which the correlation between lower-class status, race, and school failure was largely accepted—a system that had been conceived for a land-based, entrepreneurial nation with local economies.

The Earth's human population is expected to continue to escalate so that by 1998 there will be an estimated six billion persons. How should the school system respond as human beings multiply? How should education change as many cultures with competing needs and values are linked via global communications and economic systems; as undeveloped land and resources decline and the amount of overdeveloped, depleted land expands; as violence increases within and between nations? Developing an approach that can embrace those who have been marginalized by the current educational system is becoming a matter of survival since the number of disenfranchised persons will expand as the population grows and the need for and cost of education escalates. At issue are the traditional concepts of "progress" and "success" that gave direction to public education throughout this century but seem inappropriate to the current global context.

Until now educational debate has centered around not *what* progress should be but *how* it should occur, with some critics believing that the betterment of society would result from productive workers and others believing that it would result from inquiring minds. Fundamentally, this has been a win-lose debate because it is based on the assumption of a hierarchical social structure in which only a few can succeed, whether by hard work or by rational thinking. As educational theorists Martin Carnoy and Henry Levin (1985) explained: "The contradictions in education arise primarily because education is inherently part of the conflict over resources—who will get them and who will control the way they are used" (pp. 24–25). However, as the population expands, not only does the mainstream definition of success become more elusive to lower-income persons, the costs associated with a middle- and upper-class lifestyle are increasingly questioned by those concerned with the wasteful use of resources. The following are just a few of the most startling facts regarding the material excesses deriving primarily from the values and norms of mainstream society:

- In 1989, the top 1 percent of U.S. households held about 36 percent of the nation's wealth, giving this country one of the highest contrasts in the distribution of economic resources in the industrialized world—a distribution that almost matches India's.
- With only 4 percent of the global population, the United States consumes 30 percent of the world's resources and contributes 50 percent of its waste.
- The United States produces fifty times more pollution per capita than an undeveloped country.
- Suburban households are major sources of pollution, averaging ten automobile trips a day at a cost of forty to seventy cents per mile, much of it federally subsidized.
- Every twenty-four hours, the number of new drivers and the number of new cars increases by 10,000; in the same period, twelve square miles of farmland are converted into low-density, auto-dependent development.
- Energy usage has doubled since 1960 due to increased use of electrical appliances, cars, and other items once considered to be luxuries.

Poor children worldwide will become increasingly disadvantaged as such material inequities and excesses are left unquestioned, or even reinforced, by the educational process. To improve the lives of children who have been labeled "underprivileged" or "underclass" requires an essential transformation in the consciousness of privileged persons, including educators, who set the norms for U.S. society's unlimited consumption of the Earth's resources. Such changes in consciousness are necessary not only because of the environmentally destructive patterns of behavior among middle- and upper-income groups, but because of the media-driven impulse among lower-income groups to imitate their materialistic lifestyles. The countless murders that occur as impoverished youth gun one another down to obtain the status symbols of consumerism—and their unwillingness to work for low wages—might be interpreted as an incapacitating lust for the widely publicized, multimillion dollar salaries of corporate executives, Hollywood idols, and superstar athletes. Such behavior has been written off by some as the deviance of the so-called culture of poverty that lacks proper family values, the capacity to delay gratification, and a work ethic. However, the proliferation of crimes of personal gain among middle- and upper-income groups suggests that a continued longing for things will surely result in a widespread social and ecological disaster.

In speaking to a group of educational administrators, environmental justice advocate James E. Crowfoot (1994) summarized the limitations of operating within the current hierarchical structure:

> Unmet human needs are increasing as the number of people grows and as the wealth of some of these people continues to increase. The natural environment is being fundamentally altered and damaged due to these human pressures. Awareness of inequities and patterns of exploitation or oppression continues to increase. Violence is part of these patterns, and violent behaviors are increasing. Technologies continue to be developed that have many powerful potentials including violent and other life-threatening uses. In the face of these changes . . . concern is growing that if we continue our present lifestyles and relationships, we will so damage the natural environment and each other that life as we have come to know and value it will be negatively impacted even to the point of not being possible [pp. 22–23].

As citizens of a country that is in a highly visible leadership position, educators would seem to have a moral responsibility to consider whether consumptive lifestyles are being reinforced by the schooling process. Many young persons already feel a sense of protection toward the natural environment. The question is whether educators can embrace a language of inclusivity—an inner belief system—that will be strong enough to extend their caring for nature to encompass more conserving behaviors. Can we overcome the limitations of our own privileged view of the world and transform, not the educational system, but the win-lose, hierarchical values and assumptions upon which it is based? Can we break the cycle of teaching each student, directly and indirectly, to get more than others, whether in a socially sanctioned or a deviant manner?

BEING SOCIALIZED INTO DESTRUCTIVE ROLES AND BEHAVIORS

The scope of the environmental/population crisis brings into question the adequacy of Western culture and the assumptions upon which it rests. Of particular concern are the cultural assumptions underlying the belief systems of the developed countries whose technologies and patterns of consumer-oriented living are depleting the world's energy resources at an alarming rate. The core values of this belief system—abstract rational thought, efficiency, individualism, profits—were at one time believed to be the wellspring of individual and social progress [Bowers, 1993, p. 3].

What core values are being conveyed to children through the social practices and physical spaces of the classroom, school, and neighborhood? The propositions I laid out earlier suggested that children learn socially and environmentally destructive roles and behavior through environmental observations, a hidden curriculum of separateness, and hierarchical power structures. Since these three concepts form the principle screen for viewing the situations described in this book, I explore each one in greater detail in this section.

Environmental Observations

The physical environment is potentially a tool through which to encourage independent thinkers; however, if observed casually and without critical analysis, the messages contained in the environment might have the opposite effect. Consider, for example, what is communicated through the segregated, low-density settlement patterns that prevail in this country. Such settlement patterns derive, in part, from the nation's vast acreage and the federal government's support of single-family suburban living through income-tax deductions for home mortgage interest payments, grants for roads and sewers, and energy subsidies to heat large homes and make travel by private car affordable by middle-income commuters. Paralleling the support of suburban development was a systematic disinvestment in cities by government and commerce.[2] Between 1950 and 1960, such factors combined to create one of the largest internal migrations of this century as millions of middle-income families vacated urban areas to reside in suburbs (Ehrenreich, 1989, pp. 42–43). Left behind in decaying urban areas were persons with few options, and race and class were undeniable factors in these migratory patterns, as Darden et al. (1987) and other scholars of urban poverty[3] have pointed out:

In Detroit and other large urban areas, metropolitan fragmentation has emerged as an important variable in understanding the uneven spatial distribution of various racial and social population groups. This fragmentation, which involves a decentralization of economic and political activity, enables those who are financially able and white to reside in municipalities in the urban fringe (i.e., the suburbs), where they can isolate themselves from the racial and class mixture of the central city [p. 77].

Under the guise of maintaining property values, suburban zoning laws further ensure that economically diverse groups are isolated from each other, an isolation that frequently results in a segregation not only by class and race but by age. Rental properties, industry, and commerce do not intermingle with single-family housing in many of the subdivisions that are sprawling out from urban areas; nor do smaller affordable homes blend with larger luxury ones, thus guaranteeing unidimensional landscapes. The issue being considered here is what children learn about their roles in the social order by observing the spatial segregation of various populations.

Children's environmental observations also include how neighborhood environments are governed as miniature social systems with their own patterns of authority and norms for communication. Contemporary urban and suburban neighborhoods function in varied ways depending on the particular geography, density, physical design, and socioeconomic makeup of residents as well as their sociocultural habits and attitudes toward neighbors. For example, some people still carry out all their life-sustaining activities within a defined geographic area and consider their neighbors to be anyone who lives close to their home, but many others have few local activities and relationships. The governance of these varied neighborhood contexts "can be roughly divided into formal processes which depend on the state, such as the police and the courts, and informal processes which are part of the social fabric of social groups" (Merry, 1987, p. 38).

Informal processes work best when people share similar values and norms, and when they have a physical relationship with one another that supports socializing and the informal surveillance of public areas. The vibrancy of this form of governance in older urban ethnic ghettos is well documented in the sociological literature; however, during the last thirty-five years profound deterioration of the social and physical fabric of many low-income urban communities has disrupted such informal patterns of control. Many central cities have witnessed a cycle of decline in which areas deteriorate, more well-to-do residents and businesses leave, and the proportion of renter-occupied units increases. Older properties further depreciate as absentee owners neglect repairs or as the population ages and persons on fixed incomes cannot afford to make improvements. In some cases, property is deliberately left vacant or abandoned to create large blocks of land for future development. Continued deterioration of the housing stock contributes to even greater losses of the more stable population, resulting in greater declines in services. Lacking both formal and informal methods of governance (especially the careful screening of would-be tenants), criminal behavior increases.

This cycle of decline can occur within a neighborhood over a relatively short period of time so that a poor neighborhood with a reasonable quality of life can turn into a totally unsavory environment within a period of a few years. Such rapid decline seems to heighten the sense of loss in the collective memory of the residents who remain. Yet, studies of organizing activities in low-income communities suggest that some residents respond to decline by demonstrating a remarkable commitment to improving their homes and neighborhoods. According to Leavitt and Saegert (1990), women and older persons frequently take leadership in such efforts:

> Where housing and social services are of poor quality, they require intensive investment of usually female labor and care to transform them into supports for life. To the extent that conditions in apartments of low-income people deteriorate, boilers break down, somebody in the building gets ill, or needs help shopping, someone must transform these conditions through acts of care and labor into useful goods and relationships [p. 171].

At the other end of the spectrum are persons whose socioeconomic status allows them to live more privatized lives and use formal means to govern their neighborhoods, whether in exclusive urban high-rises, suburbs, or exurban subdivisions. In recent years, this privatized housing has become increasingly spread out. Although the density of older cities was about five-and-a-half dwelling units per acre, the newer suburbs and subdivisions are being constructed at about one-and-a-half dwelling units or less per acre, with some homes occupying five to ten acres each. On the other hand, little land is given over to the informal communal activities that occur in neighborhood parks or on sidewalks. Such privatized living requires wealth since individuals must be able to purchase more space, pay more taxes to support better services and schools, and exert more political power to ensure the economic stability and social homogeneity of an area. According to Merry (1987), communities that rely on space, privacy, and formal patterns of governance have the following characteristics:

> The social life of private neighborhoods is based on choice rather than propinquity. The neighborhood is chosen for the houses, the prestige, or the schools rather than family relationships or the accident of birth. Order is maintained by shared standards of behavior enforced by local government rather than by informal social control. People in these neighborhoods do not gossip much about each other because they do not know each other and are not particularly interested in each other. . . . This kind of neighbor-

hood is preoccupied with status, competition, individual growth and fulfillment, and constant activity. Status is defined not simply by wealth but by education, taste, individual accomplishment, and lifestyle [p. 63].

Keeping in mind the enormous complexities of modern neighborhoods, it seems reasonable to suggest that children internalize a wide range of messages about standards of behavior by observing the miniature social systems that comprise their neighborhood. Children in a low-income urban community might observe informal governance processes including instances in which community activists demonstrate concern for a larger extended family in the face of extreme hardship. Children in more affluent communities might observe a safe but homogenous environment that is heavily reliant on privacy, wealth, and formal problem-solving methods. Whereas poorer children might witness the social and physical degradation of their community, more well-to-do ones might come to accept as a given an auto-dependent lifestyle that is also socially and physically degrading to the global community.

The children described in this book live in racially and economically segregated environments, one neighborhood being more communal, the other being more privatized. Their work, which is presented in Chapter Six, provides insight into the lessons these children seem to be learning from these two different places.

A Hidden Curriculum of Separateness

The educational process teaches children in subtle and not so subtle ways that the individual is much more important than the community—that individuals are more likely to succeed if they distance themselves from others who are different. They learn early on that boys should line up separately from girls, that fourth-graders should be in a different classroom than fifth-graders, that intellectually gifted children are set apart from average ones. Students learn—through every class they take, every grade they receive, every counseling session they have—that they must distinguish themselves relative to their peers. To excel, they must set themselves apart from everyone else. Such individuality is a cornerstone of American society and the freedoms it guarantees. Individuals are free to be as good as they can be.

Yet, our emphasis on the autonomous, ambitious person may have become destructive to the social fabric as the collective life of our families and communities has become increasingly eroded. In describing the rise of a sense of isolation from others, Wachtel (1989) wrote:

For most of human history people lived in tightly knit communities in which each individual had a specified place and in which there was a strong sense of shared fate. . . . Over the past few hundred years, for a number of reasons, the sense of rootedness and belonging has been declining. In its place has appeared a more highly differentiated sense of individuality, implying both greater opportunity and greater separateness [p. 61].

The more recent reasons for the decline in the connection to a geographic community include smaller households and mobility, which minimizes the likelihood that adult children will live together in the same town. With fewer extended familial ties, children are less likely to experience the give-and-take of collective life in their homes, a situation that is magnified for those who grow up in two-career or one-parent families. Nor do they encounter it in the public sphere where the courtesies exchanged among strangers at parades, demonstrations, and open marketplaces are increasingly supplanted by isolationist home entertainment,[4] computer networking, and shopping in telemarketing carrels or the anonymous chain stores of regional malls. These changes in the functioning of the family and in public life are magnified by those persons who advocate the family as the primary unit of interpersonal exchange, thus further diminishing the role of the community. As many scholars have noted, the economic resources of more affluent persons increase their opportunities for mobility as well as their sense of separateness as compared to lower-income groups who are more dependent on mutual aid—a difference that will be quite apparent in the children's work presented in Chapter Six.

The decline in geographically distinct communities has resulted in the loss of neighborhood schools, which have been disappearing for several reasons. Not only is family size smaller, but households within a community may be more dispersed than in the past. In many older urban areas, there are lower densities due to vacant lots, abandoned structures, and high vacancy rates in decaying buildings; in suburbs, households are spread out intentionally through restrictive zoning that limits lot sizes. Thus in many nonrural areas of the country there are fewer children per acre than at earlier periods in history. Paralleling this pattern of scattered development was a trend in the 1950s and 1960s toward what was viewed as the efficiencies of larger structures, so children started traveling longer distances to centralized institutions. Finally, the creation of competing magnet schools that were a means of attracting a more well-to-do public school population took children away from their home neighborhoods, as did civil rights busing. The disconnection of neighborhood and school reinforces a message to children that their special interests and intellectual abilities supersede the need for being committed to others who are unlike themselves—an orientation that diminishes the sense of community. This fragmentation is continued into the classroom, where children are separated from one another according to their interests and abilities.

Television viewing after school only reaffirms the fragmentation that children experience in school. As Bellah et al. (1985) pointed out, the individuation and separation of our culture is exemplified by television, whose programs are disconnected one from the other, constantly broken up by commercials that contain contrasting messages. In their words:

> Television operates not only with a complete disconnectedness between successive programs. Even within a single hour or half-hour program, there is extraordinary discontinuity. Commercials regularly break whatever mood has built up with their own, often very different emotional message. Even aside from commercials, television style is singularly abrupt and jumpy with many quick cuts to other scenes and other characters. Dialogue is reduced to clipped sentences. No one talks long enough to express anything complex. Depth of feeling, if it exists at all, has to be expressed in a word or a glance [p. 280].

However, this programmatic disconnectedness, which is further dissected as the viewer uses a remote control to continuously switch channels, is quite consistent in its portrayal of materialistic ambition and middle-class consumerism. Given this fragmented societal context, being able to balance the "I" with the "We" within a classroom is becoming increasingly difficult. The tension between encouraging children to excel at their unique talents while at the same time nurturing their sense of community and ensuring their standardized performance is a paradox that surfaces throughout this book. You will see how this tension gets played out through the choice of classroom activities, daily routines, school management policies, and use of the school building—all of which seem to encourage separateness within a context of conformity.

Hierarchical Power Structures

An ecofeminist whose pen name is Starhawk (1987) defined three forms of authority: *power-over*, *power-with*, and *power-from-within*. Power-over comes from physical force or from assigned roles that entitle individuals to coerce obedience through fear, compliance, or external rewards. Power-with is a more ambiguously structured form of influence that is wielded among a group of equals; it only works when individuals take responsibility for their own actions and when the person exercising authority uses restraint. Power-from-within stems from such factors as idealism, magic, love, hope, or persistence that give individuals and groups the inner strength to persevere. Both power-over and power-with require social status, but power-from-within is available to everyone. Power-over—controlling others—is the primary form of authority in our society; it shapes most of our institutions, from the halls of Congress to the workplace, the schools, the churches, the hospitals, and even our families (pp. 8, 10). Despite affirmative action policies, the distribution of hierarchical authority within institutions continues to correlate with race, gender, and class, thus resulting in unequal access to opportunities and assets.

The objective dualistic thinking that evolved during the scientific revolution enables hierarchical authority and the predilection toward looking at the world through a lens of exclusivity. Because positivism involves the separation of phenomena, we tend to create opposing pairs in which one element is assumed to be not only different from but superior to its partner. For example, many people assume that thought is superior to feeling, change is better than constancy, abstract theories are preferable to concrete experience, and so forth. In this dualistic approach, we accept that whatever is unprovable or subjective is of less value than that which can be backed by impartial analysis. Objectivity in scientific thinking not only denies the contextual basis of all thought, it allows us to speak in the passive voice and be free of any personal responsibility—to the surrounding community, the nation, or the planet. Objectivity elevates the practical over the beautiful and relegates ethical thinking to the realm of private and religious life, leaving the conduct of education, politics, economics, and commerce without a moral foundation (Sterling, 1990, pp. 78–79).

The basis for hierarchical thinking first appeared in classical Greek civilization when concepts of ignorance and truth were differentiated. The Socratic method of teaching elevates some persons who have access to knowledge while placing others in positions of dependency. Through the pyramidal power structures found in most schools, children learn that well-educated males have greater authority than uneducated females to decide what is ignorance and what is truth. They learn that the middle class is more deserving than the poor, that Caucasians are more competent than persons of color, that adults are more sensible than young people, that youth are more attractive than elders—one person in each contrasting pair being dominant over the other. Through individualized instruction, whether remedial or advanced, children are exposed to an educational process that is more or less asocial, encompassing the mind but not the emotions or the spirit. Through grading and tracking, they come to understand that there is a favored position—that there are limited resources which the dominant person in a given pair is more likely to attain.

Since educational progress is defined and measured by someone with greater power, adults and children are encouraged to become partners in a patriarchal contract between those who exert external control and those who do not have to be responsible for their actions (Block, 1987). Instead of learning that everyone has inherent value—that your worth depends on the quality of your character, your ability to connect with others, your willingness to act responsibly—most children learn to accept that their worth is not inherent but rather is conferred by an outside authority, that status most often derives from a demonstration of superior intellectual ability, which entitles the bearer to exert power-over others.

The overshadowing of all other aspects of human existence by objective mental life is unexplored in educational reform debates because we accept intellectual ability as the preferred indicator of a person's competence and worth. As Nicholls (1989, p. 73) stated: "In Western culture, disciplines that seem to involve abstract reasoning have long been accorded special status," dating back to Plato and reappearing in the medieval liberal arts tradition. Such emphasis on intellectual achievement has resulted in the deprecation and marginalization of persons with other types of skills and abilities. To help low achievers compensate for their shortcomings within this unnatural framework—to achieve the ideal found in Garrison Keillor's Lake Wobegon, where all the children are above average—reformers propose to increase certain types of opportunities, then focus educational debate on how disadvantaged persons can access these resources. The outcome is to instill in children an acceptance of intellectual prowess as the prerequisite for a life of dignity. Those who have been credentialed to enter the upper ranks intellectually are encouraged in a competitive race to achieve (or buy) more whereas those who are assigned to the lower ranks are institutionally categorized as nonproductive citizens, each group being separated from the other by the extreme differences in their life chances.[5] Through this meritocratic process, children are socialized to see events in the world as being beyond their control, which can result in an automatic subservience to or defiance of perceived authority in others, lack of personal responsibility, excessive reliance on material goods as an indicator of human worth, and the need to exert physical or psychological power-over others.

In summary, the unsustainable roles and behaviors deriving from the exercise of authoritarian power include patterns of dominance or dependence, subservience or defiance, competitiveness, and materialism. The governance structures of the schools presented in this book will be examined to see if and how they encourage such roles and behaviors on the part of teachers and students.

WHY CHANGE IS SO ILLUSIVE

Why is it so difficult to bring about change in those hierarchical win-lose educational values, which make it unlikely that children will learn to resist the status quo? What are the inadequacies that grow out of our positions of privilege as middle-class professionals who have the power to promulgate the norms of society? How does the fragmented piecemeal quality of our knowledge make it hard to see how society can be transformed?

As the events in this book illustrate, dominant cultures and social groups are incredibly resistant to change because those with power and resources work in concert to maintain their class styles, privileges, and wealth (Parenti, 1978, p. 74). Scholars and practitioners in all fields tend to uphold the status quo from which we ourselves benefit, which seriously limits the social change aspects of our work. We take the lead in enabling the society to reproduce itself—with all its inequities in power—from one generation to the next, legitimizing and credentialing our own expertise in a way that protects our positions of privilege. We study the pathologies of poverty, but rarely do we question the abnormalities of the power structures of which we are a part. Because we see ourselves as the norm, most of our work assumes that children who are more well-off set the ideal or the standard from which less well-off children deviate. Because we are gatekeepers of upward mobility, we are highly invested in maintaining the requirements of each successive rank. The process of credentialing serves to differentiate and isolate individuals with different levels of accomplishment while continually escalating the need for higher levels of achievement and also securing the positions of those who are doing the credentialing.

The habits of mind that we bring to our work also tend to uphold the status quo, our theoretical and applied work producing three forms of knowledge—technical, interpretive, and critical—that have varying status in the intellectual community. Technical knowledge is based in positivism and objectivity, and "is used to expand power and control over people and the environment" (Maguire, 1987, p. 14). Technical inquiry—making what already exists work better—is by far the dominant research paradigm. Interpretive knowledge does not seek universal laws but rather illuminates the cultural specificity of situations. Its purpose is "to create the conditions for mutual understanding and consensus between members of different social orders as well as to produce practical knowledge" (ibid.). Far less pursued is critical knowledge that combines self-reflection with a historical analysis of social inequities: "Critical inquiry is used to help people see themselves and social situations in a new way in order to inform further action for

self-determined emancipation from oppressive social systems and relationships" (ibid.). Since scholars and practitioners are beneficiaries of
these power imbalances, they are unlikely to participate in their own
undoing and instead accept the social order (and their position in it) as
a given:

> When grounded in positivism, interpretive and technical knowledge takes
> the political, economic, and social structures as unconnected "givens." The
> importance of power in social relationships is largely ignored. In this case,
> both knowledge forms claim to be neutral and value free, to support the
> status quo, to separate theory and practice, and to adhere to the formal
> methodological requirements of the scientific method [ibid., p. 15].

In this book, I diverge from such a normative perspective on the social
order. By beginning with the assumption that there are deficits in the
knowledge and worldview of both poor *and* well-to-do children, I
attempt to find a way of understanding education not as a series of
rational, progressive steps toward the realization of individual ambition, but as a reiterative engagement of individuals and groups in the
multiple dimensions of knowing and feeling within a global context
that requires our interdependence. Because transcending the pitfalls of
our own culture requires radical self-examination, I seek to engage
educators in a reciprocal critique—of ourselves and our privileged role
within the social system and, at the same time, of the system itself. I risk
this broadened scope of analysis knowing that "such approaches frequently are characterized by empiricists as ideological and not schol-
arly, impressionistic and not factual, or overly simplistic and
inadequate as the basis of informed policy-making" (Sutton et al., 1995,
p. 7).

ATTEMPTING TO BREAK THE PATRIARCHAL CONTRACT

How can a focus on the physical environment serve as a point of
departure for critiquing materialistic, competitive values? How can
children learn to work collaboratively to improve their surroundings
while gaining a sense of responsibility for each other? To what extent
can practical problem solving in one's community help low-income
children become empowered social activists? Can an analysis of the
assets and deficits in the outside world assist affluent children to share
their entitlements? Since "few external objects are experienced as so
central to the self as those representing the outcome of our own efforts"
(Rosenberg, 1979, p. 36), it would seem that hands-on creative activities

provide a unique opportunity to help children feel confident that they can make a difference in the world. For disenfranchised youth, consistent efforts to bring about beneficial changes in their surroundings promise an expanded sense of control and self-efficacy as well as actual increases in resources, skills, and choices. For privileged youth, an ongoing process of critical reflection and socially responsible action might open the door to understanding social injustices as well as to a willingness to share resources, redefine skills, and accept reduced choices. For both groups, community-based problem solving can lay the groundwork for greater participation in public life as adults and decrease the tendency to look to higher authorities for solutions.

The Urban Network instructional approach involves youth in such environmental activism. During a one-year sequence of activities, students, teachers, parents, neighborhood residents, and volunteer professionals work as a team to envision, organize, and implement improvements in their school community.[6] They study their environment, select an area of focus, develop a plan, then raise money to implement the plan. Successful projects include a cleanup campaign in New York City, a celebration of urban life in Detroit, an assessment of local businesses' responsiveness to consumers in Minneapolis, a re-creation of indigenous mural motifs in Watsonville, a tree-planting in Atlanta, an archaeological dig in a vacant lot in Brooklyn, and a wild-flower center memorializing two dead children in Chicago, among others.

In addition to providing guidance on making physical improvements, a unique aspect of the Urban Network in comparison to many other design and environmental education programs is its emphasis on the interpersonal context in which activities are carried out. The social milieu the program seeks to establish was pieced together from critical education theorists, especially such persons as Kurth-Schai (1988) who looked at the conditions that support children's activism. Such a milieu would exhibit collaborative, empowering human relationships; self-governance with participants directing and evaluating their own endeavors; intergenerational learning that encompasses a diversity of skills and division of labor; an expanding, cohesive social network; and an emphasis on celebrating one's achievements. When the making of esthetic objects occurs within such an empowering interpersonal context, the process can take on a larger symbolic meaning, as occurred during traditional barn-raisings or quilting bees. In the following exhibition notes for a museum installation of quilts, one writer described the power of these sorts of activities:

> The quilting bee was a productive social event, a gathering of women sharing a common goal. As they stitched, they talked and symbolically

sewed their fears, hopes, and memories into the fabric. A strong sense of community was reinforced by the quilting bee. Women channeled their creative energy not only for themselves, but for the good of society [Notes from "Homage to the Quilt"].

Children's environmental design projects seem to have the same social, community-building quality of a quilting bee in which the making of an esthetic element begins to symbolize the collaborators' caring and sense of social purpose. Since the physical environment is itself a collective commodity, its shaping—whether explicitly acknowledged or not—reflects a moral stance about how to share the Earth's resources (Tuan, 1989, p. vii). By engaging participants in a creative group process and a thoughtful questioning of the ethical dimensions of their decision-making, it seems possible that children will develop greater social consciousness. Because a variety of skills are needed to bring about changes in the environment, a broad-based multidisciplinary activity provides an opportunity to break with the narrow, competitive skill development that is the focus of most educational experiences. Projects can promote physical strength as well as patience, intellectual as well as artistic ability, advanced skills as well as rudimentary ones. For example, some participants in Urban Network activities conduct interviews, make plans, or write proposals; some pour foundations, hammer nails, or provide publicity; others plant flowers, sew banners, or clean up; still others have bake sales, contribute money, or acquire a building permit. Everyone's capacities are needed for a successful outcome. Not infrequently a child or adult loses interest in a particular phase of the work only to be a star actor in another.

Since environmental advocacy requires individual as well as collective action, it is possible that an enhanced group identity can result from the problem-solving process. "Any kind of community is more than a set of customs, behaviors, or attitudes about other people. A community is also a collective identity; it is a way of saying who 'we' are. . . . [Community] is born from this union of shared action and a shared sense of collective self" (Sennett, 1978, p. 222). It is possible to design a series of collective activities so that an expanding social network forms as participants articulate their common concerns and carry out tangible actions to address those concerns. Such feelings seem to be enhanced when the activity has the celebratory aspects of a barn-raising or quilting bee. The instructional materials of the Urban Network explained the process of community building in this way:

A successful program goes beyond individual student growth and provides a means for energizing the entire school community around issues that affect the quality of everyday life. It will result in a visible outcome that will, in turn, create a tangible focus for celebrating accomplishments. Such celebrations can generate school pride, improve the perceived re- sourcefulness of the school and its children, and increase the willingness of local residents to contribute to future activities. A successful program also will give participants a sense of belonging to a community effort and to a larger national team that is working together to enhance the quality of life in neighborhoods [Sutton, 1989, p. 6].

Numerous planning, design, and environmental education initiatives intend to heighten children's awareness of environmental issues by offering the social and technical skills that can help them to affect their surroundings in a positive manner. Persons who subscribe to them are not generally from run-of-the-mill schools but rather from innovative ones in which teachers persistently seek ways to make learning more exciting and relevant for children. However, educational methodolo- gies that truly realign hierarchical power relationships will most likely meet with severe obstacles to their implementation. Students may be so accustomed to working individualistically that they are unable to con- ceive a collaborative agenda; teachers may not have the latitude to set aside short-term, skill-based, subject-matter instruction and pursue long-term, wholistic, intergenerational learning; and both groups may be uncomfortable with an assignment in which the teacher is not the expert. The composite schools presented in this book illustrate these various barriers to breaking the patriarchal contract.

The book contains six narrative chapters that are bookended by this introduction and conclusions, that together provide the analytical framework for the six chapters. Although a scholar's perspective is offered throughout the text, its main portion is written in a storybook format to engage the reader in experiencing—and interpreting—the situations described. The narrative portion of the book begins with a snapshot of two communities: a lower-income urban neighborhood called Oak Hills, where the Frederick Douglass Elementary School is located, and an upper-middle-income suburb called San Lupe, where the Gardendale Institute of Science and Technology is located.

The first three chapters present an overview of the schools, the first one describing their neighborhood context, the second and third being devoted to the educational programs, facilities, and staff of each of the schools. In the first chapter, a brief theoretical discussion and a series of quotes from fifth- and sixth-grade students who participated in the Urban Network at both schools suggest how powerful each neighbor- hood is in shaping the mental life of children. In the second and third chapters, both Frederick Douglass and Gardendale are represented as having forward-looking approaches to education; however, the patriarchal contract is apparent in each school's teaching methods, management styles, schedules, and even in the use of the two buildings. The fourth chapter details particular events that occurred during the first semester of the Urban Network program at each school, and a fifth chapter illustrates their differing reactions to a community enhancement project that took place during the second semester.

The sixth chapter introduces the children's perspective on their neighborhoods. Through essays, drawings, and videotaped conversations, they offer insights into the impact that Oak Hills and San Lupe have on their everyday experiences. Children also disclose various social selves as they position themselves in their writing, some taking a more altruistic, nurturing role, others illustrating an orientation toward consumerism and technological innovation. What is apparent in the work of both groups of students is that poverty as well as affluence can both inspire and impair social responsibility. In the book's conclusions, I elaborate a vision of education in a sustainable society and, to illustrate that vision, offer three case studies of innovations in New York City. Although I begin the book by emphasizing the differences between the two schools, I eliminate this oppositional format in the conclusions and instead weave a tapestry in which educators in both situations can help students learn to resist the status quo.

NOTES

1. For a discussion of the concept of a hidden curriculum, refer to *Critical Essays on Education, Modernity, and the Recovery of the Ecological Imperative* by C.A. Bowers (1993); *Schooling in Capitalist America* by Samuel Bowles and Herbert Gintis (1976); *Theory and Resistance in Education* by Henry A. Giroux (1983), especially Chapter 2; and *The Hidden Curriculum and Moral Education* edited by Henry A. Giroux and David Purpel (1983).

2. As an example of how government policies give priority to suburbs in the allocation of funds, the $100 million Detroit received in 1994 for its Empowerment Zone is what it costs to build only two and a half miles of the eight-lane highway connecting that city to outlying areas.

3. For a comprehensive look at the devastating effect on inner-city blacks of federally subsidized suburban development and persistent racial discrimination, see Goldsmith and Blakely (1992).

4. As examples of the expansion of home entertainment, in 1993 video games outsold movie admissions for the first time, and the Woodstock II concert generated about $20 million in pay-per-view revenues.

5. According to the 1990 Census, persons with professional and postgraduate degrees comprise almost half those with incomes in excess of $100,000; on the other hand, it has become much more difficult for anyone without a college degree to find a job with minimally adequate pay.

6. The nationally based membership of the Urban Network comprises public and private elementary and middle schools as well as a number of individuals and nonprofit community organizations. A publication titled *The Urban Network* (Sutton, 1989) is an instrucitonal portfolio containing guides for principals and teachers, posters, cue cards, and a videotape. The portfolio—which offers techniques for environmental assessment, project development, and implementation—is intended for fourth, fifth, and sixth grades, but teachers have adapted the materials for second through eighth grades, and its mehtods have been used in numerous community settings. The Urban Network also offers *Youth & Adovcacy* (a biannual journal), consultations on program development, and numerous special projects (such as design competitions, conferences, and teacher workshops).

Cast of Characters

AT FREDERICK DOUGLASS ELEMENTARY SCHOOL IN MARKINGTON

Mrs. Delores Driskell	Principal and director of the upper school
Mrs. Patricia Vallejo	Assistant principal and director of the lower school
Dr. Harold Johnstone	Chief program planner for the Markington Board of Public Schools
Professor Tom Mintz	Department of City and Community Planning at the University of Markington; Urban Network contact
Ms. Noreen Clark	Fifth-grade social studies teacher and coordinator for the Urban Network program
Ms. Mary Quick-to-See	Fifth-grade language arts teacher in multicultural education
Miss Gail Forster	Fifth-grade math teacher
Mr. Frank Johnson	Eighth-grade master teacher in multicultural education
Mrs. Anne Bassett	Lower-school multicultural education teacher
Mrs. Diane Greene	Chester's mother and volunteer at Saint Andrew's Church
Mister Joe	Building superindentent.
Rev. Hill	Minister at Saint Andrew's Church
The Sisters	Volunteers at Saint Andrew's Church who do community organizing

Ms. Clark's Students

Carlos	Class leader and winner of a community-service award
Chester	Shy child who creates the Happy Toy concept
Georgette	One of nine children who lives in a household of thirteen persons
Jessica	The most obedient child in the class
Jimmie	Carlos's friend and volunteer at Saint Andrew's Church
Shawn	Class rebel and designer of Happy Toy; Chester's friend and protector
Tameka	Class rebel who goes to church after school to "praise God"

AT GARDENDALE INSTITUTE OF SCIENCE AND TECHNOLOGY IN SAN LUPE

Dr. Marion B. Marcus	Principal
Mr. Bob Regon	Director of science and technology at the San Lupe Unified District
Ms. Jane Andre	Art teacher and painter; Urban Network contact and program coordinator
Miss Barbara Moore	Sixth-grade teacher and Ph.D. student in communications arts
Mrs. Betty Rayburne	Sixth-grade teacher and aspiring writer
Mr. Joshua Frank	Physical education teacher and coordinator of the conflict resolution program
Mrs. Helen Hansen	Emily's mother; plays a policewoman in the homeless skit

Miss Moore's Students

Emily	Member of the enhancement team; born on Detroit's East Side
Sallyanne	Laura's best friend and member of the enhancement team; plays Maria during the homeless skit
Claudia	Member of the enhancement team and the only black child in the class
Laura	Member of the enhancement team; plays Rosa in homeless skit
Justin	Plays the news commentator during the party; member of the enhancement team

Madison	Plays the news commentator during the party. Member of the enhancement team
Peter	Plays Rambo during the party; member of the enhancement team
Robert	Plays Rambo during the party; member of the enhancement team

Mrs. Rayburne's Students

Kimsung	Class leader; member of the measuring and enhancement teams
Charles	Member of the measuring and enhancement teams
Jeremiah	Member of the measuring and enhancement teams
Michael	Member of the measuring and enhancement teams; son of a prominent architect

Staging

CHAPTER ONE

In Oak Hills

<u>Second visit to Frederick Douglass.</u> Author takes a taxi ride to the school in October. <u>Recall of first visit to Gardendale.</u> Author had taken a car ride to the school one week earlier.

CHAPTER TWO

At Frederick Douglass

<u>Second visit continued.</u> Mrs. Driskell takes the author on a building tour that ends in Noreen's class.

CHAPTER THREE

At Gardendale

<u>First visit.</u> The author meets with Dr. Marcus and goes on a building tour with Mr. Regon. Tour ends in Mrs. Rayburne's class. <u>That afternoon.</u> The author and Jane work with Miss Moore's class on neighborhood depictions.

CHAPTER FOUR

Begins with an overview of the differences in implementing the Urban Network at Frederick Douglass and Gardendale

In Markington	Preplanning during summer. Tom meets Frederick Douglass teachers and makes contact with the author.
At Frederick Douglass	First visit. The author and Tom meet with Mrs. Driskell and Mrs. Vallejo in September. Second visit continued. The author and Noreen work with all three fifth-grade classes on neighborhood depictions. Fourth visit. The author and Mary discuss conflicts over the use of space with fifth-grade students during a snow emergency.
At Gardendale	Preplanning during previous year. Jane collaborates with Miss Moore and Mrs. Rayburne to design the Aspiring Professionals program that will feature the Urban Network during its first year. Morning of first visit continued. A team of four boys in Mrs. Rayburne's class work with the author and Jane on sketches for an outdoor science laboratory. Afterward, the author has lunch with teachers and parents at a local restaurant. Second visit. The author and Jane attend a party in Miss Moore's class.

CHAPTER FIVE

Begins with an explanation of the skills covered during the Urban Network, including the community enhancement project that is carried out during the second semester

At Frederick Douglass	January. The author, Tom, and Noreen decide to introduce the enhancement project by having children make journals about their neighborhoods. February. Mrs. Driskell, Tom, and Noreen discuss the focus of the enhancement project. They agree that Noreen's class will create something for Saint Andrew's soup kitchen and take a field trip to the University of Markington. Mrs. Driskell begins the process of obtaining a school bus for the trip. End of March. With the assistance of Tom's urban planning students and the sisters,

Noreen's class brainstorms problems at the soup kitchen. Chester convinces his classmates to make something called Happy Toy for the homeless children who eat there. Beginning of April. The school bus materializes just four days before the trip is to occur. The children go to the university and create several designs for Happy Toy. The class agrees that Shawn's team has the winning design.

At Gardendale

January. The author, Mr. Regon, and Jane set the direction of the enhancement project. The children will begin with the journal exercise and go on a field trip to Limone in the school van.

February. Jane and Mrs. Hansen introduce the children to the problems of homelessness by enacting a skit in the school courtyard.

Early March. Jane, Mr. Regon, and Mrs. Hansen take the children on the field trip to Limone including a visit to an elementary school.

April. Jane's students decide to save their allowance for a month and contribute it to the elementary school. They also create designs for improving the downtown of Limone.

May. During the final site visit, the author attends the school's Annual Spring Festival, which features work completed in the Aspiring Professionals program.

At Frederick Douglass

Mid-April. Noreen tells Tom that the children will not be able to build Happy Toy because of preparations for standardized testing.

May. During the final site visit, the author and Tom help the children to finish up a banner for their school entry. They show the children Happy Toy, which was built by the urban planning students. The class has a picnic on the playground to celebrate the completion of the year's work, then the author and Tom deliver Happy Toy to Saint Andrew's Church.

Environmental Texts of Poverty and Privilege

> You're part of where you live at. . . . And yes, self-esteem has a lot to
> do with it. If the surroundings ain't no good, it's just . . . you know
> . . . it's hopeless.
>
> Anonymous parent

Self-esteem—few would argue its centrality to the development of
active, socially responsive citizens. As with other educators of disadvantaged children, raising self-esteem was high on a list of priorities for
teachers and staff at the school where I was headed. By nurturing a
sense of pride and identity with African American culture, they hoped
that Frederick Douglass's low-achieving students would see themselves as smarter, worthier, and more competent to learn. Self-esteem—I
looked out of the taxicab window at a familiar inner-city landscape and
wondered whether this critical ingredient could be cultivated within a
classroom. I wondered whether children could develop feelings of
self-acceptance, self-respect, and self-worth *in* school while living in an
environment *after* school that continually challenged and undermined
these feelings.[1]

In comparison to ghetto neighborhoods in cities like New York,
Chicago, or Detroit, Markington appeared benign. Yet, the telltale
signs of poverty were evident through the taxicab window: a burned
or abandoned building; a crack house with black plastic covering its
windows; rusty, broken-down cars interspersed with sleek, expensive
ones; tall brush growing wild in vacant lots; garbage dumped by
rubbish companies avoiding costly landfill sites; adults (especially
men) milling idly about during the traditional rush hour; windows

crudely barred to keep out criminals. Overlooking this deteriorating place were the belching smokestacks of a city incinerator, lined up like a menacing army of tin soldiers.

The taxi sped out West Boulevard, the major street that formed one boundary of the Oak Hills neighborhood, past an abandoned industrial plant and a string of boarded-up businesses and convenience shops. Most of the ones that remained were liquor stores with an occasional bar, automotive repair, or grocery store, all with metal security gates and interiors darkened by out-of-date electrical systems. A low-rise public housing project stood off to the right on a dead-end street near the railroad tracks that ran diagonally across West Boulevard to form another edge of the neighborhood. The driver revealed his firsthand knowledge of the project, explaining that this was where most of the city's American Indians lived, some in apartments that were almost bare of furnishings. If you had a car, it was only about a ten- or fifteen-minute drive to the nearest supermarket, which was located in a mini-mall on West Boulevard about three miles beyond the railroad tracks. But for the many people in Oak Hills who had to rely on public transportation, the trip back and forth could take almost all day on buses that were expensive and frequently late.

My driver turned left onto a residential street, past shabby two-family homes with sagging front porches that had once encouraged neighborly socializing. Several small boys, seemingly uninterested in getting to school, were imitating a drug bust in a vacant lot, two of them instructing the others to "spread-eagle" against a car that was propped up on cinder blocks. Here and there among buildings that appeared not to have been painted for at least two decades was evidence of residents who refused to give in to the surrounding decay—the October remains of a summer's vegetable garden, a house hand-painted in many shades of lavender, pumpkins dressed as people and seated on a front porch. Up ahead was Saint Andrew's Church. White letters inserted into the black bulletin board of this once-elegant neighborhood landmark advertised a soup kitchen to the shadowy figures who lounged on its front steps.

As children edged past the shadows with deliberately diverted eyes, I recalled the direct, piercing looks of the students I had visited a week earlier at the Gardendale Science and Technology Institute in San Lupe. Quite unlike Oak Hills's discarded, uncared-for appearance, San Lupe had communicated a sense of being well tended. The lawns were green and manicured, shrubbery carefully trimmed, houses meticulously painted, windows curtained just so; and the many servants and nannies whom I had seen on the bus ride from the city were indicators of just how cared for it was. Quite unlike Oak Hills's invaded, insecure buildings, the architecture of San Lupe had seemed very private and permanent. Even the picturesque shop near the bus depot where I waited for my ride over a cup of cappuccino had seemed private and permanent—an abundant display of the commodities of fine living arranged on dark wooden shelves, a dignified shopkeeper wrapped in a sparkling white apron exchanging small talk with a customer, an expected delivery of "choice biscotti." The shopkeeper had handed a small shopping bag to his customer so graciously that their exchange of money had been all but invisible.

Quite the opposite of throttling along the unprotected, denuded streets of Oak Hills, my drive to Gardendale wound along a gently curving, satiny blacktop road. We glided past stately houses that were situated among towering mature trees on enormous lots. Somewhat reminiscent of the castles of Spain, many homes were adorned with slender classical columns and tied to the landscape with multifaceted gray or red tile roofs. Each one had seemed safeguarded, not by the prisonlike bars and gates that corseted the facades of Oak Hills, but by layers of lush landscape and the unseen presence of computerized security systems. In place of Oak Hills's unhealthy belching smokestacks and rusting cars was a rolling golf course where a few wholesome-looking, early-morning players were driving a shiny motorized cart past an artificial lake. In place of Saint Andrew's soup kitchen, which was a stone's throw from Frederick Douglass, was a magical lagoon that dwarfed Gardendale's ample schoolyard.

In commenting on the profound impact of the neighborhood environment on children's worldview, Berg and Medrich (1980) wrote:

> For children, the neighborhood is more than a physical setting. It defines a social universe. Children, like the elderly, have a particularly heavy investment in the neighborhood environment. Because they are minimally mobile and spend relatively little time away from the area in which they live, neighborhoods play a special role in children's daily lives [p. 320].

What was the relevance of the contrasting scenes of Oak Hills and San Lupe to the children who lived in each of these social macrocosms? If "you're part of where you live at," would the solidity of San Lupe's architecture versus the dilapidation of Oak Hills's result in higher self-esteem? Would a magnificent natural environment versus a polluted one improve a child's physical well-being? Would the omnipresence of servants and gracious shopkeepers versus pervasive signs of unemployment and criminal behavior increase that child's sense of stability and self-confidence?

SOCIETY IS MAPPED OUT ON THE GROUND

Scholars concerned with the physical context of human development have attempted to explain how place contributes to the individual and collective consciousness. Environmental psychologist Leanne Rivlin (1987) characterized how children develop an idea of themselves relative to their surroundings in the following manner:

> The notion of place identity . . . underlies the significance of the enduring, albeit changing, contributions of place to self. . . . If we begin with children, it is fair to say that the home and the range around it serve as the first and the most powerful context for place identity development. Children's immediate setting helps to define both the world and themselves within it. . . . The two immediate environments, the home and neighborhood, form the most repeated and powerful context for socialization and development, providing images that personally contribute to the child's sense of himself or herself [p. 10].

Urban geographer Edward C. Relph (1976) proposed that places have meaning for us not only because they are associated with our body movements and senses, but because we inhabit and project our personalities and imaginations onto them. Of their special relevance for children he wrote:

> For children in particular, places constitute the basis for the discovery of the self, and caves or trees or even a corner of the house may be claimed as "my place." These childhood places frequently take on great significance and are remembered with reverence. . . . Both remembered and currently significant places are essential concentrations of meaning and intention within the broader structure of perceptual space [p. 113].

Physical space (remembered and current) is an essential aspect of an individual's cultural identity, providing a sense of stability or disjuncture and, as city planner Kevin Lynch (1979) and many others[2] have discovered, the environment literally communicates to children their social status. Over a period of many years, Lynch had been asking his graduate students to talk about their childhood memories to make them aware of the importance of the environment in people's lives. After comparing tape recordings of these discussions, he was surprised to note how similar the students' recollections were despite differences in time, geography, and socioeconomic background—and social class as revealed through physical surroundings was clearly a recurrent theme. As Lynch explained:

The environment was seen as a social symbol. In my innocence, I had thought that young children were not conscious of social divisions. Their memories, however, were full of references to social divisions. They knew just where class changed on a street; they knew the racial divisions; they knew where it was safe to go and where it was not. They had found that society was mapped out on the ground [p. 105].

What position in society did the students of Frederick Douglass see mapped out for themselves on the streets of Oak Hills? Could vacant lots inhabited by drug pushers elicit their sense of self-discovery or inner stability? Was it possible for them to invent beauty and hope while being surrounded by images of abandonment and deterioration? Was the potential for idealism that Robert Coles (1986) ascribed to childhood sufficient for them to envision social and environmental justice? Alternatively, what position did the students of Gardendale see reflected in the streets of San Lupe? Could its gracious set-apartness nurture their sense of connectedness to persons outside this domain? Is it possible for them to question the consumerism that is overstressing the Earth's ecosystems while being surrounded by an unlimited abundance of material goods? In the absolute security of San Lupe, could these future leaders realistically imagine *any* major social or environmental problem?

How should teachers respond to the contrasting scenes of Oak Hills and San Lupe? If Frederick Douglass's teachers were attempting to raise the self-esteem of children who were surrounded by what "ain't no good," should Gardendale's teachers also try to intervene in their students' heritage of materialistic consumption? If it was reasonable to focus Frederick Douglass's curriculum on raising self-esteem to compensate for the assaults of living in Oak Hills, should the curriculum at Gardendale also attempt to counterbalance the privileges experienced in San Lupe?

CHILDREN READING THEIR WORLDS

Commonplaces about communities may well represent a fundamental way that Americans conceptualize and interpret society and the self. . . . Debates about suburbs and cities involve deeper commitments to competing values, and questions about where one lives become queries about who one is [Hummons, 1990, p. xiv].

For children, the messages about places, their underlying values, and their connection to self—the construction of a community's meaning— come primarily from parents but may also come from neighbors, the media, and direct experiences of that place. In the months to come, the fifth-grade students at Frederick Douglass would demonstrate a sobering clarity of perceptions about their life in Oak Hills. They would accurately assess its biggest problems as murder, litter, robbery, drugs, vacant lots, broken-down houses, gang fights, drive-by shootings, car stealing, prostitution, bad housing, and bad language. They would describe the effects of unemployment ("The Funky Fox is a big problem because people don't have nothing to do, so they go there and smoke cheba. Sometimes they start killing each other for no good reason.")[3] They would zero in on the harshness of being homeless ("The church keeps it a secret, but I knew some kids who lived in the basement over there because they didn't have no place else"). Despite a dearth of beauty in their lives, they would voice a stubborn appreciation for it ("I wish the whole neighborhood could be a garden. There should be a rainbow every time it rains"). At times, they would express their longing to be elsewhere ("When I grow up, I'm going to move someplace better") while at the same time sensing the importance of neighborhood and neighbors ("I like this neighborhood because this is where I live. I have all my friends here").

As the taxi moved past the small clusters of children who were trailing along toward Frederick Douglass, I asked myself whether they could compare the images of decline in their own environment with media images of affluence in the world beyond and still acquire the feelings of self-worth that are essential to growth. How would the children's perceptions of an adult world that was often uncaring and at times even violent mesh with their valuing of beauty and friendship? In attempting to develop self-esteem, how would teachers at Frederick Douglass seek to understand and unpack the baggage of social inequity that students brought to school? Was it possible that the school itself could become that safe space of self-discovery—"my place"—where children and adults could sketch out an alternative map of society?

Children in Gardendale would also provide a clear "reading" of their neighborhood. Due to their unrestricted mobility compared to the children at Frederick Douglass, they would demonstrate detailed knowledge of the vast open expanses in their community ("I don't have boundaries where I can't go except very far away"), as well as exposure to the larger world ("My parents lived in Italy, but our family vacations all over Europe") and the excitement of upward mobility ("My dad is an engineer so we live in different countries. I love learning about other cultures and eating different food"). They would reveal their appreciation of the area's symbols of prestige, especially its large, detached homes ("The houses are next door to each other. Mostly everyone has a front yard and back"); and the privacy they afford ("Our house is big, roomy, and old-fashioned. We each have our own bedroom, bathroom, and closet"). They would pinpoint the neighborhood's child-rearing benefits ("There is a playground and field where children play softball, baseball, and soccer games"); its extraordinary safety ("It's never dangerous around here so you can ride your bike anytime"); its cleanliness ("The air is clean and the town is not polluted"); and its gentle spaciousness ("It's never crowded in any stores and restaurants and that's what I like about this town. The houses are beautiful and some are extremely old. Our streets are very quiet except for the two main roads").

Although they would not mention the area's racial homogeneity, the children at Gardendale would indicate their awareness of San Lupe's sheltered quality in comparison to the not-so-nice places they had heard about on the evening news. And not infrequently would they elaborate scenarios for protecting their assets. Figuring most prominently in their descriptions would be the commercial establishments, highly formalized recreational activities, and extravagant mechanical devices that populated their lives. Listening to their words, I would wonder how they could develop an understanding of the outside world with its abandoned stores, unsafe playgrounds, and absence of the most basic furnishings and equipment. Could they elaborate an egalitarian concept of power given their intuitive valuing of their superior material assets? Gardendale's staff aimed to give their students "every opportunity for success," but could they nurture a compassionate citizenry and serve as a window to the injustices in the outside world? Could Gardendale become a safe space for learning to resist the consumerism and competitiveness of their surroundings?

Would teachers at either school be able to help children acknowledge their interdependence in a multicultural world—one with almost six billion people in several hundred nation-states being increasingly linked by telecommunications and economics? Would they be able to assist children in thinking critically about the sociopolitical context that has shaped their contrasting environmental lives? Would the curriculum of either school help students to negate those aspects of their environment that could prevent them from reaching their highest human potential? Surely an educational agenda would be needed that was as powerful as the children's observations of their physical worlds.

NOTES

1. See "Chapter I: The Nature of the Self-Concept" in *Conceiving the Self* by Morris Rosenberg (1979) for a discussion of self-esteem as one aspect of a person's total self-concept.

2. Frequently design faculty ask college students to recall their childhood homes to illustrate the dynamic relationship between quality of life and place. Such reflection on one's past relative to place—referred to as an environmental autobiography—typically contains vivid particulars of sensory and social experiences.

3. In this chapter the comments in quotation marks that are attributed to children have been taken verbatim from various students' writings except that punctuation and spelling were corrected.

2

Up Against the Odds

The taxi stopped in front of an aging four-story building that was as stately and imposing as the principal who presided over it. Built in 1918 to serve a white working-class neighborhood, the structure towered over the modest wood frame houses that faced it, bearing down on the sidewalk with only a narrow strip of scraggly grass to soften its entry. Darkened by time as if to confirm the institution's tenacity in this decaying community, the facade appeared even more jarringly aristocratic because of its round, fortresslike turrets and high-pitched, green gabled roof. Above the front entrance a wooden panel painted with the words "Frederick Douglass School" hid an inset where "Mason School" was etched in stone—the only sign of newness on the impenetrable exterior.

Two men were sharing a pint of port wine on the steps of the vacant building across from the school, obviously unconcerned with looking for work among the boarded-up businesses that could be found on most any block in this neighborhood. With almost 50,000 households, the number of persons on welfare in Oak Hills had risen by 30 percent although there had been a drop of 6,500 households in a four-square-mile area during the last decade. In the last fifteen years, the neighborhood had lost over one-quarter of its housing stock, most of its rental units being owned by absentee landlords, and another quarter were considered to be substandard. Eleven percent of the land was either vacant or contained abandoned buildings, and there were numerous contaminated sites and leaking underground storage tanks along West Boulevard. Whatever amount was spent on government assistance, fire and police protection, and emergency medical care (some said far too many tax-payer dollars went to Oak Hills), the neighborhood was clearly in the first stages of a disastrous decline. Jobs, services, and more well-to-do residents continued to disappear, housing crumbled, and criminal behavior was on the increase.

Several school buses were parked in front of the building and, farther along, a few children were getting out of cars and waving good-bye to parents. Almost 40 percent of the students made the journey to this neighborhood school by school bus or car, although some of them lived within walking distance but were driven for safety reasons. Children who walked spent up to thirty minutes each way navigating the less-than-hospitable environment of Oak Hills.

Despite the dispersed geography of the school's attendance area—despite the fact that it had been almost thirty-five years since the U.S. Supreme Court ruled against the practice of segregating schools—Frederick Douglass was clearly segregated.[1] Students were almost 90 percent black, Hispanic, and American Indian, including many children from migrant farm families. In addition to inheriting a historical ghettoizing-by-race, these students almost all lived in poverty, reflecting a ghettoizing by class that occurred as an unfortunate by-product of the Civil Rights movement. As Jacqueline Jordan Irvine (1990), who studies how blacks and other minorities are excluded from educational opportunities, pointed out:

> Before desegregation, the black community included poor, working-class, and middle-class people. . . . It was not uncommon to find black teachers and black maids attending the same church and living in the same neighborhood. This diverse community was stabilized by and revolved around common middle-class values and aspirations. Today, many impoverished black students are isolated in neighborhoods where they seldom see, not to mention know, people who work, speak standard English, or live in two-parent families [p. 126].

In contrast to the mostly white, middle-class educational staff at Frederick Douglass, only about 6 percent of parents had college degrees and only 55 percent had a high school education as compared to 75 percent in the rest of the state.[2] Twenty-eight percent of the school's children lived in poverty with 70 percent being in single-parent households, thus providing within the walls of the school a vivid reflection of the inequalities within the larger society.[3] Since academic success is strongly associated with parental socioeconomic status,[4] anything but persistent low performance by Frederick Douglass's students on standardized tests would have been highly unlikely. Oak Hills not only had the highest dropout rate in the city, it ranked among the highest in the state, yet principal Delores Driskell had a singular determination to raise the academic performance of Frederick Douglass's racial and ethnic minorities.

A tall, strikingly elegant African American woman in her early sixties, some described her as authoritarian whereas others saw her as progressive, creative, and visionary. These mixed assessments notwithstanding, Mrs. Driskell was among the many educators around the country who began in 1986 to resist the school reforms that had been generated by legislators' reactions to *A Nation at Risk*. These school reforms placed the onus for improvement on individual students and seemed to be having a negative impact by increasing the number of dropouts. In contrast, Mrs. Driskell saw the school, with its culture and teachers, as the focus of change; and her twelve years of experience in administration gave her the expertise and political savvy to broker broad-based support for her vision. During the 1986–87 school year, she organized a group of respected educational consultants who convinced the chief program planner for the Markington Board of Public Schools, Dr. Harold Johnstone, that achievement could be improved by revamping the school's graded structure and by implementing an aggressive teacher development program using culturally sensitive teaching materials. By the following school year, a demonstration project was in place at Frederick Douglass.

OUTWITTING THEIR BIRTHRIGHT

Mrs. Driskell's constituency drafted an educational plan that read like a set of architectural specifications, incorporating many of the latest instructional methods—two smaller schools within a bigger one including a nongraded lower school; team teaching; cultural awareness; cooperative, thematic learning—and stipulating parent education along with progressive methods of assessment. An immediately felt outcome of the demonstration was a reduction of the maximum average class size from thirty to twenty-four students in the upper grades and from twenty-five to twenty-two students in the lower grades. The demonstration also created support for four additional classroom teachers and three new resource teachers, bringing the total number of faculty to thirty-seven and lowering the students per teacher from twenty-one to seventeen.

The nongraded lower school advanced Mrs. Driskell's goal of increasing the students' sense of stability by allowing them to stay with a single peer group for as long as it took them to complete the first four years of school. By dividing the school's 625 K–8 children into two programs, each was more intimate with its own administrator and distinct educational life. The director of the lower school was a Cuban American woman named Patricia Vallejo whose second-grade daughter attended the school (it was no small matter of pride to Mrs. Driskell that the school's administration was female *and* of color but Dr. Johnstone, a white man, also wielded a heavy hand in overseeing the program). Although Mrs. Driskell's presence could be felt everywhere, the upper school was her main responsibility.

In the lower school, groups of twenty children were created to have a full range of reading abilities and social skills as well as a balance of gender and, to the degree possible with such a homogeneous population, ethnicity. Within these heterogeneous groups, students progressed at their own rate, accelerating or spending more time as necessary. Unless there was a personality conflict, children stayed with their group until they were promoted to the upper school in fourth grade,[5] where students at each grade level were assigned to one of three heterogeneous homeroom classes. A sense of stability was also encouraged in the upper school since one group of students stayed together throughout the day, changing classes to take double periods in math, social studies, and language arts; and single periods in music, gym, library, environmental science, and computer technology.

As in the lower school, teachers in the upper school worked in teams to provide instruction in their specialty area, sharing information on student progress, conducting conferences with parents, and collaborating on field trips and other special projects. A team of upper-school teachers stayed with their students for two grade levels following a schedule of seven forty-five-minute periods, a ten-minute homeroom, a twenty-minute morning recess, and a fifty-minute lunch break. The double periods, teamwork across classes, and absence of "pull-out" enrichment or remedial activities (except for the Title One reading program, all special activities occurred within regular classes) gave Frederick Douglass an overall sense of continuity that is so lacking at many schools.

The simple regularity of the schedule had the potential for a great deal of flexibility. Although single periods occurred at fixed times, a team of three teachers could shift the order of double periods to accommodate some special need by simply conferring with one another in the hall. This directness, and the small size of the two programs, made the days at Frederick Douglass School seem very orderly—an overriding aspect of the school's philosophy.

The centerpiece of Frederick Douglass's educational plan was its emphasis on the contributions of non-European cultures to history and lifestyle in the United States. When the old Mason School was revamped, Mrs. Driskell secured support for hiring two new teachers and recruited a third from the staff to participate in a three-year in-service program at the University of Markington called Multicultural Education Development (or MED). For three summers, the two new hires, lower-school teacher Anne Bassett and fifth-grade teacher Mary Quick-to-See, attended two-week summer seminars at MED along with eighth-grade teacher Frank Johnson, who was beginning his sixth year at the school.

The seminars were coupled with independent studies during which the trio experimented with multicultural instructional materials in their own classes and eventually shared their knowledge with the other teachers in their grade-level teams. Anne, Mary, and Frank (who had been promoted to the rank of "master teacher" as a consequence of his MED activities) had an ongoing responsibility to ensure that subject matter in both lower and upper schools included a broad racial and ethnic perspective, and occasionally they even provided intraservice training to teachers in other schools or districts. Their leadership in multicultural education had put the three at the center of public controversy in Markington over how to deal with the city's increasing diversity, and often they found themselves in no-win debates as parents, politicians, and educators pressured them to defend or denounce the Board of Public Schools' attitudes toward its changing clientele.

Despite this highly charged political context, a multicultural approach to learning seemed to be taking hold at Frederick Douglass, with teachers creating themes for lessons that drew from everyday life and spanned all areas of the curriculum. For example, one semester a teaching team had used neighborhood history as its theme, incorporating such activities as interviewing older residents, investigating the origin of street names, and calculating the age of trees. Themes—generally developed by teachers during their lunch hour since this was their only shared release time—might come from a current event or problem in the local community such as a major storm, holiday, or election.

Another vital aspect of the demonstration was its array of so-called compensatory opportunities for parents including parent education, parenting advice, volunteer training, and counseling. As in other schools serving low-income children, parent involvement was quite poor at Frederick Douglass. Only about 30 percent of the parents had any contact with the school during the year, and the exchanges that did occur were generally precipitated by a negative situation. As Patricia Graham (1992) noted, the lack of involvement was understandable among this impoverished group, many of whom were the sole source of economic and social support for their families:

> The issue is not that these children are loved less. . . . These families generally love their children deeply. But in circumstances of poverty it is

extraordinarily difficult to find the additional energy, psychic and physical, to discipline a child lovingly, to work supportively with a child on a project, to spend an afternoon relaxing with a child in the park, to take a child to a museum, to participate in an event at the child's school, or even to read the child a bedtime story or to talk seriously with the child at the child's initiative [p. 48].

Parenting classes at Frederick Douglass (so far attendance had been entirely by mothers) emphasized the importance of such activities to children's success and provided strategies for improving parent-child exchanges. To boost parents' confidence in participating in their children's schoolwork, the librarian had equipped a section in each of the two resource centers with a variety of self-help tools including skill-building kits that could be used at home. An individualized, longitudinal method of evaluation constituted another means of involving the parents, who were invited to attend teacher conferences twice a year with their children to review materials contained in portfolios. The portfolios, which teachers were required to compile on each student, comprised charts for documenting children's development in various areas, samples of work, photographs, and even videotape or audiotape recordings. In addition to providing the basis for a continuing discussion with parents, the designers of the Frederick Douglass program hoped that this open-ended method of evaluation would diminish the tracking of slower students while still providing a means for assessing their long-term growth in relation to specific developmental expectations. However, the ultimate goal of the portfolio—and all aspects of the demonstration program—was to raise scores on standardized tests.

THE STRESSES AND STRAINS OF CHANGE

How difficult it is to make audible the voice of oppression in a choir where privilege controls the resources and accepted tonalities of seeing, knowing, and being. Privilege can make choices and be assured that its choices are possible within existing institutional frameworks. Privilege is free of the need to constantly improvise and get others to attend to a more inclusive view of history. Oppression, on the other hand, is so consumed by the realities of exclusion that it has little energy left to create its own truth or vision of the future. Oppression must use its left hand to pound away at a commitment to somehow eradicate social injustice while, at the same time, using its right hand to leap octaves and gain acceptance into the very institutions that are creating injustice. Small wonder the choir is so lopsided in its performance. Small wonder that it is so difficult for the voice of oppression to initiate and sustain an agenda of social progress [Sutton, 1991, p. 12].

Even in the most ideal circumstances, changing a school environment is a painful process for the staff who undertake it. Administrators must justify the additional support by providing data on student, faculty, and even parent progress—an evaluative process that consumes time and makes everyone feel monitored. Educational innovations also require staff participation in in-service programs to learn new teaching techniques, which consumes even more time while eliminating familiar ways of working. The particular innovations adopted at Frederick Douglass were all quite time-consuming. Thematic teaching required a continuous process of invention and research (as did the short-lived open education techniques of the 1960s), whereas portfolio evaluation meant that teachers were processing large quantities of mismatched materials and, at the same time, keeping track of all the numerical data required by the Board of Public Schools. Most anxiety-provoking was the multicultural focus, which involved teachers in unfamiliar subject matter including the students' neighborhood. And Dr. Johnstone, who seemed more invested in the demonstration's failure than in its success, was relentless in adding bureaucratic regulatory procedures.

Although it was hard to imagine a more informed educational plan than the one at Frederick Douglass, the demonstration was causing no small amount of stress, in part because of Mrs. Driskell's and Dr. Johnstone's authoritarian leadership styles, in part because of the teachers' middle-class conceptions of the school's impoverished students and parents, in part because of the social and physical deterioration that existed outside the walls of the school.

As indicated earlier, Mrs. Driskell had hired only seven of the school's thirty-seven teachers at the beginning of the demonstration project; she had inherited another sixteen (or 43 percent) and hired the remaining fourteen teachers during her six-year tenure. Although the new hires outnumbered long-term faculty, the latter group formed a significant and resistant block whose negative attitudes had a damaging effect on the rest of the staff, especially those new faculty who were not specifically hired for the demonstration. In truth, there were only seven people who were unflappably committed to the demonstration, and that group had three of the school's four minority—and more junior—teachers who were less able to sway opinion.

Three teachers whom I got to know quite well during my visits that year revealed different aspects of the tensions the teaching staff was experiencing. Typical of the new teachers was Mary Quick-to-See, a young American Indian woman who had just moved to Markington. For her, the additional duties and training associated with the MED program presented an exciting opportunity. Not infrequently, she could be found working on a project after school with a few younger teachers who sometimes ended their workday by socializing late into the night. The in-service programs and opportunities for collaboration fired the idealism of this novice teacher and ensured her rapid progress in a challenging, stimulating situation. However, even Mary jokingly referred to Frederick Douglass as a U.S. Marine Corps bootcamp and noted the degree to which her work was overtaking her personal life.

Seasoned teachers, like Frank Johnson, found the military drill less humorous. Frank was one of two African American teachers and one of three male teachers in the school. Privately, he confided his discomfort at being in an "only one" status, simultaneously representing—and being responsible for—all blacks and all males among peers who were practically always white and female. Frank was honored by the leadership role into which he had been thrust, but he was also annoyed by what he felt was excessive scrutiny because of his race and gender. Being a spokesperson and mentor for a group that was so at-risk in the glass-house environment of the demonstration only increased his level of apprehension. Particularly distressing was his role as the master teacher in the MED program, which frequently placed this rather private person under public attack. Markingtonians were considered quite liberal in their views, but the issue of multicultural education had pitted various ethnic groups against the proponents of traditional Western values and, even worse, against one another. Frederick Douglass's program was the object of many black educators' criticisms, who saw it as too mainstream to help black children reverse the legacy of racism. And not infrequently their ire was directed at Frank Johnson.

Whatever Frank's negative feelings might have been, they paled in comparison to those of Gail Forster, a white woman who was fond of reminiscing about the old Mason School in which she had begun her teaching career almost thirty years ago. Beneath her outward willingness to cooperate simmered an inward rage—at being responsible for the performance of children whose parents had so ill-prepared them for school, at having to include multicultural perspectives that she viewed as confusing to the educational process, at having her workload increased at the very moment she felt she had earned a degree of freedom. Whenever I visited Gail's fifth-grade math class, she stopped what she was doing to chat with me about her students, speaking as if they were invisible. She told me how poor their performance had been at the beginning of the year, how hard she had worked to bring them in line, how important excellence was to her, as if to shake off blame for the low scores many of her students would inevitably receive. Gail's conversations with other faculty focused on her sense of hopelessness about what could be accomplished given these particular children and their unstable home environments. Her effect was numbing, even for optimists like Mary.

Those teachers who had negative or ambivalent feelings about the changes in venue were further aggravated by what many teachers perceived as an authoritarian management style on the part of Mrs. Driskell, which, they said, created an atmosphere of mistrust and unwillingness to experiment. Any equivocal feelings about Mrs. Driskell's leadership style were further exacerbated by the ironhanded Dr. Johnstone, whose role was to ensure "standards of excellence and accountability within a context of innovation." A career bureaucrat who used his position to dole out rewards to those who were most compliant, he and Mrs. Driskell actually seemed to have a workable relationship. Yet as Dr. Johnstone's coercive style filtered down to teachers through Mrs. Driskell, it resulted in a social milieu permeated with a sense of insecurity and bearing similarities to that found by Rivlin and Wolfe (1985) in a study of New York City schools:

> Teachers had a variety of fears; loss of control in a hierarchical system in which they could control only the students; poor performance by the children on standardized tests for which they could be blamed; or actual responsibility for children's failure to master academic subjects. They were afraid of the responses of principals or aware of the lack of peer support and even disapproval they received for any innovative attempts. As a result most teachers clung to the safety of traditional approaches [p. 189].

According to Parenti (1978), when salaried workers are divided vertically into specialized positions within large institutions, they tend to feel competition among themselves instead of solidarity against a more distant authority. Divisiveness among coworkers is heightened by differences in ethnicity, race, gender, age, and religion so that "backbiting, bad-mouthing, betrayal, and belligerency become common behavioral patterns" in the workplace (pp. 95–99). Such behaviors dominated the social milieu at Frederick Douglass, creating sharp boundaries between the younger minority and older white faculty while putting Frank Johnson on an island by himself. Teachers seemed to focus their frustrations on each other's deficiencies rather than on the structural causes of what they perceived as an unfair situation. Their fear of being negatively evaluated and the desire to maintain control cast a dark shadow over what was, in theory, a stellar educational program. Instead of the creative, risk-taking behavior that is needed to beat the odds, there was an unstated emphasis on conformity among teachers, students, and parents alike. Instead of the committed camaraderie that is so essential to grassroots empowerment, there was an aura of formality and, at times, ugly resistance. Instead of the delight of teachers engaged in the possibility of making learning more exciting and meaningful for children, there was a pervasive dread of knowing that all efforts would go unrewarded unless their students were able to outwit their birthright and make a radical improvement in their academic performance. Despite the opportunity presented by the MED program to broaden the cultural content of learning, teachers lacked the confidence to really find out about their students' lives and experiences, which were so different from their own. The very understandable insecurities they felt made it even less possible to reach the difficult goal of reversing the effects of the children's demeaning neighborhood environment.

IF I WERE A KID, THAT BUILDING WOULD SCARE ME

Sometimes the outward appearance of a school has relevance to the activities that take place within it; that was so in those first compulsory schools in late-nineteenth century England. It has often been so in New York; even the occasional capture of schools by progressives cannot change the assumptions that underlie their architectural design [Katz, 1975, p. xv].

The first thing scheduled for that day's visit was a tour of a building that could at least intimidate, if not scare, most children. Beyond its massive wooden entrance lay an aging quietness that was in stark contrast to the exuberance of childhood but perversely reminiscent of the deterioration on the streets of Oak Hills. Mister Joe, the building custodian, directed me to what was once the principal's office, now occupied by Mrs. Vallejo so she could be close to the lower school that was housed on the first and second floors. The space was still the main point of entry, overseen by two staff members who directed visitors, answered phones, took deliveries, and so forth. I signed in and proceeded upstairs to my appointment with Mrs. Driskell.

Perhaps her move out of the principal's office was made more palatable by the fact that Mrs. Driskell's newly painted space, shared with Julie (the school registrar), was quite private, spacious, and free of the constantly ringing phone. Yet, it was a long climb up the stone stairs past the high ceilings to the third floor where our tour of the building would begin. Waiting for homeroom period to end, I sat on one of a strung-together row of orange plastic chairs in the reception area, watching absentmindedly as the usual stream of monitors came in and out to perform morning chores. Then, I began to notice all the symbols of a behavior modification approach to learning.

Through the open door, I could see a bulletin board with Halloween decorations side by side with a display of "parents-of-the-month" who had successfully completed a parent education class during May of the previous year. About a half dozen color photos, curled at the edges and in need of replacement, were stapled to the wall in a semicircle around a certificate that was given to parents at the end of each class. Nearby were exhibits of "student stars"; then a locked glass case in the office caught my attention. Seeing my interest Julie explained that children could buy the toys that neatly lined its shelves with tokens that were issued for high test scores or other good (compliant) behavior. Diagonally across from the case was a bench—I have seen it in most of the inner-city schools I have visited—where misbehaving children wait (and wait) to receive their punishment while adult passersby confer shaming looks. At that very moment, a restless boy was sitting on this one, carefully avoiding eye contact while rolling his head from side to side and stretching his body in attention-getting, ostrichlike movements.

Mrs. Driskell emerged from her office and, after she expressed her disappointment at seeing this repeat offender yet another time, we began our tour by reviewing floor plans of the building that were contained in a brochure, *Rules and Regulations at Frederick Douglass.* Despite its nongraded lower school, the cellular architecture inflexibly mirrored the graded school system that took form in 1848 with the construction of the Quincy Grammar School in Boston. Each classroom in Frederick Douglass was about twenty by twenty-five feet and flanked both sides of a dimly lit C-shaped corridor. Communal spaces (administrative offices, gymnasium, resource rooms, science and computer laboratories, lunch rooms) were located in the center part of the C or in the basement.

When the school was entirely graded, a single grade level occupied one of the two wings of every floor, each being served by an enormous stairwell. With two grades neatly layered from left to right on all four floors, the building could be entered or emptied without any mixing of students in different grades. Boys lined up on the left and girls on the right, thus guaranteeing complete social segregation and confirming to children that they should be spatially distinct from those who are different.[6] The new educational program created mixed-age classes on the first two floors, yet remnants of the traditional spatial hierarchies were apparent. The older students still assumed a superior position on the top floor much in the same way that nineteenth-century students assumed a spatial position that expressed their rank in the one-room Lancasterian schools.[7] And teachers still used the conventions of left and right to separate boys and girls.

Mrs. Driskell was acutely aware of the building's limitations in terms of creating two distinct, and more informal, academic programs. As she explained, students in both programs used the same communal facilities, staff were divided between the two administrative offices but handled a given function for the entire school, and some teaching clusters were split between two floors. Making the library function for two schools was limited by the massiveness of the building. Even though the old third-floor library had been replaced by two smaller resource centers located next to each program office, the custodial staff insisted that parent education be held in a basement room distant from these centers to minimize the amount of space used at night. Mrs. Driskell acknowledged that, in addition to these functional constraints, the massiveness of the building simply did not have the intimacy of a small school. On the other hand, she seemed intrigued by the school's history. She was its eighth chief administrator, having won her position after a succession of seven white males whose stern portraits I would soon encounter hanging a bit askew on the molting yellow walls of the auditorium.

We passed by the computer laboratory on the fourth floor where a seventh-grade class was working in pairs, their adolescent hormones kept in check by a blanket of boredom. Rows of children stared up at screens made dim by too much eastern light streaming in through the windows. One girl's chair had been pulled to the front of the room because, explained the teacher, she was disturbing the others. Mrs. Driskell gave the girl a disapproving look and complimented the others for being on-task; then we headed next door to the environmental science lab where a sixth-grade class was gathered around projects that were sitting on a deep windowsill. The teacher began to account for her students being out of their seats but Mrs. Driskell interrupted: "I know that you are an excellent teacher, so why don't we close the door just till the children get settled."

We headed downstairs, Mrs. Driskell moving smoothly as if she were balancing a Grecian vase on her head. She pointed out four long, skinny rooms that were squeezed in between the groups of classrooms on each floor. One was always a teacher's room that was unused except as a toilet (teachers preferred to eat in their rooms where most kept their lunch utensils). The others were variously used for meager stores of ancient-looking photocopying equipment, office supplies, books, and audiovisual aids. On the first floor, the front door had been locked for safety, and Mister Joe was monitoring it while mopping the twelve-foot wide hallway, which was deserted except for a girl and her father, both with heads bowed and eyes lowered as they listened to admonitions from the girl's teacher.

In the basement, a long, dark auditorium was placed to the side with its own entry from the outside. In the front rows, small children were chanting to the animated drumbeats of Frank Johnson's junior counterpart, a diminutive, dashikied music teacher whose assignment was to develop cultural awareness during his weekly session with each of the school's twenty-seven classes. The entire lower level reeked of institutional food, and it was difficult to distinguish between the beating of the drums and the clanging of pots and pans as we left the auditorium and headed toward the lunchroom. The room was quite small because the building had been built at a time when most children lived nearby and walked home to eat. To accommodate the larger service, children in both programs picked up their trays in the lunchroom, then filed into one of two playrooms to eat under the jovial supervision of Mister Joe and his all-black custodial staff. Each room seated only about 150 students, so lunch was served in two shifts with two grade levels sharing one room. A few children went home for lunch and others (the so-called "teacher's pets") ate with teachers in their classrooms, leaving an almost manageable number of children in each of the eating spaces. Unlike most cafeterias in inner-city schools, which are physically inadequate and generally hated by children, these rooms were quite pleasant, with brand-new round tables for eight and a notable absence of teacher supervision. When I asked Urban Network participants to identify their favorite place in the building, quite a few students picked the lunchrooms.

Even without an art teacher on staff, extreme care had been taken to create an esthetic environment in the corridors and classrooms. Two-dimensional artwork of fairly high quality neatly lined every available surface, several permanent murals had been painted with the assistance of local artists to depict such persons as César Chavez and Sojourner Truth, and colorful multinational flags faced each other across the high ceiling of the gymnasium. Yet, everything seemed a bit too neat—more in keeping with behavior modification than with the artistic enterprise. Like the attempts at beautification I had seen in the surrounding neighborhood, that were dwarfed by widespread deterioration, the teachers' efforts to impose a livelier multicultural atmosphere were swallowed up by the aging architecture. Despite the display of colorful drawings, what stood out were fifteen-foot-high ceilings, massive exit signs, and floor-to-ceiling oak woodwork surrounding doors and transoms. The strongest impression was created by dark woodwork and faded green walls made even more putrid by the glare of skinny strips of florescent lighting, the smell of fresh poster paints overwhelmed by the mustiness of old plumbing, peeling plaster, and an aging steam heating system.

THE SPACES OF REGIMENTATION

The building tour ended in Noreen Clark's social studies class, where I would assist with teaching an Urban Network lesson to each of the three fifth-grade classes. Her room was more spacious than most because its rectangular dimensions were extended by one of those round turrets I had noticed on the exterior. Like most teachers in the school, Noreen missed the opportunity this niche afforded for creating a more private study area, barricading it instead with her desk and a stack of supplies. She had arranged the remaining area with four clusters of six desks, each with a seventh (and frequently occupied) desk for anyone who misbehaved—a seating arrangement that oddly reflected the duality of the school's educational philosophy, combining authoritarian classroom management with the open-ended techniques associated with thematic, cooperative learning. As in the computer lab, a single desk was placed at the front of the room for anyone who persisted in misbehaving, inadvertently providing the culprit with an ideal stage for acting out.

Although the room had huge windows, the space was dark because a few of the florescent tubes, which were mounted high on the ceilings, had burned out, and because the dirty windows admitted little natural light. Everything about the room appeared old—its faded green walls, its dark woodwork lacquered with many layers of varnish, its row of letters hanging above the blackboard (they seemed to be of the same genre as those that were in my own elementary school). Noreen had arranged a neat display of children's work from previous years including a collection of papier-mâché masks that sat on a ledge above massive dark wooden cupboards. On the blackboard was a schedule for the day and, right next to it, a chart listing the children's names with spaces for different colored stars that could be earned for various accomplishments, a combination of which yielded a token for purchasing toys from Mrs. Driskell's locked cabinet.

At the beginning of the year, each cluster of students selected a family name for itself from a list of states. Noreen often spoke to the "Ohioans," "New Yorkers," "Californians," and "Washingtonians" as a group ("We won't be able to go to lunch till the Californians are ready"), but most assignments did not require the groups to function as a team since to do so would have violated the school rule of keeping children quiet and on task. However, as soon as Mrs. Driskell left the room, classroom decorum fell apart. The students were clearly anticipating my visit and, despite Noreen's shouts for order, began calling out, waving, and getting out of their seats to make personal inquiries about the day's plans. Noreen apologized for her class's unruliness and suggested that

I go say "hello" to the other two groups as she began issuing warnings to regain control.

When I entered Mary Quick-to-See's language arts classroom—also dark and aging but with more lively decorations than Noreen's room—a discussion was in progress among children who were seated at desks arranged in a square around the perimeter of the room. Mary was sitting at one of the child-size tables, but (as if not quite able to break with her training) her position was clearly at the head of the room, directly in front of the blackboard. Seemingly less perturbed than Noreen by the gaiety that erupted, she drew me into the discussion to answer questions about the day's game plan. Having assured the students that I would work with them later in the day, I proceeded next door with the assistance of two enterprising students who successfully convinced Mary that I needed a guide.

Both children quickly abandoned me at the threshold of Gail Forster's math class, where I found students lined up in silent rows, bodies slumped over a paper-and-pencil task in a room that was so bare of materials that it appeared uninhabited. Gail stopped the daydreaming that was in progress and announced that an "important" guest had arrived. Contrary to the other two groups, the children responded as Jacqueline Jordan Irvine (1990) suggested that they would—with blank faces that mirrored the repressiveness of the environment they were in.

REINFORCING THE CULTURE OF POVERTY

Many educators speculate that low-income black children bring to school a set of antisocial behaviors and traits that emanate from a culture of poverty. They rationalize their harsh treatment of these children by citing instances of an undisciplined and unstructured home life, a lack of positive male models, an early exposure to crime and delinquency, and a disrespect for adult authority figures. This victimization approach ignores other important factors such as teachers' stereotypes; attitudes about race, class, and gender; and the degree of teacher subjectivity in dispensing punishment equally [Irvine, 1990, p. 17].

On the surface, the disciplinary code at Frederick Douglass, which was written by parents and staff shortly after Mrs. Driskell became principal, was an attempt to avoid the victimization approach. Mrs. Driskell believed that a code would minimize bias in dispensing punishments and make teachers accountable for their decisions regarding the seriousness of a given incident, parents accepted any scheme that would improve their children's lives, and Dr. Johnstone enthusiastically supported any form of bookkeeping. When misconduct occurred, teachers were required to give students a chance to modify their behavior by informing them in advance of the penalty a given transgression would evoke. A detailed set of rules helped teachers to decide the terms of issuing particular punishments, all being fully documented in the recipient's portfolio. As was evident during the building tour, physical separation of children was a primary technique. Anyone who went beyond a specified limit was further separated by being sent to the office with the possibility of being suspended or, as a last resort, transferred to another school. According to the children, getting kicked out of school was not the most heinous punishment; rather, it was when parents were forced to take off from work to attend a conference because they had misbehaved, especially if parents lived at a distance from the school and were without transportation.

Despite its well-intentioned goal of fairness and accountability, the disciplinary code added endless hours to an already enormous amount of bookkeeping and made teachers seem more like wardens than instructors, especially Mr. Johnson, who was not infrequently called upon to assist with older boys who were repeat offenders. As Bowles and Gintis (1976) explained, such approaches to classroom management seemed to distance teachers from students and took away their power to make decisions independently:

> The once highly personalized authority of the teacher has become a part of the bureaucratic structure of the modern school. Unlike teachers in the chaotic early nineteenth-century district schools, modern teachers exercise less personal power and rely more heavily on regulations promulgated by higher authorities. . . . The very rules and regulations that add a patina of social authority to his or her commands at the same time rigidly circumscribe the teacher's freedom of action [p. 39].

Nor were strict rules limited to students. On the first day of classes, children took home the *Rules and Regulations* brochure, which was anything but encouraging of parent participation. Written in stilted, commandmentlike language, it contained a list of the behaviors that were required of both parent and child, and even the punishments that could be expected for failing to obey the list. And although Mrs. Driskell had increased the number of parents visiting the school from 30 to 40 percent in the last year, their primary reason for coming there was to participate in enforcing the disciplinary code. Such a coercive approach to classroom management seemed all the more unnecessary since the children seemed comparatively polite and well behaved. Of course, there were name-calling exchanges, pushing contests, and even fistfights. However, there was no extreme behavior such as rapes in the toilets, use of weapons to resolve conflicts, or physical assaults on teachers to justify the degree of control that perked down to the children from the indisputable authority of Dr. Johnstone. The outcome was to ensure children's assimilation of a top-down approach to power in which praise goes to those who are most adept at playing by the rules of the game. In combination with the toys that could be earned for good test scores, the *Rules and Regulations* specified the terms of the patriarchal contract at Frederick Douglass.

NOTES

1. Meier, Stewart, and England (1989) attribute the lack of effectiveness of the 1954 *Brown* v. *Board of Education* ruling to (1) a Supreme Court that provided loopholes that local school officials used to circumvent segregation; and (2) black parents who preferred segregation over placing their children in hostile environments. Even after the 1964 Civil Rights Act made it possible to withhold funds from noncomplying districts, schools found ways to maintain racial isolation. For a discussion of the persistence of educational inequities, see Chapter 2: From separate schools to desegregated schools. In *Race, Class, and Education: The Politics of Second-Generation Discrimination*.

2. According to the 1990 Census, 20 percent of the U.S. population has a college degree and only 24 percent has less than a high school education, placing Oak Hills far below the national average.

3. In a book documenting the relationship between race, class, gender, and poverty, Goldsmith and Blakely (1992) wrote:

> The burden of poverty falls disproportionately on women with children, especially on African American women with children. Women head 10.9 million families, 7.4 million with children. Of these families, 43 percent are poor; just over half of these poor, female-headed families are white, just under half are minority [p. 38].

4. Bowles and Gintis (1976) presented data indicating that educational attainment and economic success are not related to IQ, but to parental socioeconomic status and noncognitive personality traits such as orientation to authority, discipline, and internalization of work norms. See Appendix A in *Schooling in Capitalist America*.

5. For a discussion of the organization of nongraded education, see Goodlad and Anderson (1987), Chapter 4: The nongraded school in operation. In *The Nongraded Elementary School: Revised Edition*.

6. Meier, Stewart, and England (1989) explain how students are additionally sorted into homogeneous groups according to ability and through the use of disciplinary actions, both of which are clearly associated with race. In their book *Race, Class, and Education: The Politics of Second-Generation Discrimination*, they wrote:

> Within the regular curriculum, ability grouping is used to sort students according to academic potential. At the top of this spectrum are the

honors and gifted classes; at the bottom are remedial classes. . . . Different academic groups receive vastly different educations, with the greatest resources and the highest-quality education provided for the highest academic groups. Schools also use disciplinary actions to sort students. Corporal punishments, suspensions, and even expulsions seek to encourage students to conform to school rules and regulations. Those who fail to do so are sorted out via expulsions. . . . The sorting practices of schools are associated with racial disproportions [pp. 4–5].

7. In these schools, as many as 1,000 students were seated in rows in one large room. On a daily basis, they were advanced toward the front of the room or demoted toward the rear according to their performance on assignments.

3

The Chosen Ones

Despite its diversity, the term *suburbia* calls to mind "a place of free-standing single-family homes with lawns where everyone is white, middle class, and has children" (Palen, 1995, p. 101). Sociologist David Hummon (1990), who attempted to unravel people's attitudes towards different types of communities, found that suburbanites tended to characterize their neighborhoods as clean and quiet with open spaces and access to nature. Suburbanites saw themselves and their neighbors as being interested in family life and children, and believed that their communities were places where children could get a good education within an environment of freedom and security. What differentiated cities and suburbs—in suburbanites' view—was safety, which in turn allowed them to realize a family-oriented existence. Curiously absent in their descriptions was any mention of race or housing segregation even though many of them lived in racially homogeneous communities (p. 120).

San Lupe epitomized the white, middle-class, family-oriented suburban community where the distant issues of race and segregation were left unspoken. And Gardendale Science and Technology Institute, the largest of San Lupe's three K–6 elementary magnet schools, was a magical fit with its surroundings. A model of the clean, safe, and open suburban school where it is hard to imagine anything amiss, this rather large building appeared small—somewhat like a gingerbread house—with its various wings nestled almost invisibly into the landscape. Begun in 1924, the two-story brick structure had been added onto twice, the truncated C shape of the original building graciously stepping back from the street to accept a lush, green lawn and silvery white flagpole.

Arched openings, deep recessed entries, colorful ceramic tile inlays, and sloping red clay tile roofs all mirrored the classical Spanish architecture that was found throughout this affluent suburb of 19,500 people. Although this portion of the school had been constructed just five years after the Mason School in Oak Hills, it had none of the sense of deteriorating impenetrability that Frederick Douglass had. Instead age had added character—like an old wine or a vintage car—and the freshly painted multipane windows confirmed that the school was as well kept as the surrounding neighborhood. The brightness of the exterior carried to the inside of the old portion of the building in which a fifteen-foot-wide corridor borrowed light from classrooms via broad transoms, the doors at either end left open to the breezes of San Lupe's temperate climate.

In 1948, the communal spaces that had been housed at opposite ends of the old building were enlarged and relocated to two new extensions built on either side of the rear of the structure, changing the C to an I shape. The renovated south side faced out to a thirteen-acre wooded site that bordered the San Lupe Lagoon—a treasured nature area for both children and adults. In 1966, when the school board decided to consolidate the district's seven smaller schools into three larger ones, a new building was constructed in back of and parallel to the original one so as to create a large courtyard. Although this structure was built in the flat-roof modern style of that era, it blended comfortably with the existing ensemble. The links between the new and old buildings served as entries, the east one for children and visitors, the west one for staff and service deliveries to a small kitchen located in the basement of the original structure.

The consolidation of schools that had occurred as family size decreased meant that travel time to each of San Lupe's three elementary schools was increased for many children, but it was still a manageable distance to Gardendale from anywhere in the area. About 75 percent of the students were dropped off by a parent or nanny, others walked or rode bicycles as evidenced by the overflowing of eighteen-speed mountain bikes and helmets that were piled against a bike rack next to the east entry (for those few children who were without a means of transportation, the school provided a van for door-to-door delivery). Although consolidation meant that students were drawn from a larger geographic area, the socioeconomic homogeneity of Gardendale remained intact. San Lupe was 96 percent white[1] with the average household income—solidly six figures—being bolstered by real estate assets and capital gains. The area directly around the school (where most students lived) was 97 percent white, with Asians being most of the few persons of color.

As a group, Gardendale's parents were as extraordinarily well educated as Frederick Douglass's parents were uneducated. Eighty percent of the fathers and 72 percent of the mothers had undergraduate degrees; 55 percent and 25 percent of fathers and mothers, respectively, had graduate or professional degrees. As might be expected with this educational level, parental involvement in the school included practically every family (there were virtually no single-parent households) having some form of contact with Gardendale's teaching staff during the year. Among the members of the Parents Association were physicians, professors, attorneys, architects, bankers, business persons, and so forth—many of whom were second-, third-, or forth-generation professionals. In recent years, this group had made a number of major contributions to the school including purchasing audiovisual equipment, renovating the library, refurbishing the school playground and, this year, creating an outdoor science laboratory. The presence of successful parents who held high expectations for their children's futures seemed to have as much, if not more, impact on the culture of Gardendale as its educational program and teaching staff.

If Frederick Douglass's students were unlikely to encounter middle- or working-class persons, so were Gardendale's students unaccustomed to any realistic contact with economically disadvantaged persons or with middle-class persons of color. The costly express buses to San Lupe made it a dubious destination for anyone without a private car, limousine service, or bus pass provided by a well-to-do employer. Practically all the persons of color whom the children encountered were uniformed servants—out of context, on their turf, and in a dependent situation. Some of these domestics could fit in with the norms of this upper middle-class community, others could not. When behaviors did not gibe with the children's perception of ordinary life, their reactions usually were similar to a ten-year-old's observations of a family servant, as quoted by Coles (1977) in *The Privileged Ones*:

> The poor woman [the maid] doesn't look very good. She weighs too much. She's only forty, my mother thinks, but she looks as if she's sixty, and is sick. She should take better care of herself. She said my sister and I make big messes in the bathroom. But that's because we *use* the bathroom! And her breath—God, it's terrible [p. 382].

I would learn later that viewing domestics as deviant meant that the students at Gardendale had an exaggerated view of what an impoverished life was like. Influenced by the media's excessive reporting of sensational events, they would project images of extreme violence, drunken people, and gangs of youth marauding in garbage-strewn streets. I would also learn of their enormous fears about the harm this "other" existence might bring them.

In addition to the perspective provided by servants and the media, Gardendale's staff provided another glimpse into the outside world. As was the case at Frederick Douglass, the staff were in stark contrast to the student body. Although Gardendale's teachers were of comparable educational status to the students' parents, many were first-generation professionals, their economic rank was far lower, and they lacked the mannerisms and style of affluence. Frederick Douglass's teachers would not have chosen to live in the devastated streets of Oak Hills, but Gardendale's teachers could not afford to reside in San Lupe since private homes averaged over a half-million dollars and only one-fifth of the dwelling units were rental (at a median cost of $834 per month). Thus, both Frederick Douglass and Gardendale teachers were working out of context in socioeconomically homogeneous situations from which they were apart—the former group being in a superior position to students most likely to fail, the latter in an inferior position to students most likely to achieve. Whereas teachers at Frederick Douglass were attempting to help their students beat the odds, those at Gardendale were well-trained servants, facilitating their students' progress along an ensured route to success.

A MILIEU OF SELECTIVITY

These [privileged] children learn to live with choices: more clothes, a wider range of food, a greater number of games and toys, than other boys and girls may ever be able to imagine. They learn to grow fond of, or resolutely ignore, dolls and more dolls, large dollhouses and all sorts of utensils and furniture to go in them, enough Lego sets to build yet another house for the adults in the family. They learn to take for granted enormous play-rooms, filled to the brim with trains, helicopters, boats, punching bags, Monopoly sets, Ping-Pong tables, miniature tea sets, stoves, sinks, dining sets. They learn to assume instruction—not only at school, but at home— for tennis, for swimming, for dancing, for horse riding [Coles, 1977, p. 26].

To attract the district's best students Gardendale had to mimic the spirit of exclusivity and abundance the children experienced at home, which was accomplished by creating an aura of high-powered energy and choice in mapping out one's day. Having above-optimum enrollment with 865 children divided into six classes per grade level, the school boasted the highest ratio of resource teachers in the district. Augmenting its classroom teaching staff of forty-two were another fifty-five persons who were specialists in math, science and technology, reading, art, music, computers, library, physical education, nutrition, and speech. Although Gardendale students scored well above average on standardized tests, there were always a few children in need of special instruction. For this purpose, four specialists were available to teach "independent development classes for those students who were unable to participate at the level of their peers."[2] A varied menu of enrichment activities (some free, others offered for a fee) were held both before and after school, extending the curriculum with advanced classes in math and science but also including such offerings as swimming, ballet, French, or music and art appreciation.

Officially class size at Gardendale was limited to a maximum of twenty-four, but in reality the average was about sixteen children per class with academic subjects being taught to groups of two to eight or nine children, except for reading in the early grades which was one-on-one. Although the classroom teacher was the choreographer of the day's activities, most instruction occurred in small specialized groups that formed around the interests and abilities of specific students who were guided by classroom and resource teachers. Thus, a child's social group at Gardendale was not a constant as it had been at Frederick Douglass. Rather, the relationships among individual students and teachers were fluid, and frequently children had to compete for acceptance into a particular activity by citing their qualifications in a letter of application. Through this procedure students learned to identify and promote their special characteristics.

In 1979, the San Lupe Unified School District implemented magnet schools throughout the area primarily to ensure its attractiveness to parents who might opt for private schools (despite the exemplary education offered in the district, only 63 percent of the district's students attended public school), but also because of the prevailing interest in specialized education. Given the national concern about the lack of scientific and technical knowledge among youth and, in particular, the need for helping girls to feel more competent in these areas, a technological focus was the first choice among parents and educators for a magnet offering. Mr. Bob Regon, hired as director of science and technology for the district, secured a federal grant of $893,000 that was expanded by contributions from parents. The funds were used to support the efforts of a consortium of educators and advisers (including parents) from the business and university community. Over a three-year period, the Science and Technology Consortium (STC) defined the content, pedagogy, and evaluation procedures for linking two of the district's schools, Gardendale and Tall Pines, a grade 7–12 selective public high school. The STC's activities included overseeing the hiring of new faculty who could contribute to their long-range vision of the magnet program and the piloting of various curricular innovations in each school.

The science and technology curriculum that evolved drew on the everyday experiences and concerns of students, using San Lupe and its proximity to the lagoon as a laboratory for studying the positive and negative effects of technology on nature. During extensive in-service training, teachers gained a historical perspective on how wildlife, plants, and people in the area had adapted to one another, and they developed a variety of day and overnight field trips to introduce students to science and technology through environmental concerns. Such issues as recycling, pollution, transportation, and energy conservation served as themes for all areas of learning. Despite the goal of making the subject matter more accessible to girls, the STC had thus far endorsed hiring an all-male team of teachers to implement the curriculum. There were only five male faculty at Gardendale, three of them making up the entire science and technology staff, the other two men being physical education teachers.

TEACHERS BY COMPETITIVE CHOICE

Whenever Dr. Marion B. Marcus, the school's principal, was questioned about the concentration of men in the technical areas, she turned the potential criticism into an opportunity to boast about the high degree of selectivity for teaching positions at Gardendale. There were never fewer than two hundred applications for each available position, and sometimes the response was as high as three hundred. All hires were made through a rigorous screening process that not only involved review by the consortium but a peer evaluation. Once hired, new faculty members were offered a wealth of options to ensure their continued growth as members of the Gardendale community. Junior faculty were matched with more seasoned teachers in a formal mentoring arrangement, and a number of other informal sources of support happened spontaneously. For example, this year a group of teachers from Gardendale and Tall Pines who were interested in poetry were meeting at a restaurant in the city once a month to discuss women poets. They had developed a bibliography for their meetings and sometimes invited a professor from the University of Markington's Department of English to attend. Financial remuneration for such efforts was not insignificant, coming through direct compensation and merit increases in salaries. Not infrequently did the Parents Association sponsor a particular activity by providing a stipend to cover the group's expenses. Dr. Marcus exuded confidence about the high quality of Gardendale's teaching staff, and her outlook was certainly supported by evidence of a vibrant collegial atmosphere.

The degree of professionalism among teachers was no surprise given the competition for positions and the numerous perks that were offered to them including a wood-paneled teacher's workroom equipped with a half dozen computer terminals, a teacher-to-student ratio of approximately 1:9, numerous financial incentives, and a general milieu of respect. To ensure the continued performance of her faculty Dr. Marcus supervised the publication of a quarterly newsletter documenting the activities of teachers as well as students and parents. Mrs. Betty Rayburne, a would-be writer with whom I would work and one of Gardendale's most exemplary employees, had been featured in the last issue when one of her short stories was included in an anthology published by a popular press. Having taken a furlough while her children were young, Mrs. Rayburne was honored to have been hired at Gardendale ten years ago after only one year back on the job at another, less prestigious school. Traveling an hour and a half both ways from the blue-collar suburb where she lived with three teenage sons and a plumber husband, she was responsible for mentoring two new faculty members. Despite her responsibilities at home, Mrs. Rayburne was never caught short in earning continuing education credits, preparing for classes, or meeting a parent's demand for special attention while consistently working on her own writing.

Her demonstration of discipline was unmatched except perhaps by Mr. Regon, who, having found one of San Lupe's rare rental apartments, made himself available throughout the day and evening to the constituencies of Gardendale and Tall Pines. A boyish-looking, impeccably dressed single parent of a toddler, Mr. Regon was eager—anxious, even—to succeed in his first administrative position. Unlike the feared Dr. Johnstone, he appeared more like a well-trained aide, on call to facilitate the efforts of Gardendale's staff who were, in turn, on call to parents. At the same time, Mr. Regon was enlisted as a ceaseless emissary of goodwill, responsible for elevating the status of public education in an area where parents demanded that children be well prepared for the finest higher education and employment possibilities. His relationship to the Gardendale staff was part of a class-based pecking order among parents, children, staff, and the district that was the exact inverse of the one I had observed at Frederick Douglass, a pecking order in which parents, not the district, were the overseers of professionals. Parents' role at Frederick Douglass was one of inadequacy—as persons who needed basic instruction in parenting. In contrast, mothers and fathers at Gardendale were clearly leaders in the school, furnishing daily lessons in the exercise of power and authority. And Mr. Regon was the technical assistant who made their role go smoothly.

Though masked by gentility, the social distances between the levels of the school's pecking order seemed even greater at Gardendale than at Frederick Douglass because of the emphasis on the educational credentials of the various faculty and administrators, and the subtle—and not so subtle—pressure to continue advancing one's career. Even though there appeared to be official sharing of authority through peer evaluation and mentoring, the aura of competitive excellence that hung over the school gave Dr. Marcus a chilling power-over teachers and solidified the remoteness of their ranks. Their position of servitude to well-to-do parents whose children would have far greater opportunities than their own also confirmed their lesser position and, for some, created a sense of frustration about their role as educators. Ms. Jane Andre, the art teacher who would be coordinating the Urban Network program, was one such teacher.

Jane was a painter whose large canvasses dealt with the social ills of Limone, a farming community with a large population of migrant farmers where she lived, located just fifty miles up into the mountains that surrounded San Lupe. Even though she had some stature in the artists' community, Jane's own farming background stood out as an oddity among the other, more outgoing and stylishly dressed teachers. Furthermore, Jane was the only unmarried, childless teacher at Gardendale and was at a loss to contribute to the exchanges on family life that were the main discussion in the teachers' workroom. Many of her colleagues were clearly uncomfortable with Jane's artisan style and wondered aloud how such a "laid back" person had ever gotten through the hiring process. This attitude filtered down to the children, who seemed simultaneously fascinated by and put off by her difference. In a milieu where social conformity to the standards of the upper middle class was in contradiction to the emphasis on developing individual talents, perhaps they intuitively understood Jane's embodiment of one of the paradoxes of their privilege. Certainly, she did not measure up to those unspoken codes that would gain them access to positions of power; yet, she seemed to exemplify the magic of a creative spirit—a person who had enough power-from-within to follow her own vision. At least, so it seemed.

WHERE LIFE WORKS OUT FOR THE BEST

It was the beginning of October when I first visited Gardendale. Mr. Regon was waiting on the steps at the east entry as my car pulled up, a smile on his face that was as bright and pleasant as the day itself. Since we had talked several times by phone about the Urban Network, my day would begin right away with an orientation to the school. Mr. Regon helped me to sign in and secure a visitor's pass—something that seemed as out of place in this genteel setting as the security monitor that was strapped to the ceiling of the principal's office. Occupying a good portion of the center bar of the original building, one entire wall of this cheerful space faced onto the courtyard with enormous multi-paned windows providing a sunny backdrop for children's mobiles and a homemade plant collection. Low partitions formed two comfortable work spaces for four staff persons and a receptionist who shared her desk area with the coffee service. Making sure I clipped the large orange plastic visitor's pass in a visible place, Mr. Regon served me a cup of freshly brewed coffee and whisked me past the refreshments and through the open door of Dr. Marcus's office.

A plump woman with curly gray hair highlighted against a bright plum-colored suit, Dr. Marcus greeted me with piercing blue eyes and a quick smile. She stood up from behind a carved antique desk over-flowing with papers and extended her short arm for a handshake in one energetic, welcoming move. After a bit of polite conversation about the weather ("It rains so often this time of year—I'm glad you have a nice day") and the University of Michigan ("One of my nieces went to school there. She just *loved* it"), Dr. Marcus launched into a brief overview of the school's educational approach. The curriculum was focused on individualized instruction, and teachers were encouraged to pursue a variety of innovative projects in the classrooms. Each child was treated as a unique person with special talents. I would find, she emphasized, that Gardendale's mood was warm and friendly but highly structured in standards of dress, deportment, and performance for teachers as well as students. Without question, it was assumed that students would graduate with the academic skills as well as the personal characteristics, aspirations, and self-concepts that would ensure their success. Gardendale was a total child-centered learning environment in which children were introduced at an early age to the rewards of deferred gratification.

Behind Dr. Marcus's mask of gentility, I sensed her unrelenting expectations for perfection as she explained the rigor of the social and intellectual milieu. Although the students were only on the first rung of the climb into their inherited social class, the grooming for conformity that sociologists Cookson and Persell (1985) observed as a vital force in America's elite boarding schools[3] seemed to have already begun. A different sort of disciplinary code than Mrs. Driskell's, Dr. Marcus used the "carrot" of maintaining one's privileges rather than the "stick" of not improving one's lot. Because privileged children have daily confirmation that "good" behavior will yield a good life,[4] and because the aspirations of the school culture and the aspirations of the child's family are in sync, this carrot generally is quite effective.

> A child whose parents are poor or of working-class background may have heard a mother or father (or, rather often, a teacher) say that anyone can be President in this country, or rise to the top of a company, or become a doctor, a lawyer, a "success"—given "hard work." But the child has seen and heard much evidence to the contrary. The child has seen his or her parents curbed, scorned, exhausted, frustrated, embittered. . . . In contrast, privileged children, far fewer in number, are destined for quite another fate. . . . Life works out "for the best," mostly—and one has a right to conclude that if one has had ample confirming evidence [Coles, 1977, p. 396, 399].

Dr. Marcus was quite clear in laying out the ground rules for my performance during that meeting. Having been well briefed on who I was, she laid out her expectations for my relationship to the school. The Urban Network appealed to her, she explained, because architecture was an unusual profession that not many people knew about although one of the active participants in the Parents Association was an architect. Because architecture was both a science and an art, she felt that the program could open up an exciting new dimension to Gardendale's magnet offerings and noted that there were several sixth-grade students who had shown talent in drawing and would benefit from my tutoring. My primary responsibility would be to equip Ms. Andre with the skills she would need to continue an innovative program in the future after my one-year visitation period. When I explained that a variety of talents could be incorporated into an Urban Network activity from drawing to sewing or public relations, Dr. Marcus assured me that the teachers would make sure I got the very best students for whatever activities Ms. Andre and I were planning. What I should realize is that Gardendale's policy was to give students as much individual attention as possible, so I should expect to be working one-on-one or in small groups. Even though I would be introducing teachers and students to exciting new concepts, I should respect the school's policy that work be initiated by individual children.

Her pleasantly stated, uncompromising ground rules complete, Dr. Marcus repeated her welcome and directed Mr. Regon to show me around the building before taking me to my first class. The sprawling building was quiet, filled with calm busyness and small groups of children using brightly colored instructional materials on carpeted areas under the watchful eyes of teachers. We walked up to an unfinished attic underneath the eaves of the building's original section; this space would be developed next summer as a computer-assisted learning laboratory because the smaller classrooms (900 square feet in the renovated spaces and 700 in the original building as compared to 615 square feet in most rooms at Frederick Douglass) in this part of the school could not accommodate modern equipment. Small groups of children would come to the laboratory with a resource teacher to work in carpeted areas that would be specially designed for their height and grasp. Underneath the attic on the second floor were housed the third and fourth grades along with the teacher's workroom and an adjoining large storage area, both directly above the principal's office. The first and second grades shared the first floor with the principal's office and a lounge area by the front door.

Because of a dropoff in the land, the kindergarten rooms could be tucked into the lower level of the original section of the building, each with a direct opening onto a fenced-in play area flanking the east wing. The remaining part of that level contained a number of large communal spaces including a skylit multipurpose room underneath the courtyard, which was entered via its own grand staircase from the lounge area. The lower-level hallway was lined with students' art projects that had been executed on fine art papers and were displayed in an almost gallerylike fashion. As we passed by several workgroups, Mr. Regon said hello to the teachers and students by name as he was reminded of various special school functions to which he was invited. At the end of the corridor, Mr. Regon opened the doors of two high-ceiling spaces to reveal sensual feasts that would engage the imagination of any child. Facing one another across the hall were the music and art rooms, both stuffed with all the necessary ingredients for learning to appreciate the finest aspects of Western civilization—shiny instruments, photographs of ballerinas, compact discs of classical music, paper models of famous buildings, and glossy picture books such as Jansen's *History of Art*, among other stimulating instructional resources.

Inside the art room, five children were diligently painting many small posters under the supervision of Mr. Joshua Frank, a physical education teacher who was also coordinator of a newly implemented conflict resolution program. At Mr. Regon's prompting, Mr. Frank explained that the children had been elected by their classmates to serve as peer mediators for disputes occurring during the midmorning recess. His job was to provide the mediators with clear guidelines for resolving disputes while making the rest of the students in the school aware of the mediation process. The posters, all replicas of imagery contained in Mr. Frank's conflict resolution manual, advertised the mediation team ("When a fight starts, call for help! See the Mediators") and defined the expected behavior ("Don't retaliate. Mediate a win-win solution"). The guidelines and rubber-stamped posters, which seemed more akin to token participation than to the child-initiated involvement that Dr. Marcus had just described, seemed to confirm the existence of a patriarchal contract at Gardendale, albeit in a very sophisticated guise.

At most schools, lunch is normally the time when fights occur, but not at Gardendale. Here parents (mothers) were encouraged to prepare lunch for their children at home and most did so, leaving the school's tiny dining room to those few children who were without stay-at-home mothers or nannies. Although educated well in excess of the national norm, a large majority of Gardendale's upper-middle-class mothers were not career-oriented, choosing instead to exercise their talents and training for high-powered volunteerism in the school and in the broader community. That morning a number of congenial moms were overseeing not only the social, but the intellectual and economic life of the school, adding a certain level of civility and further reducing the already low adult-child ratio. Some were facilitating small study groups, others were in the hallway baking aromatic sweets in little portable ovens, still others were discussing fund-raising initiatives or escorting children through an experiential history museum that had been installed in one area of the library.

Through their presence, all these women seemed to be furnishing a lesson more powerful than Dr. Marcus's all-male science teachers. In addition to authenticating the female role of nurturance, these grown-up debutantes also seemed to be confirming the limitations of less well-to-do teachers to transmit the values and cultural capital of their class. If gaining a sense of collective identity is a necessary part of learning to justify one's superior status, as Cookson and Persell (1985) proposed, perhaps these mothers were offering their children an introduction to the feelings of social distance—in this case from lower-status teachers but eventually from any persons who might undermine their right to dominance—that are a prerequisite to maintaining asymmetrical power relationships.

BRIDGING DIFFERENT WORLDS

The fifth and sixth grades were housed in the 1966 flat-roof building at the far end of the courtyard, which held Gardendale's largest rooms (960 square feet), arranged on both sides of a tall, skylit corridor. The sixth-grade students had the choicest spot in the entire school—rooms with deep windows along the south facade of the building looking out to a spectacular view of the lagoon. Most teachers had arranged a collection of houseplants in this space, providing a delightful backdrop for children's daydreaming. On the opposite side of the building, flush windows of the fifth-grade rooms faced north to the courtyard through a row of coniferous trees—also quite a pleasant outlook. A thick wall lining both sides of the corridor contained wooden bookcases and cubbies that were interspersed with child-height wooden seats and colorful pillows. Above this built-in storage area was a transom that brought sunshine into the classrooms from the skylit corridor. A wet area containing a water closet, slop sink, and coat rack linked two 30' × 32' classrooms and provided the exit to an outdoor work area. All the rooms in the new building had four or five computer workstations that adjoined the storage wall, and each pair of classes shared a fully equipped media cart that could be rolled to wherever it was needed, making these large spaces seem comfortably overflowing with technological gadgetry.

Of the six sixth-grade teachers, only Miss Barbara Moore and Mrs. Betty Rayburne had expressed an interest in working with Jane on the Urban Network program; three of the others were overbooked with numerous enrichment activities, and the sixth person had release time to participate in a teacher development program. The low rate of participation was not unusual given the school's policy of involving teachers in many different activities so as to offer children a range of competitive choices. Although Mrs. Rayburne and Miss Moore had been assigned linked rooms at the beginning of the year because of their intention to participate in the program, there seemed to be very little exchange between the two teachers, who each had a distinct way of working with their students.

Miss Moore's room looked somewhat like a small library, its centerpiece being a movable loft situated toward the rear of the room by the wet area. Constructed as an intricate beehive that offered personal carpeted spaces at several different levels, it would have served a vital need in the crowded, regulated classrooms of Frederick Douglass. At Gardendale it was simply an added amenity in the spacious and individuated environment of the school. A large imitation Oriental carpet that Miss Moore had purchased from a secondhand shop in the city covered the open area where four round tables were arranged, each with its own low storage unit overflowing with supplies. The blackboard—unused for writing—was covered by richly colored travel posters from Japan, India, Mexico, and other faraway places that Miss Moore hoped to visit some day. A thirtyish Ph.D. student in communications arts, Miss Moore had some degree of notoriety as producer of a weekly ten-minute radio spot on teenage health issues in which she presented commentaries by University of Markington faculty on such controversial topics as AIDS, abortion, and homosexuality. Not unlike Frank Johnson, Miss Moore found herself treading a narrow path between presenting diverse viewpoints (a mandate of the station for which she worked) and holding up the "family values" that were so important in the Gardendale culture.

Mrs. Rayburne's room was divided into four quadrants by a low, pinwheel-shaped shelving unit made of blond maple-veneer wood. A talkative and somewhat nervous women in her early forties, Mrs. Rayburne had constructed the unit herself with assistance from her plumber-husband and three sons—an indication of the degree to which she attempted to bridge the two worlds in which she lived. Above the shelving unit danced larger-than-life cardboard cutouts of characters (dubbed Mrs. Rayburne's Ruffians) posed in various stances, all wallpapered with bib overalls, red checkered shirts, white neckties, and red shoes. In addition to adding an air of joviality, the hanging figures provided greater privacy for the four work areas they overlooked. Children in Mrs. Rayburne's room were clearly not intended to meet as a class, but to work independently in these cordoned-off study areas.

As I would hear on numerous occasions, neither Miss Moore nor Mrs. Rayburne was without her share of stress. Yet, theirs seemed distinct from that experienced by Frederick Douglass's teachers because they were at Gardendale by choice, and the pressures of their day most likely derived from a high-powered drive to distinguish themselves in a privileged situation. Conversely, most teachers at Frederick Douglass were there by assignment, their tension probably resulting from the excessive regulation of an institution that was considered deficient. The commonality between teachers at both schools seemed to be that they were communicating to their students, though in different ways, a sense of dissatisfaction and need for having something else—something more than what they had. As Wachtel (1989) noted: "It is not what we have that determines whether we think we are doing well, it is whether we have *more*—more than our parents, more than we had ten years ago, perhaps more than our neighbors" (p. 17). At Frederick Douglass students had to improve their performance to catch up with the growing demands of mainstream society, and the increased education that teachers were held accountable to deliver made them, as well as the students and parents, seem inept and devalued in their day-to-day lives. At Gardendale, children had to achieve more to maintain their status in an upwardly mobile society, and the increased education their teachers were competing to offer involved all parties in a frantic race to keep ahead of all those other people who were trying to catch up. Neither group seemed to be at peace with where they were. Neither group was engaging in an activity that could be indefinitely sustained since increasingly higher levels of education would be needed to fuel the spiral of catching up and staying ahead.[5]

THE CARROT OF MAINTAINING ONE'S PRIVILEGE

Miss Moore's sixth-grade class was organized so that ideally it would model a democratic society by the end of the year. Each year, she asked students to agree on a name for their "society," designate its locale and climatic conditions, and evolve their own system of governance. At the beginning of the year, the society was an autocratic one, with Miss Moore playing the role of dictator. As the year progressed, students were to realize they could increase their power and demand better conditions by organizing into tribes. This year, the students had christened themselves the Geeks who inhabited a place called Ant Artica. When Jane took me into the room that first afternoon, three tribes (the fourth was involved elsewhere in another activity) were going over a homework assignment that children were to complete in preparation for my visit. Miss Moore was chastising Laura for not having done hers (apparently Laura's second transgression this year), and Justin had been put on notice once more for doing sloppy work.

Miss Moore drew us into the discussion, explaining that Jane had assisted the children in making diaries, which they would use to write "many, many wonderful essays about their neighborhood." Last night everyone was to make the first entry—a short story about spending a day in San Lupe. Toward the end of the class, each tribe would make a small presentation of their essays—an ingenious scheme that Miss Moore had worked out with Jane for allowing the children to introduce themselves to me—but today's class time would utilize my expertise, drawing. Miss Moore would continue to provide individual consultations on the homework assignments while Jane and I helped each tribe to create a large drawing of a favorite street in the neighborhood. Perhaps because it was only the second month of school, progress toward democratic decision-making was not yet evident. As the more vocal children began dominating the discussion of what to draw, Miss Moore asserted her role as dictator and reminded the teams in a pleasant but stern voice that they were to be quiet and hard at work.

Miss Moore sat at her desk and began calling children, one by one, for consultations on their essays. Joining my first group, I could overhear her supportive but demanding feedback as she prodded children to think harder and explain their point of view with greater specificity. "Think about what you are saying here. Does that make any sense?" "This is a great idea but you need to push it a little more. Don't be a such lazy thinker." "Remember what I told you about the first sentence of an essay? What's wrong with your first sentence?" Correcting spelling, grammar, punctuation, and even style, each child was first given positive feedback followed by explicit instructions for improving the next assignment.

In this air of professionalism, I settled into working with a tribe of two boys and two girls, all eleven years old, who were engrossed in drawing an elevation of a street containing large detached homes. Jane already had told me quite a bit about this pre–World War II suburb, so their drawing had an air of familiarity. I knew that the Village of San Lupe, which was the largest of the three sectors that formed Greater San Lupe, had developed around a turn-of-the-century stucco railroad station, now converted into an elegant restaurant since the town was no longer a stop along the new high-speed track. Unlike those suburbs built in the postwar era, when unlimited expansion conceded the countryside to sprawling development and multiple-lane express highways, San Lupe was compactly laid out. Initially, most village residents had been able to walk to the train station or to the shops that were clustered along the perpendicular street that bridged over the railroad tracks.[6] Gardendale was situated in San Lupe North about three miles from the Village's center. This sector was the most affluent one in Greater San Lupe and had the oldest, most elegant homes in the municipality, although by modern standards, they were on very small lots. Almost half of the land in this sector was still undeveloped and wooded, giving the area a parklike feeling. San Lupe East, which bordered on the gulf, was the least affluent of the three sectors with the smallest lots and the most rental properties; however, the entire area still numbered among the wealthier suburbs in the nation.

I mentioned to my tribe that I had been told that San Lupe had a number of sectors and wondered if their drawing represented a street in the northern part of the area. Justin, plainly the leader, nodded, proclaiming that it was going to be a picture of Forest Avenue where the very best homes in the whole town were located. Claudia (the only black child in the class) and Laura giggled; Justin and Peter jostled one another as each child deliberated which markers to choose from an elaborate watercolor set. As they drew and became increasingly absorbed in their work, there began a halting, introspective conversation, as so commonly occurs during hands-on artistic endeavors:

Laura	I'm putting in the trees along the street . . . ver-y big trees . . . lots of bushes . . . won-der-ful flowers.
Claudia	What I like is that it's so-o quiet around here. . . . Sometimes I think we're the only ones here. . . . I hope we will never have to move.
Laura	This town is so-o nice and so-o pretty. . . . I wouldn't want to leave here . . . ever.

Justin	(Standing up to interrupt the introspection of the drawing process). I'll bet someday you *have* to move, and you're going to move to a gang neighborhood.
Peter	(Putting down his marker). Well *we* could move to L.A. for really complicated reasons. It might be one of the nice towns with pure air . . . or maybe it could be the RI-OT CI-TY.
Justin	I'll bet someday Claudia *has* to move to a gang neighborhood where there's lotsa pollution.
Claudia	(Invoking parental assistance to overcome Justin). Mother says that it's not true that bad things could happen. I will always have a nice home and many friends. Now get back to work, you guys!

Toward the end of an extended and very intense session, Miss Moore interrupted. "Class, we have only twenty minutes before school ends today, so please get seated quickly in our discussion circle." The children fitted their chairs into a small circle just inside the area made by the four tables. "Now, which team would like to make the first presentation?" As children read their individual essays and held up their team drawings, Miss Moore corrected their pronunciation and pushed Jane and me to be more specific in providing techniques to improve the drawings. The essays—most of them a full page—were carefully scribed and, in several instances, quite imaginatively framed. Two of the three drawings qualified as absolutely exquisite, one being boldly colored, the other being in pastels, both presenting the neighborhood in a highly fanciful manner.

Jane and I collected the work and went to her art room to lock up for the day. We matched each of the drawings that had been done by the three teams with the essays written by the children on that team, and soon we could see definite themes, especially with respect to safety, privacy, and spaciousness. Two of the drawings contained detailed images of San Lupe's rather modest commercial establishments, which seemed odd since the outdoor environment was so distinctive and since a number of studies call attention to children's fascination with nature.[7] Jane recalled Justin discussing his lengthy essay with Miss Moore. He had been quite specific in describing a variety of high-technology items to "improve what San Lupe had to offer"—a push-button park ("Push a button and out pops whatever you want"); flying cars that work on batteries; mechanical grass ("You can make it grow wherever you want it"); a moving walkway between the bathroom and the bed; a built-in machine that does your homework ("It's on your head connected to the spinal cord and brain so we don't always have to be so dumb");

voice-activated mechanical servants to bring you whatever you want ("We need robots so we don't have to do anything"). Miss Moore had intervened in Justin's long-winded elaboration of his essay to ask whether he might not become overweight with so many robots, especially since there was so much good food in San Lupe. Justin had assured her that he would exercise ("But not doing chores. Just fun kinda game exercise").

On the way to Jane's house, where I would stay that evening, we continued to talk about these drawings and essays, wondering what they were telling us about the children's perceptions of how the world should be. Unquestionably, they were keenly aware of San Lupe's existing amenities and could readily be engaged in imagining an even more commodious environment, but the children's fascination with material goods and high technology made us wonder what values they would bring to the positions of leadership that lay ahead in their future. Would they be able to conceive of the struggle for mere survival in impoverished existences if their norm was a gadget-filled consumer lifestyle? Would they be able to imagine themselves as a distinct and privileged minority within a multicultural society if their norm was a white upper-middle-class existence? How would their isolation in an environment of exclusivity and entitlement shape their perception of persons who were culturally different from or less well off than themselves? How can a sustainable society ever be achieved if these and other privileged children grow up to write or support legislation that ensures their own consumptive, technologically sophisticated lifestyle despite evidence of increasing despair among the masses of have-nots?

CULTIVATING PARTNERS IN THE PATRIARCHY

> Community ideologies enable some individuals to define a community identity: a sense of being a city person, a suburbanite, a small-town person, or a country person. Within the ideological context of a shared perspective on community, people are able to identify with places . . . [and to] characterize themselves as having particular personal qualities, drawing on shared conceptions of community residents to elaborate conceptions of self [Hummons, 1990, p. 40].

The portrait that Miss Moore's class had painted of itself mirrored their upper-middle-class suburban environment and the values that created it. Their conceptions of self, gained in part through their reading of their surroundings, will enable these children to maintain their privileged lifestyle of material goods, occupational success, and political power. Being isolated from others in an environment with few, if any, constraints is their first step toward developing the strong sense of entitlement and expectation for access to the positions of stature that most of these children will inevitably attain. This birthright will give Gardendale's students a great advantage in gaining control of major corporations, nonprofit organizations,[8] and the media. These positions of power will, in turn, increase their likelihood of exerting control over the lives of Frederick Douglass's graduates—their future housing, neighborhoods, jobs, education, healthcare, way of life, and perhaps even their conception of reality.

What roles were teachers at Frederick Douglass and Gardendale playing in intervening into the community identity of their young charges? What concept of "other" children were Gardendale's teachers helping their students to acquire, given their seclusion in such a socially and economically homogeneous suburb? Since Frederick Douglass's students will grow up thinking that their lot is deficient—at odds with the norms of a good life—were their teachers helping them to distinguish what is of value in their own culture and what is destructive in mainstream traditions? If schooling is an antidote to the negative influences in children's lives, what were teachers at both schools doing to counterbalance the negative effects of poverty or affluence on their students' existence? Are the programs of cultural awareness and compensatory parent education at Frederick Douglass enough to inspire those students' leadership in countering mainstream norms and bringing about a less materialistic, conserving way of life? Are the conflict management program and Miss Moore's demonstration of democratic principles sufficient to ensure Gardendale students' social activism in the powerful positions they will most likely inherit?

What role was the physical environment of the schools and their surrounding neighborhoods playing in shaping their students' community identity? For the children at Frederick Douglass, the aging building could have been a refuge in an otherwise threatening world, a place that was kept locked and mopped by the reliable Mister Joe—elevated by the sheer force of Mrs. Driskell's elegance and dignity. As is true in many low-income communities, Frederick Douglass was more commodious than most of their homes (more than a few children were homeless, many others were living doubled up with other families, and most of the neighborhood's housing was substandard) despite the building's crowded conditions. Their classrooms were less menacing than the streets of Oak Hills and many students at Frederick Douglass seemed to have an unusual sense of connection to their community, perceiving amenities that an outsider would overlook. Even though teachers used space as a punitive measure, despite the disciplinary code and the children's negative assessment of their schooling experience, both the school and neighborhood constituted very significant elements in the children's worldview. After all, this is where they spent their entire lives since vacations or even trips to other parts of town were rare. One of Noreen's students—a boy named Shawn who had lived in the same apartment building since he was an infant—described how he would miss his neighborhood and even the school if he moved from a place that most people would assume was uninhabitable.

> If I was moving, I would be mad because I like Oak Hills. I would have to leave my friends. I would miss my friends. I would miss baseball and basketball. I would miss Oak Hills. I would miss my apartment. I would miss even Frederick Douglass even though some of the teachers are mean. I wouldn't be happy at all. I would be very sad.

For children at Gardendale, the comparatively well-equipped school was one of many amenities in their lives, which also included homes filled with fine woods, untold equipment, and servants. Despite the plethora of courses and enrichment activities offered at the school, they had many more opportunities for learning outside of school, especially through foreign travel. And the freedom of choice they had for directing their own classroom activities paled in comparison to their options as consumers in San Lupe's uptown or as adventurers in the nearby lagoon. Since these children were widely traveled, most had a rather detached view of San Lupe and Gardendale, which were among the many places they frequented. They valued the neighborhood's assets, but they also had knowledge of many other situations and frequently saw mobility as advancement. As Charles, a student in Mrs. Rayburne's class, explained about a move his family had made a few years earlier:

> Once my mom and dad were thinking about moving because my dad was looking for an offer on a better job and more money than his old job. So he asked my older sister and I where we would want to live if we moved someplace else. I said Japan because I would like to live in a different culture than the USA. My sister said Hawaii because it's warm there and a lot of water is there to go swimming. My dad said: "Thanks for your opinions."
>
> The next year we ended up moving to Japan because my dad got a job as a business man. I met a lot of new friends at the International School and so did my sister. We ate a lot of different food and did a lot of different things and shopped in many different stores. Then the next year we moved here to San Lupe. Moving isn't so bad after all.

The Gardendale children's global perspective came into play as they responded to my pretest questionnaire. "If you were the principal of Gardendale, what one thing would you change?" elicited responses ranging from getting robots to tutor children to going to the opera or

on a trip around the world. The best places that children in both Oak
Hills and San Lupe identified were taken from their own experiences
but these experiences were vastly different. For the former group, they
included the ice cream parlor, the circus, the baseball stadium, a friend
or relative's house, and many mentions of their own city, neighborhood,
and homes. For the latter group, responses included France, Spain, the
Grand Canyon, Disney World, Hawaii, Hollywood, Yosemite Park, and
also quite a few mentions of their own neighborhood, homes, and very
elaborate rooms. Whereas the worst places identified by Oak Hills
children tended to be things that they had experienced firsthand (you
will see that many identified Frederick Douglass as the worst place),
most Gardendale students focused on things they knew about indirectly through the media or through dinner-table conversations with
parents. Sometimes students chose the Third World countries that were
being discussed in the news as threats to democracy (Haiti, Cuba,
Panama, Ethiopia), or, as Claudia wrote: "The worst place is . . . well
I've never been any place that wasn't nice."

Thus Oak Hills and San Lupe seemed to have different meanings for
their young residents. One group was more contextually bound to a
school and community that, despite its state of deterioration, elicited a
full range of positive and negative emotional responses; the other was
more detached from their local surroundings since they had the economic wherewithal to sample the good life in many other places. Yet, it
seemed that neither of these life-spaces was instructing children in the
roles and behaviors that are required in a sustainable society—neither
was enabling them to develop a community identity based on a sense
of shared responsibility for one another and for the Earth. Although
Shawn was committed to his deteriorating community at age twelve,
he would soon learn that his connectedness with that place would also
bring the stigma of failure, lack of choice, and perhaps even a premature
loss of his life. Surrounded by a landscape of decay, it might be difficult
for him to evolve an ethos of sacredness toward the Earth. Though
larger than life in Shawn's mind, Oak Hills contained few of the messages that are needed to comply with a middle-class conception of
success. Its decay and material conditions would restrict his mobility—
his willingness to venture into the unknown—and distance him from
the affluence that is the dominant culture's measure of human worth.

Conversely, Charles's global outlook and understanding of community as a rung on the ladder of success would confirm that he can leave
the disadvantages (or destruction) of a particular place behind by
moving on to something better. Able to sample the benefits of lavish
environments, he might find it difficult to realize an ethos of conservation toward nature or comprehend how extravagance by a few results

in misery among the many. With material possessions providing concrete proof of his own worth as a person, he would have little reason to question his participation in the domination and oppression of those persons who are without such possessions. Shawn might be diminished by an inability to project himself into a mainstream lifestyle, Charles by a lack of social awareness and commitment to a specific locale.

NOTES

1. Despite increasing numbers of middle-class blacks in suburbs, nationally suburbs are still 95 percent white.

2. Unlike at Frederick Douglass, such terminology as "remedial classes" or "low-achieving students" was studiously avoided at Gardendale.

3. In describing the hard realities of being socialized for a position of privilege, Cookson and Persell (1985) wrote: "The external gentility of the schools often masks an incredibly demanding and sometimes unforgiving life style. . . . Students discover that power and pain are inseparable and that to a large degree the price of privilege is the loss of autonomy and individuality" (p. 19).

4. As reported by Bowles and Gintis (1976), a national study of non-Negro males from nonfarm backgrounds, aged 35–44, revealed the powerful effect of socioeconomic background on future economic success. They wrote:

> Indeed, there is a strong independent association between family background and economic success. . . . For the large national sample represented there, children of the poorest tenth of families have roughly a third the likelihood of winding up as well-off as the children of the most well-to-do tenth, even if they have the same educational attainments and childhood IQs [p. 141].

Thus, even if the children at Frederick Douglass could rise above their environment, they still were still far less likely than the Gardendale children (who were surrounded by expectations for success, wealth, family connections, and upper-middle and upper-class lifestyles) to reap economic rewards.

5. Wachtel (1989) made the point that the comparative value of education has decreased as people are required to obtain more years of schooling to achieve the same advancement in economic status:

> It must be acknowledged as a sad truth that for many people education is more of a cost than a benefit. And for this rather substantial group, the effect of making education more widely available by a process of growth has been to increase the effort required to get ahead, to place greater rather than less obstacles in the path of economic advancement [p. 25].

The frustrating illusion of growth weighs especially heavily on poorer persons who have the fewest resources to overcome these increasingly steep obstacles, especially in light of the widening economic gap between the rich and the poor.

6. Wynne (1977) and others have argued that older, pedestrian suburbs had less of a negative effect on human relations than the newer auto-oriented ones, which are designed for a homogeneous group of home buyers and built around a shopping center (see pp. 6–8 in *Growing Up Suburban*).

7. Moore and Young (1978) asked eight- to twelve-year-olds to map their favorite places around their home and neighborhood, then coded the elements in the maps. In describing their results, they wrote: "Perhaps the most impressive finding is the collective rank of natural systems, accounting for just over a quarter of the aggregate mention rate. Nature evidently has a powerful presence in the world of childhood" (p. 107). In contrast, only 4 percent of the mentions were of commercial establishments. Their findings were supported by an earlier study in which Lukashok and Lynch had asked adults to remember childhood spaces, suggesting that "the natural environment is one of the crucial continuities in human life, giving adults a recollected 'grounding' in their childhood years" [ibid., p. 111].

8. Data collected by Cookson and Persell (1985) on 289 leading secondary boarding schools showed that "for everyone in all categories of educational background, having high social origins was positively related to attaining high corporate positions" (p. 196). Furthermore, women's volunteerism ensured a parallel control over private institutions that men enjoyed in corporations and nonprofits (see "Chapter 10: Preps at play in the power structure" in *Preparing for Power*).

Learning Compliance, Learning Leadership

The story of how the Urban Network program began at Frederick Douglass and Gardendale not only offers insight into the different positions of teachers and students at these schools, it foretells the possibilities for a successful completion of the year's work. At Frederick Douglass, the program was brought in by Tom Mintz, a professor at the University of Markington who had encountered three of the school's teachers at a required in-service activity; at Gardendale, the program was initiated by Jane Andre, an enterprising art teacher who recognized the need for carving out a unique niche for herself in the school's science-oriented curriculum. In both cases, the Urban Network was accepted because of its fit with a special initiative in the school, but at Frederick Douglass that initiative had been framed by the principal and a team of educational consultants who devised an intervention into students' deficient performance; at Gardendale parents had played a leadership role in determining a magnet offering that would add to the distinctiveness of the school. Thus, whereas the Urban Network was associated with an enforced requirement to improve performance in one situation, it was connected to an elected chance to excel in the other.

Because of this fundamental difference in motives, the timing of activities and utilization of resources occurred in a very different manner at each school. At Frederick Douglass, Tom and I used up an entire site visit in September to obtain permission for implementing the program so that classroom sessions did not begin until October. The nature of the work was determined by us, with teachers being assigned by Mrs. Driskell to a rather passive apprenticeship role. At Gardendale, sessions began in September after Dr. Marcus encouraged a voluntary teaching team to plan a program that would utilize the Urban Network to address a particular interest in the school. By the end of the previous year, that team had already received funding for this program from the STC. When I arrived at Gardendale for the first time in October, my role was to provide input on work that was well underway. The differential capacity of teachers (and students) at Frederick Douglass and Gardendale to control what happened to them during the course of a school day continued throughout the school year. In one school, Tom and I assumed the role of "experts" who were needed to work out the day-to-day details of *our* program; in the other, I was a resource person who helped participants to implement *their* program. At Frederick Douglass, the participants' degree of dependence on Tom and me and their sense of ownership for the work affected their ability to complete a major project during the second semester. At Gardendale, a major project was carried off and added a new dimension to the students' yearly display of successes.

The following is an account of the events that led to implementing the Urban Network at both schools as well as what transpired during my visits to each school that first semester.

BEGINNING THROUGH LAYERS OF BUREAUCRACY

Like many cities across the nation, Markington had its share of racial disturbances during the early and mid-1980s. As these tensions erupted within the university, an Office of Multicultural Affairs was formed to address what some activist faculty and students referred to as institutional racism. Among other efforts, this office created the Multicultural Education Development (MED) program, in which Frederick Douglass was participating, and also provided support for faculty to design courses that would take university students into the city's public schools. Tom Mintz, a professor of city and community planning, was among the first group of faculty to receive funding, and that is how he met the Frederick Douglass teachers.

Tom had proposed a course called Citizen Participation in the Planning Process, in which "first-year urban planning students will teach low-income children techniques for environmental assessment, project development, and action-taking. The process will help the children to be effective citizens while making them aware of a nontraditional career. At the same time, it will allow the urban planning students to gain a first-hand understanding of problems experienced in low-income communities and to foster a sense of social responsibility for addressing those problems."

During July, Tom attended an open house at MED to look for an elementary school in which to implement his course. One of about a dozen presenters, he explained to the attendees (including the three teachers from Frederick Douglass) that the classroom teacher and his urban planning students would determine the exact nature of class-room activities, but in general children would be involved in identify-ing a problem in their neighborhood for which they would project some solution. For example, suppose the children decided that a street corner needed a stoplight: they might find out what agencies controlled the installation of streetlights and petition them. His students would come to class every week or so and show the youngsters how to read maps and do other things that urban planners do, and the university would provide a small amount of money for such things as photography, photocopying, and various other materials. What he needed in return was one or more teachers who would be willing to work with his students on a community planning project and who could follow through on weekly assignments. When Tom offered his business cards, Mary Quick-to-See reached for one, saying she was fascinated with the community-focus aspect of his proposal.

After class, Mary intercepted Frank Johnson and Anne Bassett to canvass them for their interest in Tom's proposal. Over a cup of coffee at a nearby sandwich shop, the three soon agreed that the course concept fit well with their thematic approach to multicultural education and that the urban planners could give them some real expertise in the type of neighborhood history project that teachers had tried earlier. Frank was especially drawn to Tom's career-development angle and the possibility of having more male role models in Frederick Douglass's mostly female-headed classrooms. Since Mary was the most interested in working with Tom, Frank suggested that she telephone the other two teachers in her grade level to discuss the idea. Pending their interest, he would approach Mrs. Driskell, who would most likely have to get permission from Dr. Johnstone. Her spirits somewhat dampened by a glimpse of the red tape that lay ahead, Mary graciously accepted Frank's assurances that, as master teacher, he would help her navigate any hurdles. Even though she would not be able to make a commitment, Mary decided to telephone Tom the very next day to describe Frederick Douglass's curriculum and reaffirm her interest in participating.

Tom responded favorably to Mary's call, explaining that he had done some volunteer consulting a few years back in Oak Hills and even thought that he could recall the location of this particular school. His course would certainly match aspects of Frederick Douglass's demon-stration so the school seemed to be a real possibility. However, as the summer months flew by, Tom procrastinated on selecting a host site until the fall when classes were in session and instead focused his attention on developing the syllabus. One day, while perusing his professional publications for materials, Tom happened across an article on the Urban Network and telephoned my office for more information. After an extended conversation about our two programs, in which we uncovered numerous mutual acquaintances and interests, the idea occurred to us that we could work together at Frederick Douglass. After all, collectively we seemed to have all the ingredients for success—an enthusiastic teacher who was part of a teaching team; a school curriculum incorporating multicultural, thematic learning; my instructional program with its tested activities; Tom's on-site expertise and cadre of students; and the university's purse to cover materials for the children's work. It was also advantageous that Frederick Douglass was a neighborhood school so that our work could be focused on a discrete geographic area—a situation that was becoming less and less likely to find given the proliferation of magnet schools in urban areas. Since the Urban Network was a year-long commitment, the teachers and I could build the children's planning skills and ability to work in teams through short projects in the first semester, thus preparing them for the more expansive activity that Tom's students would implement during the second semester.

Seeming to be old friends and a bit euphoric about the serendipity of our conversation, we agreed that I would send him an instructional portfolio and he would send me his course proposal, an exchange that solidified our mutual interest in working with each other. Since Tom was in Markington, he took the lead in making the initial contact with the school, explaining to Mrs. Driskell his previous encounters with Mary. Mrs. Driskell recalled that this idea had come up in a discussion with Frank Johnson and suggested a meeting with the two of us, Mrs. Vallejo, and herself for the beginning of the school year. Once the administrators had agreed on our being at the school, Tom and I would be able to talk to Mary and the other teachers about specific classroom activities.

A MATCH MADE IN HEAVEN

Deciding to go to Markington during the second week of the school term was probably a mistake, but Tom and I were hoping to get approval for implementing our joint venture so that Urban Network activities could start by mid-October. I had sent an instructional portfolio to Mrs. Driskell via overnight mail with a letter recommending that interested teachers and staff review its seventeen-minute videotape before our meeting to ascertain the suitability of the program to their

needs. Tom also had sent his course proposal along with some information on the university's outreach program. He and I had wanted to get
together beforehand, but both of us were completely inundated with
work due to the beginning classes at our own colleges, so a suitable time
could not be arranged. We decided to meet outside the school just before
our appointment and hope for the best.

After a brief wait in the reception area, during which time Tom and I
quickly planned our approach, we were ushered into Mrs. Vallejo's
office, a long and narrow, high-ceilinged space that was the old
principal's office. Mrs. Driskell was already there, seated on a love seat
that faced a dingy institutional-blue wall, which Mrs. Vallejo had attempted to enliven with a Guatemalan wall hanging and drawings done
by her second-grade daughter. It was lunchtime and Mrs. Vallejo was
unwrapping a tray of homemade sandwiches, which she placed on the
coffee table, explaining that the only food that could be ordered in was
from a nearby McDonald's. Positioning two old-fashioned oak chairs
for us next to the turquoise plastic love seat, then pulling her own
wooden chair from behind her desk, she sat down and the meeting
began. As Tom and I helped ourselves to lunch, we began to realize that
no one had reviewed our packages of materials, nor did Mrs. Driskell
have a clear recollection of having received them. While Julie searched
the upstairs office for the missing parcels, I launched into an overview
of the Urban Network and its relationship to Tom's course.

Both efforts, I explained, were intended to provide children with a
better understanding of their neighborhood while helping them to feel
more empowered to influence it positively. The Urban Network program would begin in the fall with hands-on projects lasting three or four
weeks. Children would practice working together in small groups while
learning discrete principles of how neighborhoods function as social
and physical spaces. Tom and his urban planning students would arrive
in January and continue using the Urban Network structure to guide
the children through a process of identifying a problem, then planning
and realizing a solution. Depending on how things went, a number of
exciting projects might result, for example—.

Mrs. Driskell interrupted to say that she had been wanting someone
to make some banners for the school's entry, then suddenly both administrators pounced on how these programs would improve the students'
academic achievement. The children were very low achievers, they
explained via a well-rehearsed script, who could not afford to spend
time on activities unless they directly contributed to their academic
achievement. Could we ensure the children's improved performance?

Seeing Tom's arms fold across his chest out of the corner of my eye
and wondering about my sanity in deciding to fly to Markington when

I should have been preparing my own classes, I struggled to remain cheerful. Unfortunately, I responded, no one could guarantee that programs such as ours would enhance the children's academic skills since few systematic studies had been done. However, many people around the country had informally observed that environmental education programs brought a sense of excitement to a school. The Urban Network's unique strength was in helping young people learn about the environmental conditions that impact on their lives and in putting parents into a leadership role. In this particular situation, the program would complement the school's use of thematic learning and its portfolio approach to student evaluation. In other schools, the activities had unquestionably added a positive dimension to the children's experience of schooling, but I could offer no proof of improved academic performance.[1]

Unfolding his arms and leaning forward, Tom interjected his own passion about what could come out of our involvement with the school. The children would be introduced to a new cast of characters who could make them aware of other ways of working, they would be engaged in making some practical improvements in their surroundings, they would have the experience of feeling that they could make a difference, *and* they would learn about a career that was extremely relevant to low-income urban children. In addition, just consider what the children would be contributing to his students. Seeing that he had caught Mrs. Driskell's attention with that remark, Tom launched into his sales pitch on the value of community-service learning at the university level. Coming to Frederick Douglass would force his students to demystify urban planning concepts and communicate in a straightforward manner; it would engage them in giving something of themselves, which meant they would get something in return; they would learn that knowledge does not always come from so-called experts but can come from people in the community. . . . Sensing that Tom could go on with this argument ad infinitum, Mrs. Driskell interrupted once more.

She recalled that the artists-in-residence who worked with children on a set of murals created quite a lot of excitement and, yes, children did complete their classwork despite this added activity. She was intrigued by the possibility of using urban planning as a theme for their multicultural lessons and acknowledged the importance of this being a project that teachers had sought out. And it would be wonderful if the project created some banners to reinforce the goals of the demonstration. Mrs. Driskell and Mrs. Vallejo began to discuss a possible strategy for getting Superintendent Johnstone's approval ("If we say that the program improves the environment of learning, perhaps he will agree to it"), but Tom reminded them that his course was part of an officially sanctioned program between the university and the Board of Public Schools. They need only explain that our joint venture was an extended application of the university/K–12 collaboration, which would result in children having a heightened exposure to a beneficial experience. It would give the Frederick Douglass children access to expertise at not just one, but two universities. Nodding and taking a few notes, Mrs. Driskell began considering the nature of the fifth-grade teachers' participation.

Although it was Mary who had spearheaded the partnership between Frederick Douglass and Tom, Mrs. Driskell was concerned about her lack of experience. Given Noreen Clark's seniority, her previous experience in curriculum development, and her subject matter—social studies seemed the most appropriate context for a community-based project—she was the best person to take charge of the project. Depending on the teachers' wishes, all activities could take place in her social studies class or they could occur across all three classes, but, yes, Noreen should definitely coordinate. Tom and I looked at each other and silently shrugged in a mutual agreement not to make an issue of Mary's leadership. Glancing at Mrs. Vallejo for her support, Mrs. Driskell used the public address system to summon Noreen to the office. Soon a sturdy, intense-looking woman in her mid-forties, who would have been just as comfortable working the fields of a farm as she was in this inner-city school, appeared in the doorway. Mrs. Driskell apologized to Noreen for interrupting her lunch, introduced Tom and me, then explained her new assignment. Clearly confused at being asked to coordinate an effort that had been Mary's idea, Noreen stuttered to object, but Mrs. Driskell assured her that Mary could have an important role with the children. However, her organizational skills were absolutely necessary to the success of this program. Noreen soon acquiesced and offered me her phone number so we could plan our first class session. As for Mary, neither Tom nor I would know for sure how she felt about having her role usurped by Mrs. Driskell since there was no time during the rest of the year to speak privately with her. In retrospect, we guessed that we had missed an opportunity to have a truly committed program coordinator and regretted that, in our anxiety about whether the program would be adopted, we had chosen not to intervene on Mary's behalf.

WHERE DISCIPLINE OUTSTRIPS DELIGHT

Noreen and her colleagues decided that all three teachers would take turns teaching the weekly Urban Network lesson during a double period in their specialty subject. One week, activities would be taught in relation to language arts, another in relation to math, and so forth. They would get started two weeks before my first session with the children in October so they would be oriented and I would have something to build on. Mary would have the pleasure of introducing children to the program in her language arts class, but Noreen would be the person to work with me during my visits, her assignment being to transfer the knowledge gained in our sessions to the other teachers.

After reviewing the options for short projects in the Urban Network instructional portfolio, the teachers elected to begin with a series of exercises called "The Good and the Bad" that involve students in critiquing the assets and deficits of their community. Noreen and I had several telephone conversations about how that lesson might be pursued, and I soon realized the degree to which classroom activities would be constrained by the school's educational policies. I had proposed a series of activities beginning with a neighborhood tour and culminating in a single class project to not only heighten the sense of community within the class but to increase the children's collective problem-solving skills. Noreen insisted that this approach was inappropriate since children frequently were absent or changed schools altogether, would not be able to concentrate on a single idea over a period of weeks, and were too unruly to work together on a class project. Certainly, the teachers could not be responsible for taking children out into the neighborhood, which was overrun with crime. We would have to think in terms of stand-alone lessons around the theme of good and bad neighborhoods, preferably with tasks that could be completed by individual children for their portfolios. As a compromise, we agreed that students would work in teams on the day I came since it would be difficult for me to have a hands-on exchange with each child.

Given these parameters, Noreen and I developed an outline for a sequence of activities. Mary began the program with a language arts lesson in which students imagined themselves as good or bad buildings in the neighborhood, then wrote poems in the voice of the building. Gail continued the next week with a math lesson, asking the students to draw what they perceived as the boundaries of the neighborhood on a map and measure the area circumscribed. The lesson that Noreen and I planned would focus on the subject of what makes a good or bad neighbor. We agreed to teach the lesson together, with Noreen leading the discussion portion of the class and me guiding the hands-on portion. Noreen would engage the children in defining the concept of "a neighbor" and in talking about their neighbors in Oak Hills. She would ask the teams at each table to write slogans describing the good or bad qualities of these neighbors, then I would show the children how to turn their slogans into posters by creating visual images to reinforce the written words. I had brought along photocopied photographs of various urban neighborhood scenes so students would have a choice of making their posters by collaging images or by drawing.

As I walked back into Noreen's room that too-warm October day following the building tour with Mrs. Driskell, I remembered that I had left my shopping bag of supplies in her office, sitting on the floor next to the orange plastic chairs. I raced downstairs to retrieve it and, in the few moments before the first class was to arrive, squeezed examples of brightly colored, beautifully designed posters onto the blackboard next to the day's schedule. Noreen seemed nervous and pressed me to clarify our work plan. How would we distribute materials and in what order? Did I bring enough paper in case some children needed a second sheet? How much time would we allow for each step? She emphasized that it would be difficult to allot additional time if students did not finish the assignment since there was no leeway in the schedule. Realizing how much more casual my teaching style was than Noreen's, I sat down and wrote out a timetable, silently reminding myself not to get sidetracked by any serendipitous opportunities.

Gail's homeroom students soon filed in and progressed through the project exactly as planned with minimal engagement, either positive or negative. They wrote slogans (or got Noreen to write one) that simply repeated what had been said earlier during the discussion period, then mechanically picked out a photograph and got my approval that it would work for their slogan. One team took my suggestion to alter or combine the photographs (no one responded to the idea of drawing their own image), but the others simply glued down the whole picture and lettered in the slogan, one or two children doing all the work while the others absented themselves from time and space. The activity was completed, posters were neatly stacked into the supply cabinet, materials were collected and placed in boxes ready for the next class, and children (obviously expert at acquiescing to regimentation) were called to order. The bell rang, classes changed, and lines formed for recess with the homeroom teacher—every step occurring in a whirlwind routine carried out as if speed and efficiency were the main purpose of our being there.

I followed Noreen's homeroom class on their journey outside to observe a scene that seemed an exact rerun of recess at the elementary school I had attended forty years earlier. Bodies bursting with energy headed down the stone stairs, breaking rank when the door was in sight and flying into the freedom and brightness of the outdoors toward that portion of the playground that was assigned to their grade level. The street people who had been lounging on the playground vacated to more peaceful territory as a group of boys began a game of marbles.

Others joined the volleyball toss that Frank Johnson was supervising or pretended to be cops making a drug bust. A few girls played hopscotch on the cracked concrete or tossed a ball against the blank wall of the auditorium. A few others pounded away at a rapid-fire double Dutch, but most of the girls giggled in small groups or chased each other in circles. Too soon, the bell rang, whistles blew, megaphones shouted, lines formed, and sweating children were corralled back into the musty darkness of the building as the street people reclaimed their living space.

Noreen got her homeroom class settled down and we began the lesson a second time. In addition to being energized by the fresh air, this class was obviously more expressive and enthusiastic about the assignment than the previous one—and much more adept at ignoring Noreen's shouts for order. Early on in the lesson, I spotted a pretty child with a broad grin, a long braid pulled to one side with a big purple ribbon, and a personality that easily matched Noreen's determination to keep order. Tameka (I soon knew her by name since it was being repeated so often) momentarily considered the assignment to write a slogan describing the good or bad qualities of Oak Hills's neighbors, then began insisting that there was a difference between "bad" and "very bad" ("You know the people that hang out over by Saint Andrew's? They bad, but them people on the corner with the 'Beware Dog' sign on the fence—wuh-o-o girl, now those people is *real* b-a-a-d. My mama dared me to go near them people 'cause they got guns 'n stuff").

Noreen demanded that Tameka stop showing off or move to the seventh seat. But the rest of the class had already picked up on Tameka's cue and soon various students were calling out to announce their own comparisons of the badness of particular neighbors ("Those people ain't nothing compared to what's at the Funky Fox. They dope heads"). "Great," I said. "Why not focus on the extremes. You know, why not think of *the* absolute best or worst kind of neighbor—not the people, but what they *do* that really helps or hurts the neighborhood. That way we can make very interesting pictures that will be a bit like cartoons." Noreen interjected: "And don't just focus on the bad people. What about all the wonderful people in this neighborhood?"

Far more excited with the idea of making cartoons of *the* absolute best or worst neighbors than they were with the more neutral focus on good or bad qualities, the children soon seemed to be engaged in a contest. Mimicking Tameka's humor, some children vied for the most extreme ideas while others rummaged through the photographs to figure out how to portray these exaggerations. Tameka's male counterpart, Shawn, became convinced that "these silly ole pictures" (my collection of photographs) could not possibly show his idea—he would need other materials to make a drawing of his idea. Time slipped by as the poster-making became more and more complicated and, just as Noreen had predicted, the class got thoroughly "off track." By the end of the period, Tameka was ensconced in a seventh-position chair, as was Shawn, and Tameka was being threatened with banishment to the front of the room. At the sound of the bell, monitors were collecting unfinished posters with half-glued-on bits of photographs and unfinished drawings, I was sorting out materials, and Noreen was assuring insistent students that she would find time for them to complete the project next week as she hurried to line them up for lunch period.

When Mary and Gail came into the room, it still seemed to be ringing with the children's voices, even though our brood had already joined Mister Joe and his crew in the basement cafeteria. Sitting before a delicious homemade repast that magically materialized out of a collection of wrinkled paper bags, Noreen and I began to describe how the day was going. Noreen seemed frazzled, but she was clearly delighted with her students' spontaneity and inventiveness. Mary was sorry that there was no way for her to observe. However, Gail soon zeroed in on the scheduling problem that the morning had created. With her complaints as a basso continuo ("It's great for them to learn about their neighborhood, but you know that the bottom line is the kid's test score"), the lunch conversation soon fixed on the constant pressure that teachers were under to perform ("These people who are so keen on accountability should spend just one day in our shoes") as the three tried to figure out when Noreen's class could finish its work. Our feast devoured, the lunch bags were restuffed with empty containers, and the dining space just as magically reverted to a classroom.

The afternoon was even warmer than the morning had been, and Mary's homeroom class arrived in a hyperactive state as Noreen whispered that this was a "problem class," mostly because of Mary's lax disciplinary techniques. Noreen got through the discussion session with some difficulty, pausing frequently to admonish various misbehaving children. However, all progress halted just as I began the hands-on portion of the lesson when two girls began pushing each other in violation of the school's behavior code. Noreen shouted for the children to get quiet, then summoned the girls to her desk, where she spent the remaining class period, alternating between filling out the required discipline forms and quelling other minor disturbances. The students, whose morning friendliness toward me had vanished, were united in enacting a well-rehearsed resistance, sulkily tearing up their work and pretending not to understand the assignment. By the end of the period, no team had finished the assignment, nor had any enthusiasm been generated about the project. Noreen expressed her extreme disappointment with the class's performance as she reran the routine of getting materials collected, calling children to order with hands folded on desks, waiting for the bell, lining them up, and overseeing the changing of classes.

As Noreen and I said a weary good-bye that day, we both wondered whether students had benefited at all from the effort we had invested; then Tameka reappeared in the doorway, still wearing her wonderfully impish grin. She apologized for "getting in trouble" and asked in a hopeful voice if I would be coming back the next day. With a reassuring twinkle in her eye, Noreen laughed and said: "Oh, no. Tomorrow it's just you and me, kiddo."

Worn out by all the interpersonal tension of the day, I left the darkness of the building, got into the taxi Mrs. Vallejo had ordered, and tried to relax against the hard brown plastic back seat. During the journey to the hotel, I pondered the day's events, particulary the children's strikingly different relationships with Noreen. Gail was clearly the most disgruntled teacher in terms of both the student body and compliance with the educational program; but Noreen seemed to be the most emphatic enforcer of the disciplinary code, perhaps because of her dedication to improving the children's academic performance. Each class appeared to respond to her in a particular manner, depending upon the expectations established by their more significant homeroom teacher. Her own students seemed to accept her strict regulation of their behavior, possibly because they also benefited from her intensity and willingness to extend herself as a teacher—for example, I discovered through casual conversation that she provided a variety of niceties for her students, such as bringing in homemade goodies or serving a special lunch in class. These children appeared to know how to stretch their freedom within the context of the lesson; though there were a few disturbances, all in all I felt that this class period had been rather cheerful. In contrast, the session with Gail's homeroom students was quite depressing, those children being so subdued that they elicited few reprimands as they plodded through the assignment without evident interest or enthusiasm. Maybe Noreen's greater creativity and respect for children provided them with a space of retreat from Gail's anger at their perceived faults. On yet another hand, Mary's students seemed to expect (demand) the freedom to which they were accustomed in their homeroom, resisting Noreen's authority and living up to their designation as a "problem class."

Thinking about variations in the children's reactions to Noreen, I recalled the work of the ethnographer Peter McLaren (1993), who studied differences in the behavioral styles of working-class Portuguese students in a Canadian middle-school. McLaren contrasted the behavior occurring in the local neighborhood ("streetcorner state") to that occurring within the classroom ("student state"), proposing that the streetcorner state is manifested by physical contact and boisterous, unpredictable, and kinesthetic activity, whereas the student state is characterized by passivity and dependence upon standardized cues provided by teachers.

> Following their entrance into the building, students realign and readjust their behavior, shifting from the natural flow of the streetcorner state to the more formal and rigidly sequestered precinct of the student state. It is here that the students give themselves to the powerful controls and enforcement procedures available to teachers—controls that allow teachers to dominate students without recourse to brute force. Students move offstage from where they are more naturally themselves to the proscenium of the [classroom], where they must write their students' roles and scenarios in conformity to the teacher's master script (p. 90).

Although each class exhibited differing degress of compliance with Noreen's expectations for the appropriate student state, my overall impression of Frederick Douglass that day was that it presented a very stressful, unnatural environment. Some educators, notably such functionalists as Talcott Parsons (1959) and Robert Dreeben (1968), have proposed that the artificiality of school is necessary to children's later participation in the world of work and politics. However, I wondered how these particular children could reconcile the highly mechanistic management of their behavior in school with the fact that they were living such an improvised existence outside of school. To survive on the strees of Oak Hills, they required an extraordinary capacity to deal with unfair situations and to engage in the very physically assertive behaviors for which they were being punished at school. Furthermore, they were growing up in a society that glorified violence through sports, movies, and political leaders whose rhetoric was peppered with confrontation. Surely the compliant performance that was being asked of them must appear quite abnormal.

As the year went on, I would learn that the children at Frederick Douglass had to constrain not only their more boisterous physical nature but also their more communal social attributes. The disjuncture between what was needed to succeed at school and the requirements of life in the real world would make this school into a place of conflict and contradiction. I would also realize that the streetcorner and student states of Gardendale's children were far less contrasting, since teachers accommodated a degree of obstreperousness (especially on the part of males) and minimized the dulling effect of mechanistic classroom management through highly individualized instruction. I would observe Gardendale's students being more naturally themselves while at the same time conforming to the white middle-class expectations of the institution in a way that would prove quite inconceivable at Frederick Douglass.

As the taxi edged through early rush-hour traffic, I opened the envelop containing the sixty-three questionnaires that students had completed at the end of September, just before the program started. I turned to the question that read: "If you were the principal of Frederick Douglass, what one thing would you change?" The children's responses made a great deal of sense—more time to play, fewer rules, nicer teachers, less work, no teacher's pets, and lots of toilet paper. Looking at their responses to "What is the worst place in the world?" I saw that about 30 percent singled out the school whereas an equal number said that the one thing in the world that should be changed was teachers. I wondered how such negative views of the school and its teachers could help children liberate themselves, as Parsons (1959) proposed, from the inheritance of low family status, and prove themselves afresh as achievers or nonachievers. More to the point, how could they develop feelings of self-acceptance, self-respect, and self-worth in a place that more than a few students identified as the worst place in the world—worse than streets filled with burned and abandoned buildings, crack houses, broken-down cars, vacant lots, garbage, belching smokestacks, and the pervasive terror of unemployment?

FOR CHILDREN OF CRISIS, AN EMERGENCY WAS EASY

It was my fourth visit to Markington and, since that Indian summer day in October, my visits had occurred during snowstorms. This particular day, the weather was so severe that neither Noreen, Gail, nor Mrs. Driskell had been able to get to school. Mary and I listened to the public address system as Mrs. Vallejo mustered a stern voice to announce that snow emergency plans were in effect. Teachers should go at once to their regular places in the auditorium to pick up the children for whom they would be responsible until other teachers arrived. Any anger that Mary may have had about not being allowed to coordinate the Urban Network program was not apparent as she and I hurried downstairs to find twenty or so fifth-grade students standing in line wearing snow-laden coats and dripping boots. Since conceivably there would be a lot more children in the room before the snow emergency ended, we decided to take our charges into Noreen's larger room.

Mary got the children seated, and I volunteered to initiate the social studies lesson that Noreen and I had planned for that day on the problems of sharing space. I walked to the front of the room as Mary took a seat atop a child's desk at the rear of the room, pleased to have a chance for a firsthand observation of the Urban Network in action. Hoping for the best, I faced a group of shivering children whose names I mostly could not remember and asked: "Does anyone here share a bedroom with someone at home?" Practically everyone raised their hands. "How many of you have two roommates or more?" Still most of the hands stayed up. "Well, do any of you ever have any problems with the persons who share your bedroom?" Now the hands started to wave as children begged to be called on so they could tell their stories about siblings who snored, had smelly feet, blasted radios, or left their belongings all over the place.

As we talked, Mary left her post to direct new arrivals, who were still wearing wet coats and boots, to the few remaining empty desks. After welcoming the new group, our conversation progressed to other spaces in the house. "Are there any problems at your house when you try to share, say, the bathroom or kitchen?" The stories became increasingly lively as the newcomers joined in with ease, then Shawn began waving his hand wildly in the air, pleading aloud to be called upon. Once acknowledged, he burst out with a story of how he had to wait for *hours* for his sister, Amanda, to get out of the bathroom, standing up to demonstrate her primping to the other amused boys. Not to be outdone, Georgette got the floor and rivaled him with a story directed toward her female classmates, explaining how she and her sisters had to clean up the messes her five brothers made all over the kitchen. Above the gaiety, Mrs. Vallejo's voice could be heard making an encore on the address system. "Ms. Quick-to-See, if you could possibly come downstairs, I need your help escorting children to their rooms." Her dark eyes lit up by the flow of adrenaline, Mary inquired whether I could manage alone. By this time, I was looking into the faces of about thirty children whose names I did not know, but what the heck. "No problem!" I said and continued the discussion.

We ventured on to talk about conflicts in the neighborhood as Mary led more coated, booted children into the room. Every desk was now filled, including the seventh seat at each cluster, so newly arrived students began to carry in chairs from Mary's room, placing them wherever they could find a spot. "Teenagers think they own the streets." "There's no place safe for us kids." "Cars drive through here goin' like crazy." "Homeless people think my building's a toilet." By the time Mrs. Vallejo's voice came on the speaker to announce the end of the emergency, the discussion had progressed to global problems. "Countries go to war sometimes." "My brother went to fight in Panama because there was this guy down there with drugs." At last, Noreen arrived and poked a snow-covered head in the door to see a room crowded with about sixty students who had carried on a discussion for almost ninety minutes—far longer than children are supposed to be able to pay attention.

How was this possible? How were children able to sit in a very crowded room, wearing wet clothes, and talking with a relative stranger with only intermittent supervision by an inexperienced teacher? Was it that they sensed my terror and wanted to help me? Was it the novelty of the situation that engaged their attention? Was it that the snow emergency allowed the children to demonstrate the superior skills to manage crises that they had gained through their everyday lives? More than likely a variety of factors came into play, but certainly the physical discomfort experienced that morning was a familiar type of challenge that fortuitously matched the subject matter of the lesson. Being squeezed together in a chilly, crowded classroom while talking about their experiences of living in incommodious places seems to have thrown the children into an unusually creative frame of mind. Every time Mrs. Vallejo spoke the word *emergency*, a grown-up attentiveness seemed to overtake the room that complemented the liveliness of the discussion.

In his studies of English miners, George Orwell (1958) noted how modern institutions tend to eliminate the motivational benefits of trying situations: "The truth is that many of the qualities we admire in human beings can only function in opposition to some kind of disaster, pain, or difficulty; but the tendency of mechanical progress is to eliminate disaster, pain, and difficulty" (p. 193).

Middle-class professionals, including teachers, are part of this increasing tendency to bureaucratically manage the challenges of everyday life while defining both progress and human worth in terms that legitimize our own positions. Professional status brings with it certain privileges—the right to make choices, to judge and interpret experience, to exercise influence over our own fate as well as that of others. Entitled—through our positions of authority as news reporters, journalists, educators, and policymakers—to define the reality of disadvantaged persons, our prescriptions tend to further validate our own ranks or roles. For example, service-providers are likely to define their low-income charges as helpless rather than as persons who have been strengthened by the harshness of their lives, because maintaining a dependency/caretaking relationship is essential to the service-provider's sense of worth. At the same time, the client's helplessness is characterized as so intractable that the provider is absolved from being accountable to rectify the condition.

The middle-class teachers at Frederick Douglass might have recognized those inner resources that would have enabled their impoverished students to access the power of their own imaginations. But allowing children to express power-from-within would have threatened Frederick Douglass's top-down social structure because the strength that comes from a sense of inner agency is not based on officially sanctioned merit but is available to all persons. Children having power-from-within would have been on a more equal footing with teachers, thereby undermining the authority of the educational bureaucracy to ignore—and even erase—the skills and abilities they were acquiring on the streets of Oak Hills. Thus, instead of perceiving qualities that might have provided a wellspring of motivation for their own self-determination, teachers tended to characterize their charges as "unstable" and "at risk." In the carefully controlled environment of the classroom, children were not given the opportunity to use their well-oiled talents for adapting to chaos in their homes and neighborhoods because paternalistic professionals placed them in a role of passive dependency to validate their own caretaking status. With such bureaucratic management of their lives, children were systematically indoctrinated into another aspect of the patriarchal contract, learning that institutional authority can override the initiative and creativity that exists within themselves.

In an analysis of the relationship between education and work, Carnoy and Levin (1985) pointed to an ongoing struggle in public schooling between the tendency to reproduce the prevailing power-over relationships by training children to accept their niche in life, and an opposing drive toward educating children to achieve equality. They wrote:

> The State bureaucracy is . . . the scene of conflict both between the dominating and dominated classes and within the dominating class. . . . The State not only develops its own dynamic, it is subject to the competing dynamics both of a capitalist class attempting to reproduce capitalist relations of production, and of social movements trying to expand their economic power and social and political rights [pp. 45–46].

Although frequently alluded to by liberals in educational circles, this ongoing conflict is an extremely lopsided struggle that has been defined through the lens of middle-class norms. Historically problems such as poverty and ignorance have been framed by persons who are without any direct knowledge of these states of being, as occurred during the social movement of the 1950s and 1960s. For example, it was John F. Kennedy who solidified the concept of a helpless, childlike culture-of-poverty that needed benevolent care from the government. Subsequently, the Johnson Administration selected the aristocratic Sargent

Shriver, who had no experience whatsoever in the matter, to lead the so-called War on Poverty. Viewing poverty from a position of privilege, he seemed more invested in the social uplift of those who were being charitable than in the end of impoverishment. As social critic Barbara Ehrenreich (1989) pointed out, categorizing poor people as a deviant and dependent group affected how middle-class persons conceived solutions to poverty, and, not infrequently, the solutions ensured the superior status of the professional care-giver:

> But even in what we now think of as the liberal sixties, the notion that the poor were alien members of a culture of poverty had a profound effect on how middle-class people viewed the poor and plotted solutions to their distress. Some antipoverty warriors saw the culture of poverty as an excuse for a middle-class–dominated, technocratic approach to ending poverty. If the poor were so shiftless and disorganized, they could not be expected to help themselves [p. 55].

Such stereotypes have only intensified in the intervening years due to the country's increasingly skewed income distribution, the progressive confinement of the underclass to central cities or prisons, and a more hostile attitude toward the less fortunate. Despite a commitment to multiculturalism at Frederick Douglass, the staff reflected a middle-class no-win conception of poverty as an aberrant condition in need of treatment by more knowing persons—poverty that is, at the same time, untreatable due to inbred defects in its victims. The power-over context through which the multicultural curriculum was being injected into students invalidated the skills, values, and ways of being that children acquired after school in their homes and communities. The social processes in the school not only negated using the children's experiences as a source of inner strength to resist those environmental conditions that were shaping their inferior self-conceptions, they magnified the children's subordinate status.

BEGINNING AS AN ACT OF INDIVIDUAL INITIATIVE

Though lower middle class by virtue of her educational status, Jane Andre had been raised, the youngest of six female children, in a rural farming community in the southern Alleghenies—a way of life to which she felt a deep sense of connection. Jane's parents could neither read nor write, but both had taught her to use her hands and rely on her common sense and capacity to view the world with a critical eye. Unlike her young charges at Gardendale whose environmental lives were defined by luxuries, Jane's childhood esthetic experiences encompassed the practical necessities for survival in a harsh mountainous landscape—a thoughtfully placed sequence of kitchen gardens each responding to a different climatic condition, a drafty farmhouse sheltered by an earth berm on its northern side, an unlit cold cellar lined with the colorful canned goods of harvest, crowing roosters providing a melodious wake-up for a hard day's labor. Unlike San Lupe with its symbols of extravagance, her childhood space was shaped by her parents' stubborn determination to fashion a special domain in which to resist the ravages of being poor—a stubbornness that Jane would inherit in the form of idealism.

Jane's first artistic activity (apart from her ceaseless carving of little scraps of wood) involved cutting patterns out of old newspapers to make her own clothes, a skill she learned from an older sister. Jane's artistic talent eventually allowed her to be the only child in her family to rise out of a lower-class existence and attend college. After working as a clerk for two years, she saved enough money to enroll part-time in a state college and, after graduation, she even traveled to New York City to intern in an artist's studio. Leaving home but never allowing herself to become alienated from its lessons of struggle, Jane persisted in wearing the legacy of her upbringing as a badge of pride. To stay connected to this other self, she took up residence in Limone when she was offered a job at Gardendale, and made her rural neighbors the subject of her paintings.

Jane and I had made each other's acquaintance during the period when she lived in New York City. She and I were among a group of feminist artists who got together on occasion during the 1970s women's movement to provide support for one another, and later Jane attended a workshop that I offered at a summer institute for teachers who were interested in using the design arts in their classrooms. Jane moved to the San Lupe area to earn a master's degree and became an elementary school art teacher, and I moved to Ann Arbor, but we continued to correspond. Quite naturally, this old acquaintance was on the initial Urban Network mailing list. Upon receiving an announcement of the program, Jane responded with a personal order for an instructional portfolio and telephoned later to discuss her concerns about implementing an *urban* design program in a suburban school. Jane explained that her goal would be to use the outreach focus of the program to increase her students' awareness of social issues since their only exposure to poverty was most likely during the yearly food drives that Gardendale sponsored at Thanksgiving and Christmas. Knowing about my commitment to inner-city minority children, she inquired whether I would be willing to work with an all-white upper-middle-class school.

Would the exercises even be workable in a suburban setting? The program seemed to emphasize collaborative all-school projects. How would it work in a school that underscored small-group and individual work?

The target audience for the program had been fourth-, fifth-, and sixth-grade students living in urban neighborhoods, but I was quickly learning that suburban schools had more resources for carrying out projects. Some adjustments would be necessary to implement the program in her school, however, I would be willing to consider Gardendale as one of the three pilot sites that I would accept outside of Michigan during that year, especially since I so valued our old working relationship. Perhaps the intention to involve children in their local community could be expanded to encompass a disadvantaged community. Perhaps a small group of children could organize some volunteer activity, like the food drives, that other students could join. Privately, I was asking myself whether I wanted to use up my meager resources at an affluent school, but I knew that Jane would be an engaging partner. Then, too, I might be forming a skewed understanding of children's environmental lives by only talking to urban children. At any rate, it would have been foolish to exclude such a talented and committed teacher, so I encouraged Jane to pursue her interest with her principal.

This telephone call coincided with and solidified my first attempts to look at the social issues associated with poverty less myopically—to conceive of poverty and privilege (including my own) as interlocking issues within the emerging environmental crisis.

BEING ENCOURAGED TO THINK BIG

During the springtime, Jane arranged a meeting with Dr. Marcus and Mr. Regon to discuss her hopes for implementing the Urban Network program at Gardendale the following year. She described our New York relationship and showed the videotape and other instructional materials, explaining that I had agreed to work with her on adapting the program to a suburban site. Although Jane emphasized her intention to use the Urban Network to expand the students' social awareness through some sort of community-service project, Dr. Marcus was most intrigued by the possibility of bringing an architect from a prestigious university into the school. The children might very well elect to do an outreach activity, but a hands-on exposure to a nontraditional career and alternative methods of visual problem-solving were what excited her. Such an offering could bring even more distinction to Gardendale as a magnet public school. Mr. Regon pointed out that although the science and technology curriculum was focused on nature, it could be broadened to include study of the area's elegant architecture. There was also the possibility of using Gardendale's various building renovations (such as the outdoor science laboratory that would be built the next summer) as the focus of an architecture program, and most likely the teachers and students would be able to think of any number of other exciting projects.

"What grade level would you think is most appropriate for this Urban Network?" Dr. Marcus asked. Jane worked with fourth through sixth grades, but thought the sixth-grade students would benefit most from the career education focus Dr. Marcus was implying. "And how would you propose to interface with teachers and students?" Jane would have to consider this further, but her initial understanding of the Urban Network was that visual activities should be integrated by classroom teachers into the various subject areas. Dr. Marcus asked Jane to write a one-page description of the program as she tentatively envisioned it, then instructed Mr. Regon to review the proposal with all the sixth-grade teachers to ascertain their interest in participating. He should arrange for release time so that Jane could meet with these teachers to develop a full three- to four-page proposal for review by the STC. On their approval, some funds might be dedicated to the project. Dr. Marcus then fixed her blue eyes and smiled directly on Jane, expressing her delight and encouraging Jane to think expansively, not just about this particular year and this particular Urban Network program but about the long run. She might conceive an ongoing career education effort, for example, that would bring in a variety of professionals related to the visual aspects of science and technology to regularly mentor select groups of students. Dr. Marcus impressed on Jane that whatever plan she evolved, it should utilize the Urban Network implementation as a one-year jump start for a larger effort that would add a new offering to the school's current array of choices.

Jane practically floated out of the meeting, incredulous that she had wandered into the prospect of inventing a special niche for herself at Gardendale. She was well aware of the obstacles to merging her orientation to social responsibility with Dr. Marcus's career education emphasis. However, Jane was expert at maneuvering as an outsider-within the numerous mainstream institutions that had lined her path to Gardendale from the South Alleghenies. Though white, the remembrances of her past history gave her a perspective on the social construction of reality similar to the one offered by bell hooks (1984) regarding her own poor African American community:

> Living as we did—on the edge—we developed a particular way of seeing reality. We looked both from the outside in and from the inside out. We

focused our attention on the center as well as on the margin. We understood both. This mode of seeing reminded us of the existence of a whole universe, a main body made up of both margin and center [p. ix].

Jane was only too aware of the difficulty of taking on a role in which she would simultaneously attempt to advance her privileged students within mainstream culture while, at the same time, exposing them to experiences that would help them to resist its oppressiveness. The obligation that she herself felt to both advance within the ranks of a competitive society and fulfill her own commitments to social change created no small degree of ambivalence about her choice to work at Gardendale.[2] Yet the prospect of enabling just a few students to see multiple social realities—to acknowledge their position on the inside, to look out from that position to those who live in the margins, but also to get outside and look in with critical eyes—these were the goals that made Jane's job at Gardendale acceptable. Unless she could challenge herself to achieve them, she surely should leave and use her talents elsewhere to improve the lot of her own kind.

In the next few weeks, Barbara Moore and Betty Rayburne accepted Jane's offer to collaborate on what came to be called the Aspiring Professionals program. Together, they crafted a proposal that would give students an intense exposure to a variety of science and technology disciplines, including the design arts, environmental fields, and engineering. During the first year, Miss Moore and Mrs. Rayburne would participate, but in other years different teachers might sign up, each being free to develop an individual way of utilizing Jane's esthetic input. For instance, Miss Moore's entire class would participate in activities planned jointly by herself and Jane during the first semester, then a few of the most interested children would continue working in Jane's art class on a focused project during the second semester. Since children in Mrs. Rayburne's class did not typically work together, she preferred a mentoring relationship for a few select students during the first semester; then her students would team up with Miss Moore's group to do the focused project. My role throughout would be as a role model and informational resource for both teachers and children. However, one of my primary obligations would be to lay the groundwork for a continuing curriculum by helping to define the consultant's role and identify other professional associations and programs that might serve as resources in the future.

These deliberations occurred at the end of the year with Miss Moore, Mrs. Rayburne, and Jane meeting after classes ended to confirm their concept and budget. The proposal had already received an enthusiastic approval from the STC, so the project was set to begin the following school year in September.

PRACTICING FOR THE BOARDROOM

A sign lettered with the words "Aspiring Professionals" was among several brightly colored placards taped to the door. Mr. Regon ushered me inside, where the first period of Mrs. Rayburne's sixth-grade class was already in progress. White children (the number of students of color at Gardendale was only 3 percent, so many classes were all white) were busied in small clusters around tables and on a carpeted area in one corner of a spacious airy room that was about one-third larger than those at Frederick Douglass. At first, Mrs. Rayburne was not to be seen, but her head soon poked up from one of the tables and she extended a cheerful greeting, briefly introducing me to the students and reminding them of what was in store for that week. As Mr. Regon excused himself, Mrs. Rayburne explained in a hushed voice that I would be working with a few children who had a special interest and talent in architecture. Seven students had applied to the program and just four had been selected on the basis of essays that Jane would show me later on. This foursome was working with Jane to assimilate the materials I had sent and already had successfully completed one project—a scale drawing of the classroom. The group would accompany me to the courtyard so that we could begin doing the "blueprint" for the outdoor science laboratory that was to be built there. Jane was finishing up something with another group of children, but she would join us shortly.

I was pleased—overwhelmed—by the extraordinarily professional atmosphere and advanced preparations, but I was also quite thrown off by the prospect of working in such a solitary manner, perhaps due to my previous experiences in the arts-in-education community of New York City. The goal in those situations had been to expose as many children as possible to an outside resource. Instead of being a unique event in the school, it almost seemed as if I was in a college situation, competing with other professors to attract enough students for a course. As I was struggling to overcome the same feelings of insecurity I have in such contests at the university level, Mrs. Rayburne introduced me to my protégés—four boys wearing baseball caps as if to imitate old-fashioned draftsmen. Charles, Jeremiah, Kimsung, and Michael led me to their work area in one of the room's quadrants and proudly displayed a beautifully crafted floor plan they had made of their classroom complete with all its furnishings. Michael ran over to the shelving unit and returned carrying a cardboard box full of various drafting instruments (a tape measure, numerous scales, rulers, triangles, and clipboards), which was so large as to block his view. After elbowing one another in a contest to determine who would take what tools, the boys selected some equipment and we headed downstairs to the courtyard, leaving the room unnoticed by the other workgroups who were busy with equally exciting assignments.

The area that would be used for the science laboratory was just outside a lounge, which had been created during the 1960s expansion by opening up two classrooms in the original building next to the principal's office and just across from the main entry. The lounge—maintained by the Gardendale Parents Association, which would also finance construction of the outdoor classroom space—seemed something of a botanical garden. It contained the same large south-facing windows I had observed earlier in the principal's office, providing enough sunlight to grow enormous treelike plants that reached up toward the high ceiling of the lounge. Despite its central, sunny location, the courtyard itself had never been used except by one of the newly hired science teachers, who had set up a temporary greenhouse for experiments. The new installation would upgrade this makeshift laboratory and, at the same time, open up the lounge (used for a variety of activities such as displays, parent meetings, and hands-on activities) to the outdoors.

The boys charged through the door, motioning for me to look at where their project was going to be. I took a seat on a low wall that protruded from the building and, attempting to establish a more inquiring manner of working, asked what they had in mind to build. "A science laboratory," they chimed in unison. "And what *is* a science laboratory," I asked probingly. More eager to demonstrate their measuring abilities than to answer my abstract questions, they said, "It's a place where you learn about science." I persisted. "And why are you making a science laboratory out-of-doors? Shouldn't it be inside?" Kimsung and Jeremiah ignored my inquisitiveness and concentrated on vying for the position of leader. Kimsung won by appealing to the procedures of fairness that the group had established earlier ("It's my turn today. Remember we agreed to flip for who would go first. Yesterday you won, so now it's my turn") and proceeded to make assignments. In his second-in-command position, Jeremiah would be in charge of the prized tape measure; Michael would be responsible for extending the metal rule to the right spot; Kimsung would call out the measurements; Charles would write them down on the clipboard. "Okay, take your places," directed Kimsung.

Jane appeared at that very moment and reminded the boys that they had agreed to begin by discussing their architectural plans with their distinguished guest; the measuring was something they could do another day on their own. With a little prompting from Jane and me, the boys began to reveal how much they had learned about designing space, self-assurance being in no short supply. Not ready to relinquish what he felt was his rightful leadership position, Kimsung began ("It's important to figure out where kids will be walking. We'll need circulation to each of the work areas"). His competitor, Jeremiah, chimed in ("We're going to put the work areas under the trees"). Jane probed for the reason behind this decision ("Because if there's too much sun, it'll make glare and the kids won't be able to concentrate"). I inquired about how they would go about designing the work areas ("We made up an interview to find out what the science teachers want, like it says to do in the Urban Network"). Jane searched for the list of spaces they had derived in her stack of papers, explaining that the interviews suggested there should be four separate work areas. She had brought along some graph-paper pads and suggested that I assist the students in developing some scale drawings of possible arrangements of these spaces in the courtyard—a plan that Jane and I had agreed upon earlier by telephone. "Of course," I said. "That's my specialty. Now let's find one of those shady areas, out of the glare of this sunshiny day, and get to work."

The boys sat down under a tree and began sketching out plans for the science laboratory with the same intensity I would observe later that afternoon in Miss Moore's class. As the drawing process took over, the conversation turned to each boy's credentials for succeeding at the assignment: Jeremiah had seen many wonderful places in his travels around the world, Kimsung had always been interested in math and architecture, Charles was the best in the class in drawing, Michael's father was an architect. The boys buoyed up their credibility by invoking their parents' authority ("My dad once told me" or "Mother always says"), a tactic I would observe repeatedly. Interspersing their own bios with an interview, they bombarded me with remarkably sophisticated questions about my background ("Where were you educated?" "How did you get interested in architecture?" "Is anyone else in your family an architect?" "Have you done any important buildings?" "What do you teach at the University of Michigan?"). Within an hour's time, the group had produced four different designs, any one of which was a viable beginning proposal for the science laboratory. Jane was complimenting the boys on their excellent work as Kimsung's mother appeared in the doorway of the lounge. Seeing her, he dashed off without a good-bye, abandoning his large drawing pad on the green grass that blanketed the courtyard. Jane and I delivered the other boys to the front of the building to wait for their escorts to lunch, then we gathered up the supplies and headed out to rendezvous with our own lunch contingent.

Miss Moore, Mrs. Rayburne, and two parent-members of the STC were waiting for us at a large table in a Thai restaurant that was a short walk from the school. A slightly dim room, it was filled with wonderful aromas and several groups of obstreperous middle-school students who appeared to be lunch regulars. Seemingly accepting of their raucous behavior, waiters were scurrying back and forth to answer their questions about the menu while carting heaping plates of food from the kitchen and refilling large glasses with soft drinks. Over the din, I attempted to shout my beginning observations of the program. I was more than pleased with the students' preparedness and with the quality of the work I had observed so far, which was absolutely extraordinary. However, I could not help but be concerned about spending so much travel time to relate to only about sixteen children. Was it reasonable to think of a broader impact? Mrs. Rayburne assured me that engaging with small groups was in the Gardendale tradition and accomplished a major educational objective—developing a spirit of competition while allowing children an opportunity for individual exploration. Opening the program up to more children would dilute its impact since children would no longer perceive the experience as being special. The parents concurred, promising me that my presence and exchanges with Jane would benefit all the children in the long run because it would bring greater distinction to their school.

A "PARTY" TO ENSURE THE STATUS QUO

On my second visit to Gardendale, Jane and I had agreed to spend the lunch hour in Miss Moore's class where a party would take place to welcome a new student teacher. Miss Moore had given four children complete freedom to plan the event—a fact that she proudly told me several times as I was hanging up my jacket in her locker. She pointed out the party planners, whom I recalled from my first visit when students were making drawings of their neighborhood. I distinctly remembered that this foursome had deserted their assigned tribes on several occasions to get in a huddle with each other (despite Miss Moore's intention to create mixed-gender groupings, children of both sexes resisted, especially Justin and Peter, who looked for any possible excuse to work with Madison and Robert instead of with their female teammates). I also recalled that, during that first class, the Justin et al. huddles seemed to have a sarcastic, mocking quality and not infrequently had led to some sort of disruption. Yet, Miss Moore was effusive about their party preparations, which had required no small amount of effort on her part because of the planners' insistence on having the party at lunchtime. Not only did she and Jane have to forgo their lunch breaks, but it was necessary to obtain parental permission for students to remain at school, and to arrange for the food. Miss Moore had gotten several mothers to bring in dishes, but she had not been successful in soliciting volunteers for the party itself since lunchtime was when mothers were normally at home with other children.

As Miss Moore and Jane began unwrapping the food, I could sense an air of aroused anticipation among the party planners. They instructed the other students to rearrange the furniture, gesturing for them to place the chairs in rows (in more of a traditional classroom arrangement) facing the front. They directed that a chair and a round table be positioned on either side of the blackboard, then Madison and Robert taped a cardboard microphone to the center of each table. Meanwhile, Justin and Peter searched their bookbags for notebooks, which were also placed on the tables. Seeing the broadcast setup, Miss Moore made note of their degree of planning, chuckling that the boys must be trying to impress their teacher, the producer.

When the furniture shuffle was complete, everyone proceeded through the buffet that Miss Moore, Jane, and several of the girls had arranged in the rear of the room on the two other round tables. As the audience settled into their seats with paper plates of food and plastic glasses of lemonade in hand, Peter strode to the front and announced that he would like to begin the program. He was making a perfunctory "welcome" to the student teacher just as I noticed Justin covertly motioning the other boys into the rear foyer where the slop sinks and storage were located. In their sprint to the foyer, Madison managed to trip on a wheel of the media cart, knocking over a pitcher of lemonade in the process. Undaunted, the boys proceeded into the foyer and stripped down to the swim pants they had hidden underneath their regular clothes while the student teacher thanked the class for the nice party. Miss Moore seemed unperturbed by the striptease, focusing instead on getting Laura and Emily to clean up the spilled juice.

Barechested, Justin and Madison burst to the front of the room, each one positioning himself at a table in front of a microphone; Peter dashed to the back to remove his clothes, then took a seat in the audience with Robert. The news commentators opened their notebooks and began reading from scripts replete with off-color in-jokes. Although the specific details of their stories were unclear to me, I soon realized that it was an enactment of Rambo, with Peter and Robert running to the front of the room at various points to mime his macho demeanor. The news broadcast, which seemed to be most appreciated by the party planners and the two other male members of the class, went on for about fifteen minutes amid a lot of screeching and agitated activity. Miss Moore coaxed the rest of the audience to pay attention but, hormones unleashed, the rest of the class began to engage in its own private skits. When the level of disruptive behavior was clearly out of hand, Miss Moore halted the performance, complimenting Justin et al. for their creativity and independence in planning the party. In utter disbelief and thoroughly depressed by having witnessed firsthand the insidious tenacity of sexism, I excused myself and headed for my session with Mrs. Rayburne's Ruffians.

For some time after that, I was distressed by the memory of the party. How could a group of boys get away with such obnoxious behavior in a school with an impressive female principal—one that was characterized as "highly structured in standards of dress, deportment, and performance?" Could such an event even have been conceived in the regimented environment of Frederick Douglass? Or did children in each setting have a unique way of resisting adult socialization to gain peer approval? In investigating the ways in which working-class youth develop a counterculture, sociologist Paul Willis (1977) described the role of the institutional regulation of lower-class culture. According to Willis, regulation effectively elevates the misbehavior of poor children and ensures their continued low status:

> In an increasingly vicious cycle "the lads" respond to the overall pressure on their culture with attempts to hit back in any way that is open to them. . . . As the pressure increases, so does misbehavior, opposition to authority, vandalism, and the exploitation of any weakness or mistake on the part of the staff [p. 78].

An inverse situation seemed to be in operation among the lads in Miss Moore's class who enacted what McLaren (1993) characterized as streetcorner behavior within the school. Here a group of mischievous boys had institutional sanction for behavior that would assuredly have been severely punished at Frederick Douglass, if it could have occurred at all. Instead of admonishment (followed by increased attempts to resist), the ambitious details of the party earned this group praise. Being sanctioned for asocial behavior confirms the observations of Cookson and Persell (1985) who described the conditions under which privileged children learn to violate codes of good behavior. "Daring, initiative, and excellence . . . are admired in the prep world, especially if it cleverly tweaks the nose of authority. . . . When done with wit and style [rule breaking] can become a mark of distinction; when done clumsily or meanly, it can become a mark of dullness, even dumbness" (p. 138). By finding a way to express youthful impishness within the boundaries of an institution, Justin et al.—different from Willis's lads—were being instructed in how to comply with the system while using it to serve their own purposes. Since it is easier to accept authority if you know you can defy it under certain circumstances, Miss Moore had (intentionally or not) just conscripted four powerful advocates for the status quo.

THWARTING A SENSE OF IDENTITY *AND* A SENSE OF COMMUNITY

> Children act on the world by transformation of what is and creation of the new to fit their needs and dreams. It is in their active agency, their seizing of possibilities inherent in a garage or an unused attic, that children express their power to appropriate the world and to find their place. Every child searches for his or her place and needs to develop a sense of identity and autonomy [Polakow and Sherif, 1987, p. 6].

Any careful observer of children's play will agree that recurrent themes in their conversations encompass striving for control over space, being secret, being hidden from adult control. As a second-grade student once explained to me while making a drawing of an imaginary play place: "This place is my best place 'cause it's secret and I'm the boss. When I want to go there, I don't have to ask my mother or my father. And you know something else about my secret place? I can draw on the walls." Unquestionably, the children at Frederick Douglass and Gardendale had vastly differing opportunities to acquire such a sense of place-related identity. At Frederick Douglass, the lockstep scheduling and spatial structuring of the behavior of children (and teachers) thwarted any possibility for them to exert control over their actions or even achieve the minimal level of privacy that is a precondition of intellectual and creative endeavor. Mrs. Driskell was convinced that self-esteem and cultural awareness were crucial to improving her students' chances to succeed—that the demonstration with its smaller programs, team teaching, continuity of classes, and disciplinary code would improve these traits—that the school environment would provide a sense of dependability and structure for children whose lives were economically and socially unstable. But where were her students to find the space in which to appropriate their surroundings?

In his autobiography, Carl Jung (1961) spoke of his own search for a place of identity when he was a boy of ten. Describing a year-long ritual that began with his transformation of an ordinary yellow pencil case that contained a wooden ruler, Jung detailed how he had derived his own inner security by creating a symbolic space inside the case. He recalled how a young and vulnerable Carl had carved one end of the ruler into a tiny man, then used black ink to indicate a frock coat, top hat, and shiny black boots. He described how he had sawed the tiny man off the ruler, placing him inside the pencil case, and even making him a tiny bed and a woolen coat. As a final touch, Carl had added a smooth, oblong blackish stone, which he painted so that it appeared to have an upper and lower portion.[3]

This was *his* stone. All this was a great secret. Secretly I took the case to the forbidden attic at the top of the house . . . and hid it with great satisfaction on one of the beams under the roof—for no one must ever see it! I knew that not a soul would ever find it there. No one could discover my secret and destroy it. I felt safe, and the tormenting sense of being at odds with myself was gone. In all difficult situations, whenever I had done something wrong or my feelings had been hurt, or when my father's irritability or my mother's invalidism oppressed me, I thought of my carefully bedded-down and wrapped-up manikin and his smooth, prettily colored stone. . . . The meaning of these actions, or how I might explain them never worried me. I contented myself with the feeling of newly won security, and was satisfied to possess something that no one knew and no one could get at. It was an inviolable secret, which must never be betrayed, for the safety of my life depended on it. Why that was so I did not ask myself. It simply was so. This possession of a secret had a very powerful formative influence on my character; I consider it the essential factor of my boyhood [pp. 21–22].

If creating a sacred space of one's own is as potent a force in developing character and inner security as Jung claimed, then it would seem important to make this possibility a principal mission of the schooling experience at Frederick Douglass. Certainly, the streets of Oak Hills placed limits on the safe appropriation of space, and private activities were constrained in most children's homes due to overcrowding—two facts that were revealed in the children's discussion during the snowstorm. But the school environment with its mechanical procedures and cramped rooms also disallowed exploring, changing, controlling, possessing, inventing, being secret, feeling safe. The only way students at Frederick Douglass could appropriate the world was through the daydreaming that many did to great excess.

Conversely, students at Gardendale had boundless opportunities for gaining security through the exploration and control of their surroundings both inside and outside of school. Indeed, the choice that pervaded the children's personal lives was mimicked, to the degree possible, in their institutional existence. They were encouraged to choose activities according to areas of interest and had the power to rearrange spaces or position themselves in important locations at the head of the class. Large rooms and furniture arrangements were intended for privacy, but they also allowed students to get away and carry out secret (and sometimes unacceptable) activities. Not so obvious, is the negative impact of the excessive freedom at Gardendale on the development of a sense of community. Just as overregulation, danger, and lack of privacy preempted the possibility for the children at Frederick Douglass to acquire a sense of identity, fragmentation of social networks through an indulgent accommodation of individual needs ruled out the opportunity for the children at Gardendale to practice being part of a larger whole. A sustainable society requires a balance between a strong individual identity and a fervent commitment to collective life, both dimensions evolving, in part, relative to physical places.

Secret spaces, real and imagined, would seem to support attainment of the individual spirit—the person who can stand alone and rise above limitations imposed by others. By the same token, shared spaces can enable that individual to acquire a sense of personal obligation to, and responsibility for, a group of people. Both processes are essential to the formation of a democratic society. Daniel Kemmis (1993), a politician who works on the practical and theoretical aspects of community-building, described the opposing views held by Hegel and Jefferson on how a civil society might develop in the United States. The urbanist Hegel believed that the country's great expanses of land blocked the attainment of civic culture because Americans did not have to face one another in cities; the agrarian Jefferson believed that communal interests would result from the act of farming the land. Although they disagreed on how civilization progressed, both felt that a collective identity derives from the exchanges people have in and with their physical surroundings. Kemmis proposed that the dynamic act of inhabitation—living in a place and coming to know its special characteristics, becoming bound to others by struggling against these practical constraints, developing certain place-related habits and behaviors—leads to shared interests, especially if the place poses physical limitations:

> Hard country breeds capable people—capable, among other things, of genuine democracy. . . . To have this kind of competence, a people must be bound together in ways that enable them to work together. What the project of inhabiting hard country does, above all, is to create these bonds. And when I speak of bonds here, I do not mean to evoke anything particularly soft or mushy. These are practical bonds, although they do often lead to a kind of affection among those so bonded. But they are in the first instance practical. They are the kinds of bonds that made of barn-building and similar acts of cooperation something that must be understood as a culture. It is a culture bred of hard places, nurtured by the practice of inhabiting those hard places [p. 282].

The limitations of communal life were discussed in a different manner by Sennett (1978) who traced the evolution of public space in Western society to understand our current inability to relate to one another as a community of strangers. Using historical analysis to show how our society has become increasingly obsessed with intimacy and self-expression, Sennett linked this trend to the loss of civility. According to Sennett, civility requires boundaries—limits to what people say and do. Without restraints, individuals can no longer suspend their immediate emotional needs to forge shared interests or a collective identity. Without restraints individuals lose the capacity for sociability, and they lack the fortitude to address the harsh realities—poverty, greed, ignorance, prejudice—that are part of the human condition (pp. 259–268).

Unquestionably, Sennett's view of community is an idealized one, based on geographic identity rather than on special interests or cultural identity, which have become increasingly important forms of community as "developments in science and technology allowed people to dominate and even dispense with environment and terrestrial space" (Seamon, 1980, p. 194). However, because of my interest in place as a contributor to children's individual and collective identity—and because I believe that having a sense of rootedness in place is prerequisite to a sustainable society—I tried to observe how the hidden curriculum of separateness manifested itself at both schools and see what opportunities there were for developing a sense of community after school. That is, I was interested to see whether the sociospatial practices children experienced in both schools would complement or contradict what happened after school.

At Gardendale children were encouraged to segregate themselves into a constantly changing array of special interest groups that were kept physically distinct. This policy provided them with rich choices for individual development but few occasions to negotiate with a larger group; in Mrs. Rayburne's case, it was impossible for the larger group to even be together physically. Although mothers were a constant presence in the school, they too were among the constantly changing special interest groups. After school, children rode their bikes and played with one another in the Lagoon or on the playgrounds, but frequently the compartmentalization of the day continued as small groups were driven to highly formalized activities such as golf, horseback riding, or music lessons, which took place in specialized facilities. Teacher's associations were also based on special interests, and their exchanges were so competitive and fragmented that little use was made of the architectural joining of classrooms to a shared service area. And although parents provided funding for various initiatives in the school, Gardendale children had few opportunities to observe adults working out common problems in the local community. Indeed, some children expressed the view that their community (and school) was without problems. Any difficulties that arose in the North San Lupe neighborhood were managed invisibly by the local police, private security companies, zoning inspectors, and other elected officials; most families, who were quite mobile, seemed to have few if any day-to-day relationships with their neighbors.

At Frederick Douglass, there were many wonderful possibilities for communal activities—owing to the two smaller schools, homerooms, and team teaching arrangement—and this potential for gaining a sense of community during school was extended after school. Even though the streets were dangerous, children did use them for stickball, skating, and other forms of imaginative play. Their activities were facilitated by a group of activist women at Saint Andrew's Church who organized neighborhood events in the church parking lot and generally tried to provide "eyes on the street" for young people. Children were also involved in their own activism on occasion, for example, Saint Andrew's Church involved children in setting up a recycling center and there were (unfortunately) numerous events commemorating youngsters who had been killed. However, these opportunities for children to experience Kemmis's "dynamic act of inhabitation" were eclipsed during school by interpersonal exchanges including excessive management of behavior, whirlwind scheduling of activities, and teacher's lack of support for one another. The challenges that children encountered in the outside world were studiously eliminated from classrooms and replaced by bureaucratic regulations that ensured their passive dependence, their life skills as participants in the Oak Hills extended family being unrecognized or devalued. On the other hand, the potential for enriching their individual spirits after school was under increasing assault due to rising physical deterioration, unemployment, educational failures, population loss, and crime.

Thus, Gardendale students had untold opportunities for appropriating the world and finding their unique niche as individuals both within and after school, but both school environments seemed to be lacking in communal activities requiring restraint of self-interests. Frederick Douglass students experienced the sense of mutual aid in their neighborhood and even had the potential for community-building in school, but those growth possibilities were obscured by their culture-of-poverty status. Both groups seemed to be growing up without an appropriate balance between the "I" and the "We"—without a sense of self that is limited and, at the same time, nourished by the collective. It would seem that Frederick Douglass might have enabled students to develop a sense of identity through experiences of personal control and solitude while recognizing the communal characteristics of their lived experience. Gardendale might have fabricated the prerequisite limits and boundaries of communal life as a counterbalance to the milieu of choice and self-interest that children experienced in school and in their private lives.

The reader will gain greater insight into children's afterschool experiences in Chapter Six when they tell their own stories.

NOTES

1. In a study I conducted earlier, participants showed significant improvements in social development skills but not in academic areas. For more information see *Learning through the Built Environment* (Sutton, 1985).

2. Meyerson and Scully (1993) referred to persons who simultaneously embrace seemingly contradictory roles as "tempered radicals." These persons precariously "maintain dual identities and commitments" (p. 11) in order to preserve their status as outsiders within mainstream institutions:

> We both identify with our respective organizations and professions, are committed to them, and want to pursue careers and advance within them. Yet, we also believe that these hierarchical institutions are patriarchies and need to change. At the same time, we believe that our profession is instrumental in perpetuating these forms and constraining change [p. 4].

This characterization—tempered radical—seems apt for understanding Jane's ambivalence about her job at Gardendale. She was responsible for educating students to assume their superior rank in a status quo that she was seeking both to join and to challenge.

3. Jung (1961) goes on to say that the particular elements he created—a cloaked god hidden in a crypt, the painted soul-stone (life force), the scrolls he later added—were especially meaningful because they all belong to a universally shared unconscious (p. 23).

Addressing Poverty as Insiders and Outsiders

As I explained earlier, the Urban Network provides a real-life focus for a variety of multidisciplinary learning experiences and—most importantly—encourages children and adults to be environmental advocates. But how is this to be achieved during the course of a year? In most cases, the first semester begins with short projects that prompt students to work with a variety of concepts related to the social and physical characteristics of neighborhoods as well as with the skills that are needed for planning and designing. A teacher's guide offers questions for structuring class discussions as well as lesson plans for four different projects that allow children to experiment hands-on with the program concepts and skills.[1] Although some teachers complete one or more of these projects exactly as presented in the teachers' guide, they are offered only as a point of departure. Most teachers use the program's concept to evolve activities that relate to their particular situation, and the implementation at Gardendale illustrates how this can happen. Among other things, Miss Moore asked her class to write essays about spending a day in San Lupe following discussions of that area's characteristics while Jane moved Mrs. Rayburne's architectural team toward the processes utilized in the second semester, involving them in designing an outdoor science laboratory that the Parents Association was planning to build.

The centerpiece of the Urban Network curriculum occurs during the second semester when students are to enhance some aspect of their school or community. Although the focus may be within the school or schoolyard, the intention is to take children out of the classroom to provide a service to others. The enhancement project, which comprises planning, design, and implementation, has numerous benefits for individual students, residents in the surrounding community, and the physical environment. Whereas the first semester offers children discrete skills and concepts within a structured classroom format, the enhancement project invites them to take the initiative in defining the parameters of their work. As other proponents of community-service learning[2] have observed, such instruction builds a sense of connection to others while giving students an opportunity to direct their own education and address important practical problems.

During the second semester, the Urban Network instructional materials suggest a four- to six-step process whereby students select an area of focus, develop a plan, raise money and implement the plan, then celebrate the outcome. A successful project engages participants (children, teachers, parents, and volunteers) in articulating common goals, collaborating to achieve their vision, and overcoming the obstacles that arise. Because multiple skills are needed, children and adults can select tasks that accent their special attributes, and persons of all ages and backgrounds can find ways to contribute, thereby opening up the learning environment to nontraditional participants who define the type and level of their involvement. However, the most important benefit of the enhancement project is that young people are able to make visible changes in their surroundings while getting immediate feedback on their efforts from a community of peers and significant others. In the words of an older student who was involved in a community-service learning project in Detroit:

> The purpose is not only to rebuild the city, but to rebuild a sense of community as well. We built parks and a baseball diamond. We renovated an elderly woman's house, painted a mural, and worked on antigang activities. The most important work, however, was the decreased sense of racial and age polarization between all involved as well as new feelings of hope—hope that as we continue to reform our city, we also could reform bonds among all people [Anonymous, quoted in Bryant, 1993, p. 67].

Since the designers of the Urban Network wanted to accommodate teachers' varied abilities, we developed three different methods for carrying out the enhancement project. Architectural design, which is the most ambitious of the three, requires carpentry and three-dimensional design skills as well as the financial wherewithal for buying building materials. This method—the one Tom and his students preferred—yields some sort of construction that might range in scale from a small planter to an entire playground installation and cost either a few hundred dollars or thousands of dollars. Carrying out an architectural design project generally involves professional assistance such as Tom and his students provided. Another method, environmental design, is an excellent choice for an art teacher since it produces nonstructural esthetic products (murals, drawings, posters, or exhibitions) and might cost just a few dollars. Jane selected environmental design, and Noreen ended up utilizing this method after Tom and his students completed their residency at Frederick Douglass. Advocacy is a third option, suited to schools that do not have access to planning or design expertise. This method can be accomplished by any classroom teacher and might consist of such activities as setting up a recycling center, writing letters on behalf of a cause, or holding a street fair. Depending on the activity, the investment in an advocacy activity might be quite minimal or, as is true with a fund-raising effort, it could generate monies. This is the option that Noreen would have preferred since it was the most aligned with her skills and teaching methods.

The instructions for the sample projects of the first semester are written in a standard lesson plan format. However, the instructions for the second semester are written as a series of stories told by children to engage participants in thinking through the steps of bringing about change. These narratives describe problems in schools and communities, the students' plans for addressing those problems, and the actions they took to implement their solutions. The stories end by telling how they celebrated their success, thus offering a number of suggestions for getting feedback on and feeling proud of one's work. In addition to showing how young people can make positive changes in their surroundings, the narrative format provides participants with a planning and design process that can be applied to their own needs. In this way, member schools are given a template they can use to develop unique interpretations of the assignment, and the Urban Network publishes their accomplishments in a biannual publication as an ongoing portfolio of children's environmental activism.

Just one caveat is necessary concerning the limits of children's participation. Even though students are to define and develop a solution to a problem that interests them, in all truthfulness the enhancement project is not entirely youth-directed since teachers and parents are to set its overall boundaries before posing the assignment to children. This is to ensure that children do not plan something that cannot be carried out. In particular, it is important for adults to select the option that matches the school's resources and, as the reader will see in the adult planning sessions at Frederick Douglass, avoid projects that would contradict the school's management policies. The teachers' task is to encourage the children's thinking within the established boundaries without imposing a specific direction.

Fortuitously, my contacts at both Frederick Douglass and Gardendale were strong supporters of community-service learning who were insightful in their approach to the enhancement project. Indeed, Tom's and Jane's primary reason for participating in the Urban Network was this outreach component. Tom was an articulate promoter of community-service learning for college students, and had even published a number of articles on the subject. As an urban planner, he believed that neighborhood planning should be a grassroots endeavor that includes children and adults as equal partners. Jane had been involved in many voluntary activities throughout her own schooling, often serving as a tutor or mentor for disadvantaged children. And in the community where she grew up, helping out neighbors was an absolute must. Nor was Noreen a stranger to real-world learning, having written experiential social studies curricula for Markington's Board of Public Schools on several occasions.

Though their projects evolved in different ways, adults at both schools chose the same topic of children's homelessness and impoverishment.[3] Tom persuaded Mrs. Driskell and Noreen to focus on this topic because many of the Frederick Douglass students walked by the soup kitchen at Saint Andrew's Church every day, and quite a few students either were, or knew another child who was, homeless. Jane and Mr. Regon agreed that an exposure to the poverty that existed nearby in Limone among the children of migrant farmworkers offered an opportunity to expand the students' understanding of problems outside their own protected community. As an art teacher, Jane was quite clear that environmental design best suited her needs. However, there was an ongoing tug-of-war between Tom and his students, who were drawn to the scale and public quality of architectural design, and Noreen, who preferred a more private advocacy activity that individual children could do within the confines of her class. Ultimately, the project that was completed fell into the category of environmental design, which was Mrs. Driskell's preference from the outset. The impact of these differing approaches will become apparent in the coming pages, as will the similarities and differences in the way the two schools approached the subject of children's impoverishment—one being an insider to hardship, the other being an outsider.

MAKING A NEIGHBORHOOD JOURNAL

Contrary to the Urban Network's intentions that the enhancement project snowball so as to involve a *larger* number of participants than the first semester, in reality, a *smaller* group of children continued with the second semester's work at both schools. Working with only a few students was part of the initial plan at Gardendale and in keeping with the school's policy of selectivity, but Tom had anticipated that his urban

planning students would work with all three classes at Frederick Douglass. However, during a visit to the school toward the end of the first
term, Mrs. Driskell informed him that only Noreen's class would continue with the neighborhood project. Her main concerns, she reiterated,
were the fast-approaching standardized tests and how the children
would perform. Since Noreen was a seasoned teacher, Mrs. Driskell was
more confident about her ability to produce good results than she was
about Mary, whose teaching skills were still unproven. As for Gail, her
input into the project thus far had been more destructive than helpful,
and she recently had begun taking quite a few sick days; the effort
would be better off without her. Reluctantly, Tom accepted Mrs.
Driskell's determination that the project would be more manageable if
it were confined to social studies lessons with Noreen's homeroom
class; Noreen, Tom, and I began to plan accordingly.

During a meeting that took place at the very beginning of the second
semester as we mapped out our roles relative to the children and the
urban planning students, Noreen commented on the insightfulness of
the writing produced during the first semester. She brought out a folder
and showed Tom and me several essays, which, we concurred, were
quite imaginative. Perhaps we could incorporate a writing exercise into
the enhancement project to give us a better idea of how children saw
their community and, at the same time, get them to think more about
the importance of their physical surroundings. The writing could serve
as the first step of the enhancement project because it would get children to think creatively beyond what the neighborhood *is* to what it
might be. Over time, we elaborated a journal concept that would allow
children to express inventive ideas about their neighborhood; so as to
not exclude the students with poor writing skills, it would encompass
writing and drawing as well as videotaped discussions. Initially, I
proposed doing a daily exercise during a one-week period that would
take about an hour each day, but it was readily evident that Noreen
could not possibly find that much time within the confines of the
schedule. Perhaps if we began the session during homeroom and short-
ened the activity to fifty minutes on just four days . . . Okay, we compromised; that would be our plan.

Toward the end of January, before Tom's students began their visits,
I spent four consecutive days at Frederick Douglass, arriving early
every morning to set up an ancient slide projector. For each of the first
three days, I showed a few slides of a particular type of neighborhood,
one that was clearly affluent, another that was low-income but quite
pleasant, and a third that was quite poor and horribly deteriorated. I
asked the children a series of questions about each of these neighborhoods ("What do you think about this neighborhood?" "Who lives

there?" "Where would children play?" "What would their school be like?" "How does it compare to this neighborhood?" "How would you feel about living there?").

Following the slide show each day, the children completed a writing or drawing exercise ("Write a story about an imaginary walk through your neighborhood." "Draw a future visions plan for your neighborhood." "Make a TV program about your neighborhood"). On the fourth day, children actually made a TV program as I videotaped them presenting their journal. Having set the stage for creative thinking about the neighborhood, Noreen and I ended the journal activity by facilitating a more practical discussion of their community. "What are the major problems in this neighborhood?" I asked. Hands shot up as children described what they had experienced firsthand:[4] "I seen someone get killed." "My friend's friend committed suicide." "I know this man's been in jail." "Lotsa people got AIDS." "Drug pimps hassle us all the time." "Well, what can we *do* about these problems?" Noreen asked. "Nothing!" everyone responded with great conviction as Noreen launched into her lesson for that day, a discussion of the Civil Rights movement as an example of how a few people can be catalysts for major change. By the end of class, the students had made a list of things that people do to transform their communities, and the way was paved for beginning the enhancement project.

THE HOMELESS PROJECT GETS STARTED AT FREDERICK DOUGLASS

It was already the beginning of February. Tom's students had gone to the basement with the children to check out the school cafeteria while he and Noreen had lunch with Mrs. Driskell to agree on the direction of the enhancement project. Mrs. Driskell began by saying that a large banner with a motto such as "Student Improvement through Parent Involvement" would definitely be an enhancement to the school's dreary front entrance. It would reinforce Frederick Douglass's educational goals and add color. Might this be a project for the urban planning students? Tom agreed that a banner would be effective, but pointed out that his class's focus was on involving children in the decision-making process. Since deciding what to enhance was just as important as actually carrying out the activity, we would need a broader framework for the children's idea. A banner would be too specific. "Okay, how should we begin?" queried Mrs. Driskell.

Tom suggested that perhaps Noreen's class could survey other students in the upper-elementary school to get their ideas for improving the school. Noreen responded that this would be too disruptive of the other classes even if the intrusion only lasted a few minutes. Besides, the children had to be supervised and she could not be everywhere at once. Taking another tack, Tom suggested hanging butcher paper in the lunchroom or in the corridor for students to write their ideas. "Absolutely not!" exclaimed Mrs. Driskell, moving her body to show how stopping to write on the walls would create chaos and lead to disciplinary problems. For his third idea, Tom proposed to expand on the "Good and the Bad" project by having students write stories about the positive and negative aspects of the school building. The children could read their stories to his urban planning students, then vote on a problem they would like to solve. Mrs. Driskell liked this approach and added that he and Noreen should walk around the building first to make a list of possible projects and begin discussing these during homeroom.

As enthusiasm built and a plan began to take shape, the group was interrupted by a young mother who whispered through the open door that she needed to speak to Mrs. Driskell. Invited in, she acknowledged Noreen, her son's teacher, then nervously apologized for the disturbance. Mrs. Driskell introduced the woman as Diane Greene, who sought penance once more as she fussed with her too-small coat, murmuring that she would have to miss parent education that evening. She was needed to take an unexpected turn serving dinner at the Saint Andrew's soup kitchen. There were so many people, Rev. Hill and the other ladies were shorthanded. Tom seemed interested and asked a few questions about the soup kitchen and Diane's work there. Mrs. Driskell expressed her disappointment at Diane's absence, sternly reminding her how critical it was not to miss too many classes, as the woman hurried to escape the room.

After Diane left, Tom said, "You know, I just got an idea for the enhancement project. What if Noreen's students become Diane's consultants at the soup kitchen? My planning students have been studying the homeless. What if they could work with your guys here to come up with a way of helping the children who eat at Saint Andrew's Church?" Mrs. Driskell was shaking her head, saying, "How can children possibly go out of the school to Saint Andrew's? This sounds really dangerous and out of hand." Tom assured her that the work could be done in the school by using pictures of the soup kitchen. Perhaps the director of the program would be willing to visit the school. And the children might even go on a field trip to the School of Planning to develop their design. Noreen pointed out the benefit of the topic being clearly in the area of social studies, adding that homeless people had figured prominently in the posters her students had done of their neighbors at the beginning of the year. Attracted by the fit with social studies but especially by the field trip—a rare occurrence at Frederick Douglass—Mrs. Driskell began to be won over by the homeless project. Certainly, it was a real issue for many children in the school, and the trip to the university would be wonderful. Tom offered that his students would bring in photographs of the church and soup kitchen right away so they could get the children to begin thinking about this particular issue. Mrs. Driskell would initiate the process of getting a school bus from Dr. Johnstone, and Noreen would go about obtaining written permissions from parents.

PLANNING FOR AN ELUSIVE FIELD TRIP

It was nearly six weeks later, toward the end of March, and a school bus had not yet been procured. Tom had called Mrs. Driskell many times, and she had just as insistently called Dr. Johnstone, who had yet to make a definite commitment of a bus, which, according to him, should have been processed at the beginning of the year. Tom had even investigated getting transportation from the university since time was running out on his class, which would end in another month, but this would take a big chunk of his budget. Not only were the rates high for university buses, but he would have to pay for two round-trips instead of one since the campus had to be the origination point. Renting a university bus would effectively eliminate the possibility of carrying out the plan his students had been evolving with the children, which would require about two hundred dollars or so in materials. So, Tom continued to stretch out the schedule, hoping that somehow Dr. Johnstone would relent early enough so that the project was not completely upended, either by lack of funds or lack of time.

Tom's students had already involved Noreen and her class in a number of exercises that eventually got them to the idea for their project. The children had discussed the narratives in the teacher's guide and also the pictures the urban planning students had taken. In their visits to the soup kitchen, the urban planners had discovered a group of women who not only ran the kitchen but also organized various neighborhood events and tried to look out for youth. Two of these women, referred to as "the sisters," came to class one monring to discuss their work at the soup kitchen. Notably, the children donned the same grown-up behavior I had observed during the snow emergency. Even Tameka and Shawn submerged their usual attempts to upend the class agenda, sitting angelically with hands folded as Noreen welcomed her guests. The sisters (who seemed to know most of the children by name) thanked Noreen for inviting them. They said a special greeting to Carlos and Jimmie, a white child and a black child who were best friends and seemed to be the most popular boys in class not only with the other students but with Noreen. Then, with cheery matter-of-factness, the sisters launched into an account of how the soup kitchen got started, how food was prepared, who worked there, who the clients were, and what it was like for children to eat there. Noreen asked the class to write a paragraph about what they saw as the worst problem at the soup kitchen and soon discovered the children's considerable knowledge of this place. As the sisters chimed "um-hums" and "amens," the students read stories about how people had to wait outside in the cold, how embarrassing it was for homeless children because the whole world knew they needed free food, how people had to stand up because there were not enough tables and chairs. Jimmie volunteered: "They have whole families over there and they go through a real lot of bad things. Sometimes after school, I try to help out by washing dishes and stuff." "Um-hum. Yes he does . . . one of our best helpers," agreed the sisters.

The urban planning students lettered each one of their ideas (including a few provided by the sisters) on large pieces of paper with bright magic markers, then they taped the pages up on the walls so that every square inch of wall space was covered. Through a very animated voting process, the children finally agreed on the worst problem at the soup kitchen—the lack of any place for children to play after their meal—and the sisters enthusiastically backed up this idea.

In the session that occurred just before time ran out on getting a bus ride to the university, Chester (Diane Greene's son, who had helped her at the soup kitchen on numerous occasions) had managed to overcome his shyness long enough to convince his classmates that a large Happy Toy would be the perfect solution. None of the adults had been quite sure what a Happy Toy was, but the children were unanimous that this was just what the soup kitchen needed. The next step would be for the children to figure out what Happy Toy should be like.

When Tom and his students got together with Noreen to discuss how to proceed with Happy Toy, Noreen expressed serious concerns with the direction the project was taking. More attuned to teaching students as individual learners, she was quite uncomfortable with the degree of group work that was implied by the construction effort and also by the lack of clarity on learning outcomes. "This is no small thing and it's *one* thing. How will twenty-three children be able to work on one big thing in this tiny classroom?" she said, looking around at her crowded room. "Besides, how will I know what each child contributed? How will the children have a sense of ownership for their contribution? Wouldn't it be much better to do something that each child can make at his or her desk . . . so that he or she can have something to take home . . . or put in his or her portfolio? And, it would certainly be preferable if the project relates to the children's schoolwork. For instance, why couldn't you have each child write a story and then put them together in a book for the homeless kids?"

Tom and his students agreed that a book of stories would be a great project and much simpler to manage, but they reminded Noreen that the children were to decide on the nature of their enhancement project within the overall framework set by the adults. The children's planning process had led them to Happy Toy and this idea had to be honored, especially since the teaching team had the financial resources and the skills to help the children realize their idea. And why *not* do something really big so the children could stand back and say: "Hey, I did that!" Besides, Rev. Hill and the sisters were expecting Happy Toy, not a book of stories. The onus was on the team to work out the mechanical details of getting the project designed and built without violating the school's procedures. Furthermore, they needed a plan that could be carried out in some form whether or not the bus materialized. Assured that she would have their assistance in completing whatever the children designed, a hesitant Noreen went along with the urban planners in figuring out what the steps of the process should be.

The group agreed that their focus should be on getting the children to design the toy in cardboard, either at Frederick Douglass or at the School of Planning. If the field trip came about, it would be an added experience, but they would downplay it as much as possible (although the field trip had been a main topic of discussion ever since the planning students had arrived). After the design of the toy was agreed upon, the urban planners would precut pieces out of wood so the children could assemble the actual toy in their classroom by the end of April during the university's exam week. The planners would deliver the toy to the soup kitchen and their class obligation would be over. Given this overall approach, the urban planners focused on developing the format of their design session and also a preparatory lesson related to children's play activities in Oak Hills, that Noreen would teach before the trip.

In case the field trip came about, Tom wanted to be sure Noreen understood the setting her students would have to navigate so she could prepare them for it. He pictured for her an enormous modern building with a large open atrium that served as the school's circulation core. Many students would be wandering around wearing the sort of clothes that the children were forbidden to wear at Frederick Douglass. The space would be noisy, and it would be very hard to hear. Their class session would take place on the carpeted floor of the atrium. The urban planning students would supply soft drinks, but the children should bring a bag lunch since they would arrive at the school around lunchtime. Noreen should make sure that they understood the absolute requirement to stay together in the carpeted area—if anyone wandered off, they could get lost or even hurt—and to work as quietly as possible in a spirit of creativity appropriate to a university. Time allowing, his students would take the youngsters on a building tour after the design activity was over and, of course, they should continue to stay together. As the various catastrophes that could occur with twenty-three ten- and eleven-year-olds had flashed before his eyes, Tom felt his heart beating underneath his tweed jacket. "This is Plan A," he said with a sigh. "We'll go to Plan B if—when—the bus falls through." In that case, the class would spend the entire day after recess on the design activity, beginning with a homestyle lunch together in Noreen's room.

HEY, GIMME FIVE FOR THIS HAPPY TOY

Miracles do happen. Dr. Johnstone's approval for a school bus came through just four days before the scheduled event. Tom got the news as he was signing in the tattered black visitors' book on the counter of the old principal's office. Taking the stairs three at a time, he went to Mrs. Driskell's office to confirm that everything was set to go. On the contrary, Mrs. Driskell explained, there were still major problems to resolve. The biggest one was that Noreen had called in that morning with a bad flu; she expected to be out the rest of the week. Mary could not take over for her because she was already scheduled to attend a teacher development workshop on Friday, the day planned for the field trip. If they moved the day forward till the next week, they would have to renegotiate with Dr. Johnstone and risk not being able to get the bus again. Furthermore, the semester was running out for the urban planning students. The only solution, they realized reluctantly, was to have Gail take over for Noreen.

That resolved, Mrs. Driskell turned to the problem of getting at least two parent volunteers. Tom suggested that Diane Greene and the sisters would be the perfect candidates and that perhaps they might bring a couple of homeless people. Mrs. Driskell looked aghast (she had once confided in me that Tom sometimes seemed really strange) as she explained that Diane and other staff from the soup kitchen were of course welcome to come along as parent helpers, if they had time. Taking homeless people was simply out of the question.

Friday arrived blanketed with one of Markington's early April snows and glistening in bright morning sun. One by one, the twenty-three children hopped off an old yellow school bus into the vast parking lot that flanked the College of Design Arts, where the School of Planning was housed. The sisters had not been able to come on such short notice, but Diane and two other parents were there. They helped Gail to organize the small bodies according to their height and gender so they formed two almost straight lines to advance toward what must have appeared to be the Land of Oz. Several of the planning students were waiting at the entrance to escort their guests to a sparkling, five-story space. As it was almost noon, the atrium was flooded with sunlight, which dappled the green philodendron plants that draped down a brand-new gray masonry wall. The scene looked as tasteful as it had in the photographs that had been published in all the architectural journals when the building won a major design award. Mostly white, mostly male graduate and undergraduate students were milling about with the air of feigned casualness that seems to go hand-in-hand with the high-stress environment of academia. Practically everyone, female and male, was sporting standard collegiate attire—faded blue jeans redesigned with colored patches and painstakingly frayed slits just big enough to provide seductive glimpses of pallid buttocks.

I tried to imagine how the children—whose cocoa-colored skin seemed even darker than it had in the shadows of Frederick Douglass—perceived this sparkling white place. Could they begin to understand that this structure had the same basic function as their own school? Could they imagine themselves taking up Tom's offer of a career in planning? Could they conjure up a vision of being able to inhabit this white man's palace as one of those laid-back, blue-jeaned students? Or, did the children relate to what they were seeing as make-believe? Perhaps it appeared to them as a stage set from *Dallas* or *Lifestyles of the Rich and Famous* rather than as a place to which they could aspire to belong.

Tom directed the children to pile their coats on the lounge chairs that ringed the space and got them seated in a large circle on the floor. Without invitation, they silently opened their identical brown bags (just as Noreen had instructed them to do) and began to munch on limp peanut butter sandwiches while the planning students served a vile-looking drink they had concocted with sherbet and fruit punch. Resigned to Gail's presence, Tom walked over to where she was seated facing the circle of small bodies, and offered a welcome. As if having been given a go signal, Gail seized the opportunity to loudly retell the children's quandary, speaking very properly so as to distance herself from this shabby crew. They were wild and out of control; a constant stream of kids transferred in and out of the school; some were at second-grade reading levels; many lived with single mothers who received Aid to Dependent Children; the rest were not much better off; they all got "free" lunches like the one they were now eating, which, she always reminded them, were not really free but provided by tax-payers. Then came Gail's own plight, her words bouncing off the award-winning masonry wall and crescendoing as they echoed up five stories. Mrs. Driskell had asked her to go over some questions about how children played in Oak Hills, but she had not been able to do it. There were just too many distractions—snow canceled classes one day, an unmanageable child had required a disciplinary action, the count-down was on for the state tests. Besides, she did not live in Oak Hills, so it was hard for her to lead a discussion on what children did there. In fact, it was hard for her to imagine what *anyone* did there, let alone children.

Tom found a second of space to interrupt and excuse himself so he could focus on getting the design session started. His students had selected a few slides of indoor and outdoor play equipment, which they showed along with slides of the room at Saint Andrew's Church, where Happy Toy would be installed. When asked for input on what type of play equipment might be good for homeless children, the fifth-graders began criticizing the play equipment Tom's students had shown. Plainly, they felt they could improve on that "dumb stuff" and offered ideas that were richly detailed. Not only were their comments unconstrained by the uncommonness of the situation, they seemed to have the same humorous vibrancy that had occurred during the snow emergency. After about ten minutes of brainstorming, the urban planning students brought out an enormous cardboard model they had built of the interior of Saint Andrew's soup kitchen. The urban planners placed the model in the center of the space as they explained to the children that everyone would work in their regular teams—the Ohioans, New Yorkers, and so forth—to make small Happy Toy models to add to the large model of the soup kitchen (Tom indicated about eighteen inches with his hands to show the approximate size of their models). At the end of the day, they would decide which one of the models to build as a gift for the homeless children at Saint Andrew's Church. As the children started to whisper and point at the big cardboard room, Tom shepherded each of the teams to a corner and motioned for his planning students to initiate the model-making process.

As four groups of bodies huddled around boxes of supplies to begin their work, Tom noticed that Gail and the parents were sitting at the edge of the space disengaged from each other and from the huddles. Approaching the parent group first to see if he could get them involved in the work, he reminded Diane Greene that she was the children's main client. It was very important to get her input on what would be an appropriate Happy Toy. Diane giggled with a gesture that conveyed her reluctance to assume such an important role as she and the two other women haltingly walked toward the nearest group. Tom turned his attention to Gail, but she was unrelenting in her decision that this was not her sort of activity; she was happy to stay right where she was.

Meanwhile, the work proceeded with a wonderful intensity as cardboard was cut and glued into various shapes. The parent-clients began to meander around the room observing, but not interacting with, the children; soon they were joined by onlookers from the School of Planning who folded their arms and planted themselves around the perimeter of the carpet. Other students and faculty circulated around the atrium, some looking or pointing, some just passing through. As if oblivious to all the watching eyes, the children concentrated on combining pieces of cardboard and colored paper, and soon each team had an odd-shaped element that represented their Happy Toy. Tom signaled the group to gather around the cardboard room, then invited the Washingtonians to be the first to show their model. Their faces became frozen in terror as Tom asked: "Which one of you would like to describe your Happy Toy?" Chester was pushed to volunteer by his teammates since Happy Toy was his idea in the first place. "It's basically nothing," Chester said as he shrugged his shoulders and contemplated a crumpled creature that looked as if the sculptor Dubuffet might have invented it. With some encouragement, Chester provided a halting but coherent description of a clown whose moving arms and legs would make the homeless children laugh. Tom asked, "Mrs. Greene, what do you like best about this toy? Does anyone else on this team have a different opinion? What if you were to redo this design, what would you change?"

Sheepish delight appeared on the children's faces when Tom explained that they should present their designs in a loud, clear voice because the planning students were there looking for ideas for their own work. Confidence and enthusiasm built, and the children's responses became less stilted. The first two teams deferred to a leader but by the third presentation all the members of the team joined in as the children began correcting and disagreeing with one another on specific aspects of their proposal. Then, Tom called on the last team. Six New Yorkers stepped forward and triumphantly placed a colorful model of a miniature playhouse inside the cardboard room. Confident that they had figured out the perfect gift for a homeless kid, they described the details of the house. When Tom asked what could be improved, Shawn began to strut triumphantly around his team's cardboard model. "Not a thing, man—it's perfect. Hey, gimme five," he said as his classmates cheered that this design was, for sure, the winner.

PLEASE KEEP ME SEPARATE

As with implementing the Urban Network at the beginning of the year, considerable planning for the second semester had occurred before my arrival at Gardendale. During a telephone consultation in January, I had shared with Jane the ideas generated at Frederick Douglass regarding the journal activity as an introduction to the enhancement project; Jane was enthusiastic to begin in the same way. She proposed framing this exercise as an integrative language arts, social studies, and fine arts experience (which would allow her to devote a full week to it) and suggested adding photography to the writing and drawing assignments. The children all owned cameras, Jane explained, and had some experience in developing and printing film so the journal would provide a motivation for extending their skills in this area. Mrs. Rayburne and Miss Moore had already selected a total of twelve students to participate—the four boys from Mrs. Rayburne's class who had worked on the outdoor science laboratory and two of Miss Moore's four "tribes" whom I had also met. Jane was delighted that I would spend the entire week of the journal activity, the two of us working with the students every day for a couple of hours in her art room. Similar to the plan Noreen and I had developed, Jane would take over at the end of Friday's journal activity with a discussion that would initiate the enhancement project.

The opening exercise in hand, we progressed to discussing the direction of the rest of the semester. Jane said that she had been considering my earlier suggestion to focus the enhancement project on providing a service to a disadvantaged community. Limone, where she lived, seemed an ideal community since it was relatively nearby but was quite different from San Lupe, both socioeconomically and geographically. I agreed that this approach seemed to have potential. Our challenge would be to guide the children toward some broad issue in Limone and inspire their creativity in addressing that issue while not influencing the direction of their decision-making process. In other words, once she made a plan to increase the children's awareness of a problem in her community, we would both need to support them in developing and carrying out their own solutions to that problem. Jane said she would map out an awareness-building plan and have it ready for discussion during my week-long visit in mid-January.

When I arrived at Gardendale that Monday morning, the first thing on my schedule was a meeting with Jane and Mr. Regon upstairs in the teacher's workroom. Jane had already gotten Mr. Regon's nod of approval on the journal activity. His only suggestion was that, in light of the Aspiring Professionals program, the children be encouraged to examine their photographs with a critical architectural eye. This activity agreed upon, we turned our attention to a mini-outline that Jane was just printing out on the Laserwriter. As she gave us copies of her draft, Jane explained that she wanted to make her students aware of the children of migrant farmworkers living nearby in Limone. She thought that by finding out about these children's impoverished lives, her students might envision some sort of an exchange with them. Toward this end, Jane proposed an activity that would help her students understand what it means when families do not have control over their circumstances, especially when they do not have permanent housing. Afterward, she envisioned taking them on a field trip to Limone to observe migrant farm conditions firsthand. Possibly, the science teachers might even tap into this project and do something on agriculture. Never caught short on supportive input into teachers' ideas, Mr. Regon patted Jane's outline with genuine approval, suggesting that the courtyard might be a good place to explore the problems associated with temporary housing. Certainly, he could handle such details as reserving the school van, which would be just big enough to accommodate all twelve children and three adults on the Limone field trip. Any supplies would, of course, be covered by the mini-grant Jane had received from the STC, but she should remember that a report was needed to demonstrate how this activity fit with the goals of the Aspiring Professionals program. These administrative details complete, Jane and I finished our coffee, then rounded up the children and headed down to the art room to begin the neighborhood journal about midmorning that same day.

Following each day's slide show and writing or drawing exercise, the children spread out the photographs they had printed the week earlier on one of the large wooden tables in Jane's luxurious art room. Spending one session looking at just two or three students' work meant we could go into considerable detail not only on San Lupe's architectural qualities but on the children's feelings about living in that community. Through these sessions, which were quite intense, Jane and I attempted to demonstrate our openness to the children's ideas about residential environments while also meeting the goal of the Aspiring Professionals program, namely, to increase their awareness of architecture.

On Friday, after videotaping the children's presentations of their journals, Jane began a discussion by asking the children to describe the major problems that existed in San Lupe—or in places that were not so nice as San Lupe. The problems they identified were not unlike those named by Noreen's class except that they spoke much more abstractly about things they had not experienced directly ("We worry all the time about getting robbed." "Mother says the police protection around here is not what it should be." "I went to the city once and we drove by this housing with all the windows shot out and stuff, and kids were just standing around smoking and helping their dads park cars. It's amazing how they can do that"). Some of their fears were about their own downward mobility ("It's hard to get ahead these days. I heard about one kid in high school who cracked up because of the strain." "My dad is going to take me out of this school if they let too many dummies in"). When Jane pressed for solutions, the children became adamant in insisting on the need for more external control ("The school should be forced to give us body guards because these pitch-black gangs are everywhere." "We need more vigilantes to wipe out the crooks." "Every child in this school should get a bulletproof vest." "People who cheat on welfare and refuse to work are ruining this country. They should all be put in jail"), their level of insecurity rising as the discussion continued.

When Jane broached the idea of a field trip to Limone, the level of panic exploded among the children, who were already behaving in a disorderly manner since they were unaccustomed to group discussion. Children began calling out that going to such a place would surely put their lives in jeopardy. Then Claudia leaped to her feet, motivated either by a perceived duty to protect her white classmates or by the need to distance herself from the "pitch-black gangs." As Claudia persisted in elaborating the horrors that would occur, Jane became just as forceful in asking how she knew that such things were true. But, support for Claudia grew. Soon Justin (who was so often Claudia's antagonist) even chimed in to verify that Claudia was stating "the facts," adding confidently that their parents would *never* allow them to go to Limone. Sensing the futility of attempting to change the children's minds that particular day, Jane brought the session to an end as quickly as possible.

On the way to home, Jane fretted about the possibility of the children remaining totally unaccepting of the enhancement project concept. "Well then, we'll go to Plan B," I consoled as I enjoyed the ride to Limone. "But I think your plan is going to work."

WHERE HOMELESSNESS IS AN ADVENTURE

Jane began the second step of her awareness-building agenda by reading a story about Rosa, a young single mother who has just lost her job in a Kmart that went out of business. Rosa had saved a little money, so for a while she and her ten-year-old daughter, Maria, got along. But, as the months went by and Rosa was unable to find another job, she fell behind in her rent. Soon the landlord had no choice but to evict Rosa and Maria. At first Rosa and her daughter moved in with Rosa's sister, but the sister's husband was very abusive. Before long, Rosa decided that living on the street would be safer than living with her sister. Jane ended the story by saying, "Today is the first day that Rosa and Maria are homeless. Your assignment is to imagine being in their shoes."

In addition to the two key players, Jane had created another ten roles so that each child could assume an identity. She told the class about a second, newly homeless family consisting of a mother, father, and two boys as well as five homeless men and one woman who been living on the street for quite some time. Jane explained that she would play the part of a social worker who was in charge of providing various services, and Mrs. Helen Hansen, Emily's mother, would be in the role of a policewoman whose job was to keep vagrants off the street. Clarifying that the purpose of the role-play was to explore the feelings and experiences of their characters, Jane instructed the children to imagine that a big storm was on the way so the homeless people have a pressing need to construct some sort of shelter. The children spent a long time selecting their roles, trading parts with one another until they had the perfect cast, then headed outside to the courtyard to enact Rosa and Maria's first day on the street. Jane planned to end the activity by taking the children back inside for a discussion and writing exercise.

Fortunately, it was a bit overcast in San Lupe that day, so it was somewhat easier to pretend that Gardendale's luscious courtyard was actually a place where homeless people might have to dodge a police officer or seek refuge from a storm. Donning his role as Homeless Man II, Peter surveyed the yard and promptly hypothesized, with a look of utter delight in his eyes, that the homeless people probably had gone to live in the Lagoon with the birds and the deer. "Oh, that's awesome!" exclaimed Kimsung, flapping his arms and running in circles to imitate a bird. "Let's all go to the Lagoon to live in the trees." Without missing a beat, Mrs. Hansen (who had grown up on Detroit's East Side and had only recently moved to San Lupe from Dearborn Heights), assumed her role as Policewoman and announced that vagrants were strictly forbidden to enter the woods. Anyone caught there would be arrested and thrown into jail. The ferocity of her response took the children so off-guard that their initial giddiness rapidly turned into seriousness as Jane laid out the rules of the role-play.

Pointing to a pile of materials (cardboard boxes, bedsheets, a ball of heavy cord), Jane informed her cast of characters that they would be living in the courtyard indefinitely, so they would need to construct a shelter. The more experienced homeless people would be responsible for helping Rosa, Maria, and the other family who had just started to live outside. As Ms. Social Worker, she handed each child a shopping bag containing various smaller supplies (masking tape, staple gun, string) and a card representing a food stamp, cautioning that no mid-morning snacks would be dispensed without the food stamp. Surveying the building materials, the children's ebullience began to return as Maria (played by Sallyanne) convinced the group that the play structure would be the best place to build a shelter.

The homeless characters dragged their supplies and shopping bags over to the play structure, which was located fairly close to their classrooms, and began to plan out their shelter. Maria was quite right—the structure offered a perfect backdrop for elaborating an enclosure. It consisted of a half dozen platforms, each a different size and height, each oriented to face a different direction, each containing a unique play element. Some were rimmed by bars that were meant to swing on, others had barrels that could be crawled through, still others had vertical panels with holes cut out to form small seats or peek-a-boos. Four of the platforms rotated around a fat center post that contained foot holes for climbing; two others were less connected to that grouping. Maria hopped onto one of the set-apart platforms that was the highest perch, claiming it for herself and Rosa. The second family rushed to take possession of two of the larger platforms as the remaining homeless people clamored to divvy up what was left.

Small hands sorted through supplies to select particular elements, then they began to tie cord, drape bedsheets, and cut cardboard shapes; they taped and stapled and soon the most fanciful structure began to take shape in the courtyard. Just then, Ms. Social Worker interrupted Rosa to say that she would have to stop her work on the shelter and travel across town to look for a job. "But," objected Rosa, "I want to finish my house." Looking very stern, Ms. Social Worker explained that she *had* to look for work if she wanted to get any more food stamps, and directed Rosa to the bus stop at the opposite end of the courtyard. Resigned, Rosa headed toward the bus stop, but Ms. Social Worker called out: "What about your daughter? You can't go without her." So both Maria and Rosa, who were best friends in real life, skipped off to the bus stop, where they promptly became engaged in their own game of imagination as Policewoman delivered the next piece of bad news to the remaining characters. "This is city property. Loitering and littering are not allowed. You'll have to take down all this stuff and move along."

The shelter-building activity ended as the characters reluctantly disassembled their magnificent construction (but not before Jane and Mrs. Hansen had taken quite a few pictures) and queued up to trade their food stamps for midmorning snacks. Returning to their real selves, the group headed inside to discuss their experience in their teams. Jane, Mrs. Hansen, and I posed a series of questions to each team: "What does 'control' mean?" "Why do some people have more control over what happens to them?" "What does it feel like when you don't have control over things?" "Sallyanne and Laura, what did it feel like when you were told you had to leave the group in order to keep your food stamps?" "How did everyone else feel when you were told that you had to remove your shelter?" After heated debates among teammates, the students wrote essays, and this one by Michael was fairly typical of what they crafted:

> This was a great lesson on making shelters for the homeless. What I liked best was when we climbed up the pole and hung the sheets to keep the water out of our house. I think our house would be safe when the storm came. I also learned that architects could design some really interesting houses for the homeless, and I hope they do because it's no fun being homeless. Also I think it was really mean when the pretend police lady made us take down our shelters and leave. We should get to have more control over important things.

A THIRD TRY AT SOCIAL AWARENESS

The next lesson in Jane's sequence was to be the field trip to Limone, but first she needed to prepare the children for what they would observe. Her paintings seemed a better introduction than photographs, which might underscore the town's physical deterioration and return the children to their initial reaction of fear. The paintings, she thought, would provide a window into the personality and day-to-day life of the community. So Jane carted in three of her canvasses, one of some boys chasing after a dog, another of a school playground where children were playing a game of tag, and a third of a man standing on the porch of a shanty. With these images, she had been able to describe the kind of people who lived in Limone, what their lives were like, and, in particular, what the elementary school was like since this building would serve as the homebase for their field trip.

Using as a format one of the narratives from the Urban Network instructional materials, Jane engaged the students in writing a list of questions to answer on the field trip ("What was the best thing you saw on the field trip?" "What was the worst thing?" "If you were the mayor of Limone, what would you do to improve the town?" "If you lived in Limone, what would you do to help your community?" "What can children in this class do?" "What supplies would we need?" "How can we get information about what the community needs?" "How would we know whether the people who live in Limone would like our plan?"). Armed with questions, clipboards, cameras, and a picnic lunch, the children and their chaperones boarded the school van and headed to a place that would probably seem as strange to them as the College of Design Arts must have appeared to Noreen's class.

It was the early part of March and the fog was just lifting from what promised to be a beautiful spring morning. Jane took her usual route out of town, onto the four-lane highway that climbed sharply up into the mountains surrounding San Lupe. A sign announcing the exit to C14 appeared after about twenty miles, directing the way to Limone. The van slowed as Jane navigated the tight curves of a narrow road, her passengers delighting in a thickly wooded area that looked as if it had just burst into bloom. Farther along, Mr. Regon pointed to a bare strip in the landscape where all the trees had been chopped down, and reminded the children of a lesson they had had earlier in the year on clear-cutting. Eventually, the woods thinned out and the van descended slowly into a rolling valley of orchards and dairy farms. The rainy season had just ended, so some of the fields were being cleared and planted by large combines, others were lined with endless rows of knurled trees flowering with white or purple buds that would soon turn to grapes, still others had huge trees dangling clumps of white flowers that would become almonds. Occasionally, the orchards were punctuated by a pasture with enormous black cows and their heifers grazing near faded red barns and murky green ponds. When the van passed such a farm, an odor penetrated the van that caused its passengers to shriek, "Pee-uw, this stinks!" and flap their hands as if to force the air back to the outside.

Sometimes at a distance down a long skinny dirt road, an immense house where a landowner's family lived came into view; sometimes there were glimpses of the trailers and shanties where the families of migrant farmworkers lived; everywhere there were trucks, some shiny and new, others barely upright on their axles. A single electric line and telephone line followed along each dirt road, where an inevitable collection of dogs and cats lounged, pretending to ignore the occasional rooster that strutted by. As the journey continued, this undulating blanket of agriculture became punctuated with smaller parcels of land that were steeply banked one against the other. A few had fairly substantial houses sitting back from the road, but most had small wooden structures—perhaps with just a room or two—sitting very near to the pavement, their tin roofs slightly pitched toward the sun.

On seeing the shacks, Kimsung begged for Jane to pull over so he could take pictures. "Jane! Jane! This looks just like where I grew up in Thailand when my parents were missionaries. But, it's right here in the USA. I've got to show my dad this. Please stop!" The next few miles took about twenty minutes because of many pauses to let the students aim their automatic cameras out the windows of the van to capture on film the romance of rural poverty.

The town itself was nestled in a small valley within the mountain range, giving it a very picturesque approach. One- and two-story masonry and wood buildings lined either side of a narrow street with equally narrow sidewalks, the broken-down cars that were parked among the pickup trucks appearing to the children "like ancient antiques." Jane pulled into a parking lot at the edge of town that served all of Limone's public schools. The passengers climbed out of the van, got into their teams, each with its chaperone, and entered a miniature elementary school for a rest stop. Jane introduced her wide-eyed charges to a guard seated in a darkened corridor next to a rickety desk meant for a child. The guard, who was obviously expecting their visit, picked up his walky-talky and silently escorted the visitors to the toilets at the end of the short hallway. Sneaking peeks into the open doors that lined either side of the hallway, the Gardendale parade saw the smallest, darkest rooms they had ever seen, jammed with bodies, a din of monotone voices reciting multiplication tables or alphabets—smells and noises merging together in the corridor. In place of their cozy carpets, brightly colored materials, and shiny electronic equipment, they saw bare floors, small brown children, and larger white children sitting on chairs bolted to the floor, bent over the most tattered books they had ever seen.

Having held their breath through the torturous moments in the toilets, the children trekked swiftly back out into the sunlight, where Peter and Claudia (especially Claudia) pleaded that it would be much better to get back into the van. Jane firmly reminded the students of their plan—they would walk back down Main Street to look at the shops and a big church, make a short visit to her art studio, and then return to the school playground (the one in her painting, she emphasized), where they would have their lunch. By one-thirty, the adventure of going to Limone would be a distant memory and they would be back in Gardendale doing all their ordinary activities. Mr. Regon and Mrs. Hansen endorsed Jane's outline for the morning, and the contingent tentatively advanced into the street as if walking onto a movie set for an Alfred Hitchcock murder mystery.

Main Street, which was just four blocks long, was where Limone's more successful farmworkers lived. Some even owned small shops and lived above them on the second floor with their families; others lived in small, tightly packed houses on the side streets. The Gardendale parade trudged past the hand-lettered signs taped to the windows of El Chico's restaurant, past the tiny pink-and-white crocheted blankets in the Los Niños clothing store, past the crates of plantains and avocados, past a row of seated men with arms folded across their chests and tilted back so the front legs of their chairs no longer touched the sidewalk.

They crossed the street toward the Our Lady of Guadalupe Church, which, in relation to all the tiny shops, seemed huge, its white stucco facade enlivened by the faded blue ceramic tiles that framed a wooden door. A few steps away from the church was the police station and the town hall, a dusty and damp room lined with backless wooden benches—a room that made Frederick Douglass's auditorium seem palatial.

Reminding her visitors to take a few photographs, Jane directed them to turn right onto Los Altos where the mountains came back into view. Almost at the end of the street was her white frame house with its flower boxes and red shutters. Inside, in rooms bare of furnishings, was a space that could have been imported directly from SoHo in New York City. The children alternated between surveying the smells and sights of splattered oil-base paints, and making sure they took their turn in the bathroom so as to avoid another encounter with the toilets at the Limone Elementary School. Their visit complete, the group headed back down Los Altos, onto Main Street, and over to the school playground. Because the children of both the landowners and the farmworkers attended the same schools, Limone's facilities were a cut above what is typical in most of the rural towns in this area. The playground, though dusty and devoid of any equipment, had the luxury of being planted with most of the town's large trees. Groups of children were taking advantage of the shade they afforded to munch on one of two distinct menus—neat sandwiches wrapped in waxed paper and commercial packages of potato chips for the landowners' children, tacos and fatty chunks of pork wrapped in pieces of old cloth for the farmworkers' children. Jane waved to several of the Limone children and ushered her students to a tree they had selected as a picnic spot. Under the curious eyes of both Limone groups, the Gardendale children spread out a blue checkered tablecloth on the red clay where they placed their wicker picnic basket and Igloo cooler. Feeling suddenly tired and very hungry, they began devouring the food that had been prepared that morning by their suburban mothers and nannies, adding yet another dimension to the menu of this outdoor multicultural dining room.

LEARNING THE ROLE OF PHILANTHROPIST

> An old-fashioned name for much that gets called service is, of course, "charity"—a rubric still used by many people in this country. For some of us the word has patronizing implications—toss "them" something called "charity." But for others the word summons the greatest of moral mandates, for as a biblical word it is meant to convey the essence of concern for others and the act of making that concern concrete and generous [Coles, 1993, pp. 53–54].

To what degree could Jane, herself an outsider in the Gardendale environment, get students to begin developing a realistic concern for the farmworkers' children so that their charity would reflect not just a perfunctory need to be kind, but rather the selfless and enduring idealism that is embodied in the biblical meaning of this word? Could she get her students to imagine what life was really like for these children— sitting crowded together in a room to recite mindless information, being taught by a teacher who does not bother to learn your name, being ridiculed by the landowners' children, working long hours in a field, living in the most temporary of shelter? Or would she be accused of being "too political" and risk the opportunity she had been given to demonstrate her worthiness to direct the Aspiring Professionals program? Sensing the degree to which she herself had been co-opted, Jane realized that she could continue to talk about the quality of the farmworkers' lives, but she would also have to ensure that students accomplished the high-quality products that were expected at Gardendale.

Back in her art room, Jane began the planning phase of their work by asking teams of students to consider the questions they had written before going on the trip as a way of reflecting on what they had seen. A lively debate ensued in the teams about the best and worst aspects of the trip. Sallyanne and Justin debated about whether the luscious orchards were better than Jane's mysterious studio. Kimsung put the shanties highest on his list of field-trip pleasures, and several children thought picnic lunch was "totally awesome," but all the teams concurred that the worst part of the trip had been the journey down the hallway of the Limone Elementary School and into those stinky toilets. How, they wondered, could kids possibly go there every day and sit all jammed together in those sweaty little dark rooms? Jane explained that sometimes the farmworkers' children did not go to school because they had to work in the fields. The school was extra crowded that day because it was planting season and, since machines did that work, everyone was in school.

"If I were the mayor," Claudia told her teammates, "I would tear down that awful school and build a nice new one out in the orchards." "If *I* were the mayor I would get rid of El Chico's," countered Madison. "Did you see the food in there? That was cholesterol heaven if I've ever seen it." As Jane steered the teams toward "solutions" they could actually implement, the groups began to focus on what they might donate to the school. Two ideas emerged as the students debated whether to send their old toys or a gift of money. After considering the appropriateness of their toys (roller blades, computer games, china dolls, golf clubs, horseback riding equipment) for the farmworkers' children, the teams eventually decided to save their allowance for one month and make a contribution to the Limone Elementary School. They also decided to write letters thanking the school for hosting them on their field trip and saying how much they had enjoyed their picnic lunch. Jane would deliver the money and letters along with some used books she had collected.

That settled, Jane encouraged the group to think about what else they might contribute in their role as aspiring architects. Almost immediately, Michael said, "Let's redesign the town. That's what my dad would do." "Yeah, let's redesign the town," echoed Kimsung, beaming. Soon an enthusiastic plan evolved for redesigning Limone's Main Street as the teams considered building a model and possibly using their photographs to make either a display, a book report, or perhaps both.

Since Mrs. Rayburne's team had learned to make scale drawings during the first semester, the students volunteered to make a scale model of Main Street while one of Miss Moore's teams printed the photographs and the other used an old history book of Jane's to write an essay about Limone, past and present. Documentation of the existing conditions was competed in about two weeks, leaving the students another three weeks to develop their design and present it. They glued new facades onto the old shops, removed the old town hall and police station (replacing them with a single structure that was even larger than Our Lady of Guadalupe Church), widened the sidewalk, parked brightly colored toy cars along the street, and added a playground for the Limone Elementary School (even though the school was not on Main Street). When the model was almost complete, the children focused on making drawings to illustrate their improved downtown (ones that looked remarkably like San Lupe) and on writing essays to explain their design. Photographs were mounted, essays were word-processed, and soon the class had a variety of excellent finished products stacked in one of Jane's storage closets.

Their enhancement project complete, Jane asked the children to think back on their experience and write an essay about what they had learned. Although it will be clear in the next chapter that Emily Hansen was profoundly moved by her exposure to Limone, most of the children focused on their own processes and capabilities. As the following essays by Laura and Jeremiah suggest, visiting Limone did seem to promote a degree of social awareness, but it also reinforced a valuing of San Lupe's lifestyle.

> The Limone Project taught us about how people live in the rural areas. The kids who worked in the Aspiring Professionals program were chosen as the best from the whole sixth grade to make a new design for Limone. This is so when we grow up, we will know how to fix these towns up. This

project also taught us how to keep this world a better place and made me appreciate how nice it is to live here in San Lupe.

I think we did a great job. This was a fabulous idea that our art teacher came up with. I'm glad the teachers at Gardendale are teaching us kids about wonderful careers like architecture and how to become better citizens.

By Laura, Class 601

Hi! I'm Jeremiah and I'm going to show you what we did in the Aspiring Professionals program. Our project is about fixing up a farm town not too far from here. The town has little run-down buildings and houses and the worst thing is a really messy school. The toilets stink and there's no paper or doors.

We took pictures of the town to learn what architects do. We surveyed a broken down church and a town hall and some funny little stores with horrorful food. We also took pictures of a very interesting art house where our teacher lives. Some other kids developed the pictures and mounted them on a board. I made a great architect's (scale) model of how we would like Limone to look. It is not easy to be an architect, but I learned that it can really be quite fun.

After doing this project, I have begun to take social issues a lot more seriously. It has given me responsibility to help poor children have a better life. This is why we are sending our allowance to the school.

By Jeremiah

It is true that many activists come from privileged backgrounds; it is also true that social inequities are highly resistant to change, as are environmental problems, which are increasing to the point of crisis. The question I am raising is, What kind of early exposure to social and environmental issues would encourage adult activists such as Gandhi who begin their work by questioning their own role and way of life? Perhaps, Jane's dual commitment to increasing the children's social awareness while simultaneously reinforcing their access to privilege through the Aspiring Professionals program may have been an impossible one to achieve—at least not without some broader familial and institutional support.

CENTERSTAGE AT GARDENDALE

It was my last visit to San Lupe and a picture-perfect June day. The school was abuzz with preparations for the Annual Spring Festival, an all-school celebration of work completed during the year which would be held that evening. Every special program had a time allotted for a formal presentation as well as a place in one of the corridors to exhibit work. All the classrooms would be filled with projects and open for display, and the courtyard would be set up with plenty of delicious refreshments for the proud parents and school officials who were expected to show up that evening.

This year, the children who had participated in the Aspiring Professionals program were to be the central attraction not only because sixth-grade students were generally given a special spot in the festivities but because of their participation in the outdoor science laboratory. During the second semester, while the children were working on their enhancement project, the Parents Association had engaged Techetti and Associates, a landscape architecture firm, to develop the sketches that had been done during the first semester by Mrs. Rayburne's architectural team. The design had already been finalized and approved by the Parents Association and the San Lupe Unified School District. Tonight's celebration would begin with a groundbreaking ceremony for the outdoor science laboratory, which was to be constructed during the summer months.

When I walked through Gardendale's airy entrance, I could feel the excitement of an opening night. Children, teachers, and more mothers than usual were rushing back and forth through the halls, carrying armloads of projects, stepladders, and various exhibition supplies; voices were rehearsing parts; and even Dr. Marcus was scurrying around to finish her last and most substantial edition of the school newsletter. I spent the day alternating between helping Jane and the aspiring professionals to mount an exhibition of their work and rehearsing them to present it orally. Kimsung, Charles, Jeremiah, and Michael from Mrs. Rayburne's class had written essays to read at the groundbreaking ceremony in the courtyard, just after all the adults had made speeches and Dr. Marcus had dug into the ground with a shiny silver shovel. Michael would end by inviting everyone to take a closer look at their sketches, which were hanging in the lounge alongside Techetti's crisp blue construction drawings. Then the audience would file downstairs into the multipurpose room for the rest of the presentations, including one of the Limone project, which would happen last. Since Mrs. Rayburne's students were presenting the outdoor laboratory, Miss Moore's students would present Limone. Emily and Sallyanne had written a song about their contributions to the Limone Elementary School, which they practiced over and over in a corner of Jane's art room; the remaining six would present their redesign of Main Street by projecting slides of their models and drawings on an enormous screen. The children were well prepared as usual so that the main problem was in finding enough space to exhibit all their projects.

Jane and I stayed in town for dinner and arrived back at the school to find the gingerbreadlike building bursting with well over a thousand people. Realizing that it would be impossible to get in through the front door, we went around to the east entry, found our crew of students, and inched our way through the crowd to the courtyard just in time for the groundbreaking ceremony. Kimsung tugged on Jane's arm to get her attention as Dr. Marcus stepped onto a small podium that had been set up for the speakers. "You know what? Hey, guess what?" he demanded with great agitation. "We're going to be the beginning *and* the end. We're going to have the first *and* last word." And, indeed they did. The Aspiring Professionals program was a major success at Gardendale that evening.

WHAT HAPPENED TO HAPPY TOY

Tom's course on Citizen Participation in the Planning Process had quite a different outcome. He and his students had been quite pleased— relieved—with the stellar performance of Noreen's class during their visit to the university. But, it was already the second week of April and time was running out on them. They needed to figure out how to construct the children's design via a technique that would allow each of the four teams to build a section of the house at their desks. Then, they would have to purchase all the supplies, precut the pieces, and design a lesson that would get the children through a successful assembly process. The group was so occupied with their decision-making (should they stain the pieces ahead of time or let the children paint the assembled house? should the pieces be slotted together or permanently attached? should it be made out of plywood or Plexiglas?) that it did not occur to them to check in with their teaching partner, Noreen. When Tom finally telephoned her around the middle of April to say that everything was set to go, the bad news came. The children would not be able to spend any more time on this project until May, when the standardized tests were over. Everyone had benefited from their field trip and thanked the urban planners for all their hard work. Of course, Tom's students would be graduating and could not come to Frederick Douglass during May, but Noreen would use all she had learned that year to help the children complete some kind of enhancement project.

Even though his classes were over, Tom agreed to meet me at the school for my last visit to Markington, where I went directly after Gardendale's joyous Annual Spring Festival. The entire country seemed to be having good weather as it was another perfect June day, but Frederick Douglass still was cloaked in the quietness of winter. Tom and I concentrated on the weather, struggling to muster our enthusiasm for this final encounter. We stepped across the broad threshold, out of the sunlight and into the musty darkness of the building, signed in, and climbed to the third floor office to say good-bye to Mrs. Driskell. As we began thanking her for hosting us, it soon was apparent that Mrs. Driskell expected us to return the next year. "But I already assigned Anne Bassett to coordinate your program. I thought it would be better in the lower school where the academic program is more flexible," she objected. Tom reminded her that we had only made a one-year commitment and expressed his hope that the fifth-grade teachers would continue using some of the principles we had covered and even find a way to share them with Anne Bassett and the other teachers. Sensing her displeasure, we made an uncomfortable exit and went to Noreen's class where her homeroom's social studies session had just begun.

Noreen welcomed us as she pointed to a large piece of brown Kraft paper that was taped to the blackboard, explaining that this was a pattern for the banner the children were making to hang in the entrance of the building. The children were busy at their desks cutting small pieces of black felt into letters that would form the words: "Student Improvement through Parent Involvement." But the sight of Tom and me interrupted all progress on the banner as Shawn demanded to know what had happened to Happy Toy. Tom had already suffered through his own students' rage at the cancellation of the Happy Toy project, but he remained calm as he explained that sometimes things do not go as planned, even in the best of circumstances. He deeply regretted that the children had not been able to build their design, which was truly wonderful, but the urban planning students had done their very best to build Happy Toy exactly as the New Yorkers had designed it. " In fact," said Tom, "Happy Toy happens to be sitting in my car at this very moment because today, after lunch, I'm going to deliver it to Saint Andrew's Church. If you like, I could bring ole Happy Toy in to show you just how nicely it came out."

The class let out a cheer, and Noreen quickly focused their enthusiasm on finishing the banner. Tom and I joined in the work, helping to glue the black letters onto a piece of green felt edged in red. Dowels were inserted into the top and bottom of the banner and by lunchtime the colorful creation was complete with large ribbons for hanging it from the ceiling. The children got their lunches from the cafeteria and helped Noreen set up a magnificent picnic in one corner of the playground under a huge oak tree whose leaves were the bright green of spring. Tom and I carried Happy Toy to the playground, and Tameka and Shawn had the honor of summoning Mrs. Driskell to see their two finished projects. Mrs. Driskell moved smoothly across the broken concrete pavement, balancing the invisible Grecian vase on her head, smiling at Noreen and the children who were inspecting Happy Toy with great amazement. Clapping her hands to acknowledge both the banner and Happy Toy, Mrs. Driskell made a short speech about how proud she was of everything the class had accomplished that year as the children's faces filled once more with sheepish delight.

After the picnic, Tom and I said our good-byes and trekked down the street to Saint Andrew's Church, lugging Happy Toy and feeling totally sad. In his usual manner, Tom began ticking off our successes and failures. The children had gotten to see their idea in a completed form and no doubt many of them would see it installed at the soup kitchen; Mrs. Driskell had even seen it and, at the same time, had gotten what she wanted for her own building; and Noreen had gotten a pat on the back for her role as program coordinator. On the down side, Tom had gotten the worst evaluation ever from his students because they somehow blamed him for all the delays and changes in plans. And it was clear to both of us that there would be little if any continuation of the ideas we had tried to initiate that year because the one person who might have taken ownership for them, Mary Quick-to-See, had been squeezed out of participation.

We rang the doorbell at Saint Andrew's and soon one of the sisters cracked open the door. "Where are my children?" she asked as she opened the door a bit wider. "I thought the children were coming."

EMPOWERMENT AND EMPATHY—TWO NECESSARY INGREDIENTS

Although the power structure at Gardendale was no less hierarchical than at Frederick Douglass, the exercise of authority was quite different at each school. The rigid bureaucracy of Frederick Douglass stifled any possibility for spontaneity and made teachers and students alike feel as if they were continually rushed to meet one set of requirements while at the same time being blocked by another. This no-win environment served to reinforce a sense of failure since everyone—even Mrs. Driskell, Tom, and myself—received repeated feedback on not being able to reach their own, or anyone else's, goals. The children were not given sufficient time to realize their idea after a crew of adults had spent months trying to figure out how to overcome administrative blockages. Then, they were diverted, not to the stories that Noreen would have preferred to produce, but to the banner proclaiming the goals of Mrs. Driskell's demonstration. In contrast, plans were made at Gardendale via an open-ended informal process that made Dr. Marcus's uncompromising management style seem efficient and responsive to a variety of needs. Her unrelenting mandate for children and teachers to excel was buoyed up by a can-do attitude that magically removed obstacles. They not only were given the time and materials to refine their ideas, parents stepped in with additional expertise so that sketches could become a full-scale space in a matter of months.

Yet, neither school realized the potential of helping children to envision social change through place-related learning, which could have resulted in a greater sense of empowerment on the part of Frederick Douglass children and a greater sense of empathy on the part of Gardendale children. Just imagine the sense of empowerment that would have derived from the Frederick Douglass children being supported in making a visible mark on the Oak Hills community, especially since it showed so few signs of being cared for. Not only would they have been able to help the homeless children recapture a moment of childhood, they would have gained some sense of control over the ugliness of homelessness—a condition that many of them knew only too well. Instead of having their bodies subdued and their minds directed toward tedious individual tasks, they would have been able to spend their physical energy on purposeful collective work, which would have also engaged their intellects and creativity. Had Mrs. Driskell not been so afraid of allowing children out of the school building, they might have been able to link their schoolwork with the extended community household that the sisters oversaw, resulting in a much more meaningful multicultural education than the artificial program offered by MED. With such support and encouragement, the Frederick Douglass children might have begun to resist rather than comply with a social system that afforded them so little status.

Just imagine the sense of empathy that would have derived from the Gardendale children being supported in questioning, not the deficits of the farmworkers' children, but their own entitlements. They might have been able to go beyond donating a month's allowance to generate an exchange among their Limone peers that would have helped them value the cultural wealth of these so-called disadvantaged children. Had Jane not felt so compelled to deliver a product that met the school's standards of excellence, she might have encouraged her students to involve the Limone children in redesigning their own town or playground. The process would have been messier no doubt, but sharing their design skills with children who had so little control over their surroundings might have been a much more significant gift than the money and books that were sent. With such support and encouragement, the Gardendale students might have begun to resist rather than participate in a social system that afforded them so much status.

bell hooks (1994) talked about theorizing as a child to deal with the dislocation she felt growing up black in a racist society:

> Living in childhood without a sense of home, I found a place of sanctuary in "theorizing," in making sense out of what was happening. I found a place where I could imagine possible futures, a place where life could be lived differently. . . . [Theory emerged] from my efforts to make sense of everyday life experiences, from my efforts to intervene critically in my life and the lives of others [pp. 61, 70].

The enhancement project presents a wonderful opportunity for dislocating prevailing social values through theorizing as well as action-taking since children not only talk about places where life could be lived differently, they also construct those visions in three-dimensional form. More importantly, they can practice sustainable roles and behaviors (like taking responsibility, being inclusive, working together, being more conserving) while they are building their ideas. To have utilized that opportunity—to have helped the children at Frederick Douglass and Gardendale imagine a future without oppression or domination while practicing their roles and behaviors in that future—would have required a profound transformation in the values and habits of mind that shaped the learning processes at both schools.

NOTES

1. One of these projects, *Sharing Space*, introduces a basic premise of the program, namely, that people are interdependent in their use of environmental resources. Using the spaces of their own homes and neighborhoods as examples, children explore how one person's actions can affect another person's quality of life. This is the lesson I used the day of the big snowstorm in Markington. Another project, *The Good and the Bad*, asks children to evaluate their school or neighborhood. This project, which is the one Frederick Douglass's teachers began with, can be used as a starting point for the second semester, when children are asked to enhance or eliminate a good or bad aspect of their school or community. The two remaining projects, *A Landmark Is Something Special* and *The City Is a Circulation System*, develop design skills while focusing students on the special places as well as the infrastructure that comprise neighborhoods. Refer to Sutton (1989).

2. Educators who create learning opportunities outside the classroom use a variety of terms including experiential, community-based, and civic arts learning as well as community service, each term having a slightly different meaning. The term I prefer is *community-service learning*—a term shared by faculty at the University of Michigan—which suggests a careful balance between community service and learning. It is a partnership between the students and persons in the community who work together on a collectively defined problem; its goal is to broaden students' awareness of social problems while sharing institutional expertise with low-income groups outside the institution. Typically, such learning experiences involve regular reflection sessions to ensure that students are able to harvest the lessons of their service activities and develop critical analyses of the problems they observe.

3. Perhaps the common focus at both schools was owing to the attention the media was giving to this subject that year, or perhaps I somehow indirectly encouraged a look at the topic as I consulted with Tom and Jane.

4. Keep in mind that the comments in quotation marks that are attributed to children were recorded by me or my research assistants directly after such discussions took place and represent, as accurately as possible, the actual statements children made.

Through the Window of a Child's Mind

In this last narrative chapter, the children at Frederick Douglass and Gardendale will have a chance to tell some of their own story. But first, I would like to revisit the propositions I offered in the introduction as a screen for understanding the events just described. Recall that I began with the assumption that the development of poor and well-to-do children alike can be compromised or enhanced by the quality of their physical environment. A central proposition I put forth is that children learn directly by observing their immediate surroundings, which reflect their socioeconomic status—observations that help reinforce the status quo and children's rank and role within it. Environmental psychologists generally agree that places contribute to the formation of children's identity and believe that being able to appropriate a space of one's own is important to gaining a sense of personal control and inner security. My particular interest focuses on how children's attitudes toward social and environmental equity are shaped by their experience of the physical environment. I conjectured that growing up in contemporary U.S. landscapes—which are frequently segregated by race, class, age, and function—would discourage those personal characteristics and beliefs that are necessary to envisioning a more equitable, conserving society. Furthermore, I surmised that children would be less negatively impacted by the extremes of poverty and wealth if they were actively engaged in socially critical, place-related learning.

More specifically, it seemed possible for children in low-income urban neighborhoods to benefit from the community caretaking that sometimes occurs in these types of neighborhoods as activists organize to improve the lives of a larger extended family, often in the face of extreme hardship. Yet, these benefits most likely would be obscured by the children's experience of overcrowded, unsafe, and deteriorating places as well as by the lack of educational and economic opportunities that exist in such places. It seemed reasonable to think that observations of an unsavory neighborhood would communicate to its young residents their lack of worth and inability to access the rewards of mainstream society, a situation exacerbated by the materialistic norms that are beamed into their homes via television. Conversely children in more affluent communities would observe a safe, well-tended, and well-furnished environment but one that is heavily reliant on social isolation, wealth, and formal problem-solving methods. It seemed reasonable to think that observations of this set-apart physical environment would engender among its young residents a sense of superiority and entitlement, especially since such places also would have abundant educational and economic resources to ensure their progress. Whereas poorer children might be diminished by the social and physical degradation of their community, more well-to-do ones might be impaired by being socialized into privatized and consumptive, auto-dependent lifestyles. Both groups would seem lacking in opportunities to observe and practice the sustainable relationships that are required if life on Earth is to continue.

Interrelated with this central proposition, I speculated that teachers reinforce children's environmental observations through the values, attitudes, and norms inherent in their classroom practices, especially in the way they use, and allow children to use, space. I called such sociospatial practices a hidden curriculum of separateness, suggesting that its lessons have been magnified recently by a variety of socioeconomic forces that diminish traditional community relationships. Given the increasing fragmentation of a rapidly expanding global society, I proposed that the need for balancing the "I" with the "We"—for encouraging children to excel at their unique talents while at the same time nurturing their sense of community—was greater than ever. Whereas modern forms of community include ones based on special interests and cultural identity, I proposed that having a sense of rootedness in a particular place with a particular group of people is prerequisite to developing social consciousness. The children's stories provide interesting insights into that notion.

The third proposition has considerable support in the critical education literature, namely, that the hierarchical power relations in schools, which reflect the race, class, and gender inequities of the larger society, reproduce a stratified social order. The objective dualistic thinking that is associated with positivism and Socratic teaching methods encourages children to see learning as a disengaged, asocial process in which some persons have greater authority than others to determine their futures. Through a discriminatory practice of tracking, those futures reflect, not the child's IQ, but the parent's socioeconomic status and the child's normative personality traits. Although some teachers and students learn to resist this meritocratic system, I suggested that many more are socialized into the terms of a patriarchal contract, including patterns of dominance and dependence, subservience and defiance, competitiveness, and materialism. Some persons are credentialed to enter the upper ranks of society whereas others are assigned to the lower ranks, their unique skills and life experiences devalued.

How were these propositions informed by my visits to Frederick Douglass and Gardendale?

HIDDEN CURRICULA THAT MAGNIFIED CHILDREN'S ENVIRONMENTS

Let me begin by summarizing how the messages contained in children's surroundings seemed to have been magnified, both positively and negatively, by the sociospatial practices occurring in each of the schools. For the Frederick Douglass students, a strength of their neighborhood turned out to be a group of activist women at Saint Andrew's Church who engaged in various community caretaking activities. Children participated in these survival strategies, which seem to have heightened their ability to manage crises such as the snow emergency. Certainly in their stories, you will see that the social network at the church had a profound effect on their behavior (recall how behavior in Noreen's class improved when the sisters visited) and on their ability to conceive positive adult roles despite the social pathologies that surrounded them.

Even though its overall structure posed wonderful opportunities to extend the social milieu of the neighborhood into school, the benefits deriving from the neighborhood's informal governance structure were not reinforced by classroom-management policies at Frederick Douglass. Promoting a sense of community such as existed at the church might have minimized the assaults on individual identity that the students experienced in school (as low achievers) and out of school (as residents of a declining neighborhood). Encouraging expressiveness or bringing parents into the school in a celebratory, nurturing role might have also had the same effect. But these opportunities were missed as the educational staff strove to reflect a mainstream model of individual achievement—and failure—through a lockstep sequence of activities that failed to recognize or value the skills and experiences children brought to school. Instead of encouraging communal exchanges, Frederick Douglass's normative standards of behavior actually forbade communication among children and frequently put them into escalating confrontations with teachers and even with their parents.

Noreen had arranged her classroom as physically distinct teams to reflect the school's philosophy of cooperative, thematic learning, and she also went to great lengths to create a familylike milieu for her homeroom class by bringing in homebaked goods and arranging communal lunches. But these efforts were overshadowed by a disciplinary code that not only forced her to restrict children's movements but to specify particular positions in the room for various punishments. Her dingy classroom was made all the more unpleasant by her shouts for order and the children's slamming of furniture as they took up their punishment stations. In addition to being almost barren of visually interesting surfaces, the room was too small to afford privacy, and the one corner that might have offered a modest getaway was blocked by Noreen's desk. The daily routine—getting hands folded on desks, waiting for the bell, marching in two lines in and out of the classroom— turned Noreen's efforts at making a familylike atmosphere into a military drill. Like Oak Hills with its belching smokestacks, "*real* b-a-a-d" people, and vicious dogs, the overall effect of Noreen's room was one of confinement rather than one the children could have appropriated as a space of their own. On the other hand, both the school and the informal social network in the community seemed to constitute places of refuge for children who claimed it as their home—the place where they lived and had their friends.

At Gardendale, such regimentation was nowhere apparent. The building was humming with individualized, exclusive activities to which children had to apply for acceptance. Although the conflict resolution program clearly involved only token participation, Dr. Marcus sought to create the impression of child-centered learning, with students coming and going to activities of their choice. There were ample spaces to appropriate not only in school but in a neighborhood that was perceived as safe. Children were free to use the nooks and crannies of the school building, which was small in scale and had an easy relationship with the outdoors. Classrooms were large, especially in the newest addition where the sixth-grade students were located, and had varied private spaces in which to work simultaneously on many different projects. In addition to nicely furnished classrooms, there were also a variety of well designed specialized spaces both inside the building and outside in the courtyard.

Like the school, the Village of San Lupe provided the children with a wonderful array of amenities, yet what seemed lacking was any sense of a *working* community that might encompass children in the practical tasks of, in Heidegger's words, "making a place upon the Earth." San Lupe was more akin to what Bellah et. al (1985) defined as a "lifestyle enclave," focused on leisure, consumption, and the protection of class interests (pp. 71–95). Whereas the Frederick Douglass children had gained community caretaking skills by living in an area where neighbors had to solve real problems, many of the Gardendale children felt that San Lupe was problem-free. What the children saw were well-cared-for but empty public spaces that were effortlessly managed not by neighbors but by anonymous persons. Social life took place on the golf course, in private club houses, shops, and restaurants as well as in large private homes.

Given this bureaucratically managed, privatized, and homogeneous existence outside the school, promoting a sense of caretaking and participation with others who are somewhat different from yourself would seem essential within the school. However Gardendale—in the flow of activities and use of space—was as lacking in the sense of being an engaged community as San Lupe. Many teachers like Mrs. Rayburne arranged their rooms as a series of private work areas, and I had quickly discovered during the enhancement project how difficult it was to have even the briefest discussion with all twelve children. Although they were working on a single project, Jane and I had to go like honeybees from team to team to conduct discussions and get consensus on what the group would do.

The aura of Gardendale's public spaces (like the magnificent skylit multipurpose room and the courtyard) especially mirrored San Lupe's environment of self-interests. A more communal society like that of Mexico would have used such spaces for all sorts of performances and ceremonies, with children parading in colorful costumes to promote school or national identity. Gardendale's public spaces lacked such a social purpose and were used primarily during the day for small groups or after school for such activities as square-dancing or holiday-related celebrations. Except for graduation, the courtyard remained disappointingly sterile with its chemically treated grass, manicured bushes, and individualized play and work areas. Perhaps the fragmented culture of Gardendale would prepare the children for the alienated work environments they would encounter later in life, but would it equip them to solve difficult problems with persons of diverse backgrounds and interests?

On the other hand, the Gardendale children had many opportunities to observe other cultures and ways of life. They had traveled nationally and internationally, their families had moved from place to place, and the children were aware that their mobility resulted in higher-paying jobs, more luxurious vacations, bigger houses, and better schools. Yet while the Gardendale children appeared to have a worldly perspective, their stories will suggest that they had a somewhat abstract relationship to their own community.

HIERARCHICAL POWER STRUCTURES WITH DIFFERING EFFECTS

What events in this book seemed to contribute to the children's socialization into their class-based ranks and roles at each of the schools? How did the exercise of authority communicate these ranks and roles? At the starting gate, one group had been defined as "on track" or "needing compensatory learning" whereas the other was defined as "gifted" or "needing independent development." What was the effect of these different beginning definitions on the children's behavior?

The education of the Frederick Douglass students began with the assumption that they required extensive socialization into mainstream norms, which put them in a one-down position. Such lifestyle indoctrination of persons who are economically or culturally different has been a continuing theme throughout the history of this country. Among many examples were "Americanization" classes for immigrants earlier this century, some of which went well beyond English and citizenship skills to encompass homemaking instruction for women who were presumed deficient; the banishing of American Indian children from their homes so they could be taught "healthy" behaviors at Catholic or U.S. government boarding schools; and, more recently, housing-readiness and work-readiness programs that prepare homeless and jobless persons for what, in truth, are basic survival activities. These denigrating, superficial approaches to poverty and cultural difference affirm mainstream norms and allow well-to-do persons of the dominant culture to conceptualize themselves as superior while "the other" is perceived as deviant, each group locked into their respective positions within a hierarchical social structure.

Mrs. Driskell and her faculty reflected this historical tendency to impose mainstream norms on the other. They seemed more trapped by the traditions of reproducing a repressive system than they were liberated by the potential of using multicultural education to generate entirely new learning approaches and social relations. In a school that served children whose lives were rather chaotic, the zeal to adopt the norms of the dominant culture upended the possibility for engaging in a process that would have been truly empowering. The contradiction between being told to be proud of your own culture while being treated as second-class citizens was borne by children and their parents as they assimilated negative (and implicitly racist) messages about their social status. Given the goals of raising self-esteem and cultural awareness, I expected to see a celebration of the school community as a culture. What I saw instead were countless incidents in which staff confirmed to parents and children that they were less than normal—parents being taught how to discipline their children, children never being allowed out of their teacher's sight, children not being given control over their creative products, children and parents being reminded that taxpayers paid for their "free" lunches. Increasing cultural awareness at Frederick Douglass was an abstract process in which children learned *about* culture while experiencing their own culture-of-poverty as deviant.

The first line of diminished human potential at Frederick Douglass began with Dr. Johnstone and Mrs. Driskell's mechanistic management of teachers. Someone like Mary, who was energetic and wanted to contribute, was locked into her rank as a novice, her leadership capacities appropriated by the institution. By the time she had worked her way into the system, her freshness may have gotten spoiled by that system. Both Noreen and Frank were capable but unwilling leaders, and Gail devoted her days to self-righteous destructiveness. Frederick Douglass's teachers complained about how institutional requirements affected them, but they were too divided within their own ranks to resist the school's unfair practices, so they passed its requirements on to the children. Parents were at the bottom of the pecking order, being in the most contradictory, no-win position of all. Mrs. Driskell aggressively pressured mothers to take lessons in parenting, but the parenting they most frequently were asked to engage in was not the power-with that exemplifies the best kind of maternal influence. Rather, as persons who had already been categorized as deficient, the Frederick Douglass parents were forced to exercise the oppressive power-over of the school—a requirement that alternatively provoked rebelliousness and submissiveness among both the children and their parents. Submissive persons like Chester and his mother, Mrs. Greene, reacted to any display of authority with nervous subservience, slouching their bodies and looking generally depressed. Parents of assertive children like Tameka and Shawn were often deadlocked in confrontation with Noreen and Mrs. Driskell, having to choose between siding with the school or with their children. Despite their frequent punishments, Tameka and Shawn found ways to resist authority and used the isolation area at the front of the room as a stage for practicing their leadership skills on their peers.

McLaren (1993) differentiated active (intentional) and passive (tacit) resistance to the "rules and norms established by school authorities" (p. 83), noting that one of the means of passive resistance is through prankish buffoonery. Tameka and Shawn exemplified McLaren's concept of passive class clowns. Unfortunately, their humorous, show-off styles would probably disadvantage them as they tried to move on to other educational or occupational situations. These observations suggest an extension of Block's (1987) concept of the patriarchal contract; not only does domination result in an abdication of responsibility, it also results in self-defeating acts of defiance, depending on the particular personalities involved.

Tom and I both foolishly fell into the trap of Frederick Douglass's hierarchical power structure, becoming silent partners in Mrs. Driskell's usurping of the leadership role Mary had taken in getting the Urban Network started. Instead of becoming Mary's advocates, we aligned ourselves with the person who was calling the shots because we were so focused on achieving our own agenda. In so doing, we missed the opportunity to collaborate with a committed teacher who possibly could have shared her own empowerment with students. Ultimately, Tom and I paid for our mistake, being as manipulated by Mrs. Driskell as the other teachers were.

The children at Gardendale began from a one-up position, and their parents were in a supervisory role in the school to ensure that they maintained this position both socially and academically. Parents were everywhere, at times raising money for special programs, at times participating in the development of the curriculum, at times joining in instructional activities. Their authority in the school communicated that they, not the teachers (who were of lower social rank), were in change of their children's future advancement. Within this power arrangement, there was both subtle and blatant evidence of patriarchy. Not only were all the science teachers hired by the parent-dominated STC male, but fathers most often participated as consultants to the staff (on fund-raising, space design, and curriculum development) whereas mothers most often participated directly with children as nurturers.

Teachers, in their subordinate role, adopted the rules of patriarchy, giving male children more latitude in exercising leadership and breaking the school's codes of conduct while encouraging boys and girls in gender-typed activities such as architecture or helping to serve lunch buffets. Miss Moore in particular gave male students preferential treatment—treatment that sometimes tacitly supported their violation of the school's codes of conduct. Stated in terms of McLaren's (1993) model of active and passive resistance, the four boys who engineered the Rambo broadcast in her class would seem to have been actively *restating* rather than resisting patriarchal norms. By rearranging the room in a lecture format and assuming positions at the "head" of the class, the boys were consciously reasserting their own and the school's authority. I did not get a chance to observe whether the conflict resolution mediators (three boys and two girls) mimicked the norms of patriarchy, but feminist scholarship suggests that infractions by girls would have been viewed more harshly. Although girls and boys participated differently within this overall structure, some girls rejecting housekeeping tasks, some boys shunning macho roles, there seemed to have been far more opportunities for male children to both exercise authority and rebel against it in a socially sanctioned manner.

The motivation for excelling at Gardendale also assumed a one-up position for its teachers and students. Unlike Frederick Douglass's teachers and students, who were assigned a place in the educational hierarchy through a punitive focus on enforced teacher development and standardized testing, the Gardendale teachers and students were given the illusion of placing themselves by being able to identify and promote their talents. The teachers, who had undergone rigorous competition to secure their jobs, could invent their own development activities such as poetry reading sessions in a restaurant, and the school provided significant financial rewards for their efforts. Within this atmosphere of competitive creativity, a novice teacher like Jane could advance herself by having good ideas and working hard, and the school provided intellectual, financial, and practical resources to back up her efforts. The children were part of this same atmosphere, being offered an array of choices for which they could compete based on their interests and abilities. Through the application process, they were being trained to know their strengths and prove their worth through demonstrated achievements.

Thus, whereas the Frederick Douglass children began with the presumption of failure, having skills and ways of being that teachers neither recognized nor valued, the Gardendale children began with the presumption of success, having skills and ways of being that coincided with the values of the school culture. The experience of competing for various opportunities would prepare the Gardendale children for the hard-nosed, free-market rivalry of their future lives, but it was also teaching them to adopt the notion of scarcity—that there is simply not enough to go around, especially if individuals are not real go-getters. It was preparing them to rationalize why some people (like those in Oak Hills or Limone) just do not succeed.

In an earlier, more systematic study I gathered data that showed a significant correlation between the responsiveness of children and that of their teachers (Sutton, 1985, p. 83). Although this was an investigation of limited scope, it seems quite logical that teachers—who are so significant in the lives of children—would be powerful role models. Teachers' participation in the hierarchical power structures of these two schools provided children with vastly differing understandings of success and power, one group experiencing the conditions of being submissive and defiant, the other experiencing the conditions of being exclusionary and competitive. Both these role models seemed equally flawed.

DIMINISHED EXPERIENCES OF THE URBAN NETWORK

All service is directly or indirectly an ethical activity, a reply to a moral call within, one that answers a moral need in the world. . . . Of course, the person being called does not always take the step from having a sense of what ought to be done to making a commitment of time and effort [Coles, 1993, pp. 75/291].

As a community-service learning program for youth, a successful Urban Network implementation has at least five characteristics. Projects should be youth-initiated and action-oriented; they should grow out of a need in the children's surroundings, not out of the teacher's need to teach; they should provide a context for integrating a variety of skills and for developing social and environmental awareness; they should involve young people in community caretaking, thereby giving them the sense of giving back; and these efforts should occur over a period of time so that participants can build on a history of success in the surrounding community. How did Frederick Douglass and Gardendale measure up on these characteristics?

Since long-term programmatic activities in most school situations are adult-initiated because they stem from the availability of certain resources, the Urban Network instructional materials provided guidance on how to interface the decision-making of adults with that of children. As was discussed earlier, the adults at both Frederick Douglass and Gardendale had differing roles in initiating the program, which ultimately affected the nature of children's participation. At Frederick Douglass, where Noreen was the unwilling program coordinator, the first semester's work was totally teacher-directed, with children being locked into performing discrete tasks within a set time period. During the second semester, the adults set the direction of the enhancement project, but theirs was a very shaky consensus deriving from Tom persuading Mrs. Driskell and Noreen to focus on a community need, namely, Saint Andrew's soup kitchen. Then, for a brief period of time, what was an adult-initiated idea became intensely child-directed as the project took on a uniquely youthful understanding of what it was like for homeless children to eat at the soup kitchen. But the children's participation turned into an act of manipulation as their ideas for Happy Toy were short-circuited and their labor was used, not to address a need in the community, but to spread Mrs. Driskell's propaganda.

At Gardendale, where Jane was the enterprising program instigator, the first semester's activities were also teacher-directed, but one particular activity grew out of a need (though adult-defined) in the school to create an outdoor science laboratory. In this case, a team of boys had the flexibility to undertake a process that resulted in sketches for the laboratory. At the end of the year, they displayed their work alongside working drawings that had been done by a landscape architecture firm, and the relationship between their sketches and the professional drawings was obvious. During the second semester, Jane chose a direction for the enhancement project and immediately received Mr. Regon's support and assistance. However, one aspect of her idea—raising the children's awareness of living conditions in Limone—required a lot of aggressive teaching. The other aspect of her idea—meeting the school's requirement to produce top-quality products for the Aspiring Professionals program—also required a lot of aggressive teaching. Thus, although the Gardendale children appeared to have a grander success at the end of the year than the Frederick Douglass children had, they probably were equally manipulated in terms of how their participation occurred. Because of the exploitative manner in which both groups were involved, the degree to which they accomplished a sense of active problem-solving was limited, and neither had a realistic experience of community caretaking or giving back. Considering all the activities at both schools, the outdoor science laboratory would seem to have been the most successful in terms of its participatory, community-service quality.

In assessing the dimension related to building a variety of skills and developing social and environmental awareness, the design of the Frederick Douglass implementation had the most potential during the first semester since three teachers were to develop lessons in their respective subject areas. However, their inflexible teaching methods eliminated the possibility for children to explore ideas on their own terms, or for children to bring the social and environmental awareness they had already learned in their community (about which you will soon learn) to bear on their classwork. At Gardendale, the program was not intended to help children integrate academic subjects but rather to make them aware of a career. Within that narrow focus, Jane included a number of activities such as interviewing, measuring and drawing, designing, writing, photography, and presentation. All their products demonstrated a high level of skill; however, as their communications will reveal, the level of social and environmental awareness that the children achieved was quite limited.

On the last dimension—developing an ongoing effort to create a history of success—Gardendale clearly was a winner, not only with respect to the Aspiring Professionals program but in all their endeavors. An unspoken mandate from Dr. Marcus was to surround students with evidence of attainment, and the Annual Spring Festival was the most elaborate instance of teachers and parents celebrating the children's work. Frederick Douglass was entirely lacking in this area.

Later, in the conclusions, I briefly present two case studies in which teachers have created innovative community-service learning programs and a third that goes even further in linking school and community.

THROUGH THE WINDOW OF A CHILD'S MIND

As you will recall, the Urban Network activity that initiated the enhancement project at both schools involved the children in making journals about their neighborhood over a period of four or five days. The activity, which was done by Noreen's twenty-three students and the twelve students who worked with Jane, encouraged the children to express ideas about their neighborhood in a creative manner through writing, drawing, and speaking. In addition to discussing what it would be like to live in different types of neighborhoods, the children wrote four stories, called *My Imaginary Walk*, *My TV Program*, *My Life Story*, and *My Story about Moving*; drew a map called *My Tourist Trail* to show their existing neighborhood; and created *My Future Visions Plan* to show how they would like their neighborhood to be in the future. On the last day of the activity, the children discussed their ideas while I videotaped them making "a real TV program about this neighborhood." The journal itself contained good-quality paper and interesting graphics to inspire the children's artistic sensibilities, its assignments intentionally ambiguous to give them room to make their own interpretation.[1] So the activity would not seem like "schoolwork," I was the primary facilitator, with Noreen and Jane both staying in the background. My role was to assure the students that there were no right or wrong answers—they should simply express their own ideas and feelings about their community. If children pressed me for more instructions, I showed them examples of journals that had been done by undergraduate architecture students, and said: "Just make something as wonderful as these."

As you will see, the children's communications unmistakably reflected the material conditions of their lives, and most children seemed

to understand the embeddedness of social class in the physical environment, as Kevin Lynch (1979) suggested they would. In presenting their
neighborhoods, the children at both schools were also presenting themselves, whether realistically or with a degree of fantasy, and they took
advantage of their musings about their surroundings to project certain
images of themselves. Some ascribed to themselves a role of helplessness, others created personages that were efficacious; some were compassionate, others materialistic; some were socially critical, others
self-indulgent—and these roles seemed almost always to relate to the
children's environmental context. Their future visions drawings were
also informed by the artists' physical surroundings. Whereas most of
the poor children indicated practical interventions into their deteriorating neighborhood, many of the well-to-do children conjured up very
fanciful, high-technology futures.

But, let me now invite the children to tell their own stories about Oak
Hills and San Lupe.[2]

Reading Environmental Texts of Poverty

In describing Oak Hills, most of the Frederick Douglass children
seemed to shift back and forth between reality and romance. They
acknowledged that their neighborhood was deteriorated and not infrequently expressed hopes for living in a better place. Despite the invitation to take an *imaginary* walk, most children wrote about Oak Hills in
the here and now, describing a real place that intruded into their lives
and limited where they could go and what they could do. At they same
time, they seemed to see Oak Hills as a real "neighborhood" in the sense
of being a social place where they had their friends and people helped
one another.

You already know Tameka, who may have gotten some of the spunk-
iness you saw earlier by being the fourth child in a family of six
children—three girls and three boys. A lifelong resident of Oak Hills,
Tameka spent her time after school playing baseball, baking cookies at
her grandmother's house, and going to church "to praise God." Her
commitment to the only place she has ever called home was balanced
by a realistic assessment of the neighborhood's problems. This was
Tameka's imaginary walk:

> As I walk through my neighborhood, I see people are very nice and
> friendly. You see people planting and very happy that the plants they
> planted last year are growing. Oak Hills is certainly not the nicest place to
> live, but it's my home. There are a lot of people that smoke and drink in
> my neighborhood. Children make the neighborhood bad by robbing and

getting into fights and smoking cigarettes. I would like to clean up my neighborhood and make Oak Hills safe, friendly, and cheerful.

When asked about moving from Oak Hills, she expressed some commonly held stereotypes about urban and suburban life, indicating an awareness of the possibility of being rejected by children in suburbia:

> My mother and grandmother would want to move to get away from the city. They would probably move to the suburbs. I would feel sad and kind of exciting [*sic*] because moving is like an adventure. I would feel mad and sad about leaving my friends in Oak Hills. I would feel scared about making new friends because I would think: "Oh my gosh! What if they don't like me."

Jessica had a much broader view of the world than Tameka. An obedient child who was always the first to have her hands folded when Noreen gave the order, Jessica spent the first three years of her life with her mother, an entertainer, and both of her grandparents in Atlantic City. Then, she and her mother seemed to have lived in a variety of places including a house with "a twelve-foot swimming pool and a waterfall right by it." Four years ago, her mother got married and moved into an apartment in Oak Hills, which Jessica described as "the worst place I ever lived." Jessica speculated about whether her parents might "move to a nicer, quieter neighborhood," and, given the ups and downs of her residential life, it is understandable that she appeared to be so sensitive to the differences between good places and bad ones. This was the imaginary walk that Jessica took:

> So me and my friend were walking down River Road, and I told her how beautiful that air smelled and how helpful and nice the people were. All the streets were quiet and practically deserted. So we were walking for a while, then we came into a bad part of town. The air started to smell ugly and nasty people were messing everything up. I saw a lot of rats and buildings crowding around. Then when we got home, the air was nice again and there weren't ugly bugs and mean people. It's a big difference between a good and bad part of town.

The idea that bad people create bad places was a recurrent theme that reappeared in work produced by both the Frederick Douglass and Gardendale children, and Shawn wrote a beautiful essay on that topic. The child of a single mother, Shawn provided a humorously terse autobiography, explaining that his mother moved to Oak Hills when "I was quite a little baby. . . . My mom got a boy friend. He moved in for five years. We moved across the street from the school. My mom kicked out her boyfriend. She got a new one. My mom's old boyfriend got married and has five children." In thinking about moving, Shawn wrote: "It would be fun to move. Maybe to a foreign country so all the kids would be nice. With no Amanda [his sister], all the nice fresh wild life, and all of the scenes."

As these pithy essays and his performance in Noreen's class indicate, Shawn had no shortage of wit, but that ability blossomed as he visualized walking through a potentially nice neighborhood that was spoiled by people. This was Shawn's imaginary walk:

> As I walk through my neighborhood, I can sort of smell sweet flowers. But then all of a sudden . . . Boom! Whew! Stinky. I was just hit by an awful smelling gust of pollution. Yuk! I guess I will continue. O-o-oh! Listen to those pretty birds. Onk! Iek! E-e-e! Whow!! God what next, more cars. O-oh! Look at that pretty flower. PLOP! Yuk! Tar from the roof. All over the flowers! So as you can see, Markington is a pretty nice place to live . . . that is, until we come and mess it up!

Reading Environmental Texts of Privilege

Coles (1977) noted the esthetic objects that surround privileged children, contributing to their "sense of place, privacy, property, stability" (p. 16). Michael, the son of a prominent architect, seemed to have such a sense of place. A middle child, Michael described the house his dad had designed for his family as looking "like a futuristic house from the outside. It has a lot of large, unusually shaped windows. It is a three-story, light pink house. The inside is totally the opposite. When you walk in to the right is our living room. I call it the antique room because it is filled with antiques." Michael went on to characterize himself as "intelligent, active, and athletic." This was Michael's TV program:

> My program would be about architecture in the neighborhood and what the neighborhood is like. Children would take pictures and measure the most beautiful gardens, the biggest houses, the best swimming pools, the largest and greenest trees, and other things in their neighborhood. All the people of my town would see the beautiful and peaceful golf course, the empty town square, and the quiet streets where children can ride their bikes anytime. I wanted to make this program to show people how fortunate we are to live in the Village of San Lupe.

But Michael also expressed some insights into economic inequities in the broader society (although he does not say what he might *do* about his observations). This was how he ended his autobiography:

After school I might go uptown with my friends, but I would probably play video games, computer games, sports, and sometimes we just talk for maybe five to ten minutes about sports and other things. On a weekend, I'd definitely ride my bike or roller blade uptown and probably have lunch at Red Zingers. I'd also play a lot of sports with them. The best place I've ever been would be California or more specifically Disney Land. I'd like to go to Australia, and if I couldn't go there I'd go to Israel. The worst place I've ever been to was a soup kitchen in a poor neighborhood. It just hurt me so bad to see all these people suffering while others are living in piles of riches.

Feeling entitled to a good life means that you must protect against any threats to the sanctuary in which that life occurs. A number of stories written by the Gardendale children revealed their fears of losing the accouterments of their existence as well as their capacity to invent solutions to assaults by outsiders, and Claudia provides an elegant example of this genre. Claudia—the black girl who was taunted by Justin about having to move to a "gang" neighborhood and who was so fearful of going to Limone—expressed strong positive feelings for her neighborhood and the freedoms of childhood when she wrote her autobiography:

> I love my house and I will never move. Ever since I was three, I have lived in our house. I love our house. One of my best friends lives down the street. Her name is Sallyanne. Actually she is my best friend. We play together all of the time. My favorite place in the whole world is California. We go there every year. I just love it.

The person who lurks in Claudia's imagination as a threat to her wonderful neighborhood did not do anything atrocious like selling drugs or stealing from people. Ricardo, as she called him, put Claudia's idea of what makes a good life in jeopardy by adding several recreational facilities that are associated with a lower-class lifestyle and by bringing in his friends (who may also be Latino). Ricardo was run out of town by Claudia's neighbors because his very presence would endanger San Lupe's property values as exemplified by private swimming pools and the beauty of Crescent Avenue. This was Claudia's TV program:

> *The Bully: Channel 20*
> Once in a street called Crescent Avenue, the biggest bully of all times lived. This bully's name was Ricardo the Rough One. One day, the bully pushes through a crowd and says, "This block from now on belongs to me!" All of the people that live on Crescent got very mad because this bully was trying to make over the beautiful Crescent Avenue. The bully said "I am

going to put in a hangout, poolroom, karate club and I am going to change all of the houses with indoor pools and I am going to have a big party with all of my friends." All of the people were mad so they all made a change and stood up to this mean bully. And in a few days all the people on Crescent were all happy that the bully moved away. The people bugged him so much that he left.

To complement this happy ending, Claudia drew a picture of the members of her smiling family standing under a bright sun, each tall slender figure carefully rendered in tailored clothing. At a distance is the frowning Bully, much stockier, with long baboonlike arms, wearing a dark brown jumpsuit (see Figure 2). Claudia's possessiveness about her neighborhood was communicated throughout the journal, each of her pieces being carefully labeled with her name and the name of her beautiful street.

Feeling Powerless versus Being in Charge

Children create a cultural identity that is unique to themselves, but that identity is also embedded within a social and physical context. Two boys, who wrote almost identical texts for their imaginary walks, projected very different personalities through their stories that reflected their sociocultural and environmental backgrounds. One of the authors was Mrs. Greene's eleven-year-old son Chester, who had invented the Happy Toy concept. When he drew his tourist trail, Chester indicated a very limited area of the neighborhood where Mrs. Greene allowed him to play unsupervised—an area just the length of five houses on his block and a tiny park across the street from those houses, which did not even include Frederick Douglass or Saint Andrew's Church (see Figure 3). These were the adjectives Chester used to describe Oak Hills, where he had lived only a year and a half: "Awful," "boring," "crowded," "dirty," "empty," "filthy," "friendly," "inconsiderate," "lousy," "ordinary," "polite," "stinky," "stupid," and "ugly." In his autobiography, Chester wrote: "My neighborhood is pretty old looking," and explained that he had lived in nicer places like Oklahoma. This was Chester's imaginary walk, which he took alone.

One day I was walking through an awful, dirty, stinky, and rundown neighborhood. There was fighting, killing, and shooting going on in the streets. There was yelling and screaming as people were getting shot. Parents were crying that their kids were getting shot. As I was leaving this dangerous neighborhood, I was also shot in the arm. For the days following, I always had gloomy dreams about it.

Figure 2: Claudia's TV Program

The experience Chester wrote about might have really occurred. Perhaps, it was just such a journey that resulted in Chester being so confined in his movements, requiring him to stay within full view of Mrs. Greene at all times. The other author, Charles, did not write about reality but rather took a journey into fantasy from the safety of his San Lupe bed. Unlike Chester, Charles was able to bicycle throughout the Village of San Lupe, and the vast, mysterious woods surrounding the lagoon was one of his favorite hangouts. "I go exploring in the woods a lot of times and it is a lot of fun." Charles's mobility in his real neighborhood seemed to have helped him frame danger as an adventure. Like Claudia, Charles was able to create a happy ending for an imagined invasion of San Lupe by the terrors of lower-class life. This was Charles's imaginary walk, which he took in the company of his friend, Jeremiah:

> I woke up Saturday morning, and I got dressed, ate breakfast. Then I went outside and I met my friend Jeremiah.
>
> When we reached uptown it was the most dirtiest town I have ever seen. People were killing each other, and ugly fat women were running and sitting on people.[3] All the stores were dangerous. The people in the stores were shooting everybody. Kids were playing in garbage cans and wicked policemen were taking people to jail for no reason.
>
> When I went home, someone turned out of an alley corner and shot me. . . . I woke up Saturday morning, and it was all a dream.

Significant Others as Nobodies or Stars

The attitude toward the other as well as the attitude of the other may play a role in self-concept development. In other words, not all significant others are equally significant, and those who are more significant have greater influence on our self-concepts [Rosenberg, 1979, p. 83].

Without question, children are more influenced by what their parents, teachers, and peers think of them than they are by what the broader society thinks (ibid., pp. 168–69). However, the relative social status of their significant others would seem to affect the way children think about those others and how they project roles for themselves. The Gardendale children had significant others who were in the news, getting promoted in their jobs, participating in important activities— involvements that were frequently used to boost the children's own credibility. The Frederick Douglass children could not make such claims for their significant others, many of whom were violating socially sanctioned norms by collecting welfare or being single parents. Some were victims, or even perpetrators, of crime.

Figure 3: Chester's Tourist Trail

The following pair of TV programs illustrate the children's differing views of their significant others. One was written by Chester and another by Madison, who had played the role of Rambo during Miss Moore's party. To film his program, which featured "basically nobody . . . just some of my neighbors," Chester ventured out of his normal territory to a soccer field, which was located across the street from the police department:

> I will be filming the program at Grand and Barker. There will be basically nobody in it, just some of my neighbors will be in it. It will be about neighborhood cleanups and watches, so neighborhoods can be safer because my neighborhood is a mess. People are always drinking and that's right next to the Police Department. People with bad neighborhoods and homeless will watch. I made this because I wanted people to know that they can make a difference.

Shawn pressed Chester for more details on this TV program during a videotaped interview. Chester added police officers to his cast of nobodies "just in case something happens" and then ticked off a list of community-caretaking activities. He explained that his film would show "what you can do to reuse all the stuff, send out public service messages to tell people there's a cleanup, start recycling, put together neighborhood watches, keep police informed, and all that stuff"—stuff he had probably heard the sisters discuss at Saint Andrew's Church. When Shawn shifted the conversation to ask Chester how he felt about living in Oak Hills, Chester admitted: "If I had a choice between leaving the neighborhood and staying, I'd probably leave."

Madison had a different view of his neighborhood. He had lived in San Lupe his entire life in a house that "is not that big but has fifteen fairly small rooms." He characterized himself as "a humorous, crazy, wild person (crazy being because I've done crazy things before). I am also determined and serious." Madison did not draw a tourist trail but rather inserted into his journal photographs of his after-school activities including taking cello lessons, practicing the guitar, playing a concert, playing ice hockey, videotaping Justin doing "on-purpose bloopers," and going to the golf course putting green. In his TV program, Madison's neighbors were not nobodies, but stars, and the successful role that he created for himself was linked to a powerful father who provided equipment, doting mentors, and job opportunities. These significant others helped Madison project himself as someone to whom everybody listens. Like Claudia and Charles, Madison was in charge of the adventure he had created—an adventure in which "scary and horrorful" things have a happy ending. This was Madison's TV program:

It all started a few years back when I was playing around with my Dad's old camera. One of my Dad's office workers came and thought my film was so good that he decided to play it on the cable network, so that's how it all got started. Now I've got a new show called "Zany Days." The stars are the people who live in my neighborhood. It is very odd and 4th dimensional. Sort of like "The Twilight Zone." It is also scary and horror-ful. Everyday things happen. Then it starts getting crazy. Weird things happen. And then everything will be fine after it's over. I have many selected people to do certain scenes. I direct and EVERYBODY hopefully listens to me and does what I say and gives suggestions. I am raising money by doing chores and getting jobs at my Dad's company. It's really quite fun.

I Wish the Whole World Could Be a Garden

Even though conditions in Oak Hills were deteriorating, there still seemed to be a strong social network in place through which persons like the sisters tried to improve the quality of life in their community. The self-help and empowerment that prevailed locally were not allowed inside Frederick Douglass, yet the nurturing that children experienced after school seemed to loom large in their imaginations. Many of them pictured environments filled with people cooking outdoors, children eating ice cream, and "babies crying but at a very low voice." Nature figured prominently in their stories—bright sun-shine, singing birds, colorful flower gardens—and their characters were rescued or given career opportunities by helpful strangers. Sometimes the Frederick Douglass children themselves assumed the role of adult nurturers, for example, Georgette was one of several children who imagined what she would do later in life to improve her neighborhood. You will recall that Georgette enlivened the dis-cussion on sharing space when she complained about having to clean up after her four brothers. Georgette knew about sharing space; she was one of nine children and lived with both parents and both grandparents—thirteen people in a town house that she described as "pretty roomy" in comparison to other places she had lived. Although she demonstrated greater knowledge of Oak Hills than Chester (perhaps because she had lived there longer), Georgette also indicated a rather small area where she could go unsupervised. Her after-school activities included talking to friends, taking piano lessons, singing in the choir, and watching video movies at home; in her future vision of Oak Hills she proposed modest improvements like building a movie theater and installing playground equipment next to Frederick Doug-lass. This was Georgette's imaginary walk:

When I take my walk, I see the world. I look around and see the druggies on my block. I wish they didn't mug people. I wish there wasn't so much crime and homeless [*sic*]. I look around and see what has to change. When I grow up I would like to clean up my neighborhood. I would fix the broken windows in our school. I would fix the broken down houses. I would plant a lot of very pretty trees and flowers. The end.

Jimmie, who spent most days after school playing four square, baseball, and helping out at the soup kitchen, was another student who used the journal to project images of caring and concern among people as well as for the environment. He wrote and drew very little in his journal—Jimmie preferred action and conversation—but in the one story he did write, the theme of helping, which was so much a part of his real life, came through. In the story, Jimmie pictured courteous people who took care of the environment and even sold goods for whatever money the buyer had. This was the imaginary walk Jimmie took:

It was an awesome day to walk to the store. Birds were singing, people were laughing. A lot of people are planting things like trees and flowers to save the EARTH. While I was walking, a car drove by and ran through a puddle of mud. It splashed all over me. The car stopped, a man came out and gave me a towel to wipe the mud off. I finally made it to the store. I got some candy, but I was ten cents short. The owner said it was all right. Just go. So that's the end of my Imaginary Walk.

Jimmie created an opportunity to explore this theme further when he interviewed his friend Carlos who had recently gotten a community-service award. Jimmie's constant partner at four square and baseball, Carlos had also gotten involved at Saint Andrew's Church when he helped the sisters to set up a recycling center. Carlos was born in Oak Hills, the second of three children. His dad, who coached the neighborhood Little League team, had separated from his mother the year before, but his parents still lived just around the corner from one another. Despite all the problems in his community, Carlos seemed to not only have a real affection for it but the willingness to spend time improving it. In the interview, Jimmie asked Carlos to talk about his work at Saint Andrew's Church, but when he broadened the discussion to inquire about what Carlos might do to address bigger problems at "the projects," Carlos acknowledged that he would probably need to grow up first. This was the conversation that was videotaped between Jimmie and Carlos:

Jimmie   I heard you got an award for helping out your neighborhood, for helping build a recycling center at Saint Andrew's.

Carlos   I did.

Jimmie   What are your emotions about that?

Carlos   I feel it's very good because we need to make the Earth
            better, make the Earth more of a safer place where we
            can live longer on it so we don't need to move to
            another planet or something like that. Every little
            bit helps.

Jimmie   Would you help some other neighborhoods if
            you could?

Carlos   Yes . . . If I could I would.

Jimmie   Would you try to help the projects and all that?
            Would you try to help them?

Carlos   If I *could* I would. I would probably later on in my life.
            I would try to help some of the more worser
            neighborhoods that are more in need of help.

Jimmie   What kinds of things would you do for your
            neighborhood?

Carlos   I think there should be like a recycling center. There
            should be more community get-togethers and stuff
            like that. I think there should be more gyms and stuff
            for kids because most of the gyms around here you
            have to have cars to get to. They cost a real lot of
            money. Most of the clubs are just for adults. I'd like
            to get some sports things, teams going for Oak Hills,
            like football, baseball, basketball teams. You could
            join by just wanting to instead of paying $120[4] just to
            join some team.

Where You Can Buy Just About Anything

As I had observed that first day in Miss Moore's class, many of the
Gardendale children's journals focused on the stores in the village's
central shopping area, which was referred to as "uptown" even though
the shopping area was located to the south. They described wonderful
cakes and candies, magical restaurants, and toy stores where "you can
pick out just about anything you want." Many of their drawings contained depictions of children wearing recreational equipment, and their
essays referred to highly formalized activities—roller-rink skating, tennis, soccer, golf, softball, basketball, rollerblade hockey—requiring special equipment and facilities. Jeremiah was one such author. Jeremiah's
principle journal entry was a lengthy autobiography cataloguing the
events that had happened during each of his eleven years as his family
moved from city to city "because Dad got a promotion." In his imagin-

ary walk, Jeremiah was a tour guide for a group of "Big Guys," and made the rounds of San Lupe's stores, shopping for all sorts of sweets (Jeremiah's tourist trail showed that he actually went to these places after school). And while Jimmie required the generosity of a store owner to buy candy, Jeremiah seemed not to need money to make his many purchases. This was Jeremiah's imaginary walk:

> Hi! I'm Jeremiah, and I'm your tour guide. And I'm going to take you on a tour of our neighborhood of San Lupe. First, we're going to stop at Red Zingers and taste their wonderful cookies especially their chocolate chip cookies. Next, we'll go to Godiva and get some candy or something like that. Then I'm going to get a twinkie because it's my favorite kind of junk food. Now let's go to Mary Jane's Toy Shop. Wait, what's that I hear? Oh, it's a sea gull. We have a lot of sea gulls around here. Come on let's go to the back and look at all the toy trolls. Did you get what you wanted? Next we're off to the Sweet Shop. I think their best thing here is their chocolate covered pretzels. I think I'll buy one. Our last stop is going to be at the library where I go a lot to do homework. Yuk! Now you're free to do and go where you want Big Guys!

Laura also focused on San Lupe's consumer opportunities. Laura lived in a house that had "two rose gardens and a tulip garden. It is very green and beautiful. It's big and has most things every normal house has." An elegantly drawn tourist trailed indicated that Laura spent her time after school biking all over the Village of San Lupe, visiting friends and stopping by the golf course, tennis courts, clubhouse, and playing fields—and shopping uptown with her friends at many different stores. Her map even had an inset with an enlargement of the uptown area. This was Laura's imaginary walk:

> I am taking you to uptown San Lupe. Now we are passing by Mary Jane's. That is a little toy store. Across the street, there is another toy shop called Toys for Kids. In that same area, there is a grocery store (Bush Brothers) and a bookstore (The Little Professor). Across the street from that there is a bakery—it always smells good. All these are popular places for children to shop and ride their bikes around. It's really a fun place for kids. There is the Village Mall with all sorts of shops: Nail shops, barber, jewelry, ice cream, and things like that. This part of San Lupe really attracts you.
>
> I personally like the lagoon. It is a really wide, grassy, quiet, peacefully wooded, beautiful area. It's nice to ride bikes through the trails. Sometimes you can see deer. That's really special.

Imagining the Future

It was not surprising that the children in Noreen's class revealed an orientation toward fixing some of the many problems they encountered in Oaks Hills. There was a certain seriousness in their communications, especially the spoken ones, as they described the basic needs in their neighborhood. Even though they were younger than the Gardendale children, they seemed older, and most of their conversations consisted of one student interviewing another. The interviewer and interviewee looked at each other or at the floor, talking about real goals and real people, ignoring my video camera and the TV monitor that had been set up to allow the children to see what they looked like on the television screen.

During one such conversation, Georgette got the impish Tameka to describe her future vision proposal for Oak Hills, which focused on young children's needs. Tameka imagined herself as the owner of an ecological play equipment company. This was a videotaped conversation between Georgette and Tameka:

Georgette   What would you do to fix up the neighborhood?
Tameka   I'd like to start a company to make a lot of
            playgrounds for little kids. I'd start tearing down the
            old park equipment, to play on, because some are
            really dangerous.
Georgette   How would you build the playground?
Tameka   I'd build new equipment that's from recycled plastic.
            I think that is really good because you can't really get
            hurt unless you fall real hard.

Lacking an art teacher and the habit of experimenting with art supplies, the Frederick Douglass children's drawings were weak and, in many cases, incomplete or missing. For their future visions plans, most children redrew their tourist trails (which were very undetailed, possibly owing to their parents' restrictions on where they could go), then added amenities like nature, playing fields, and movie theaters. Chester's future vision focused within his small territory, where he proposed making the park across the street from his house "bigger and better" and adding "bigger back yards" to his own and his neighbors' houses. Shawn simply drew a building with a sign that read: "Don't smoke or do drugs" while Carlos showed some of the items he had discussed in his interview including a gym, a baseball diamond, a football field, a recycling center across from Frederick Douglass, and a park in back of Saint Andrew's Church (see Figure 4). But, Tameka's drawing indicated an extensive array of educational and social service amenities such as a library, museum of art, free bus rides, and camping trips for everyone (see Figure 5).

Nor was it surprising that the Gardendale children's work was more in the realm of fantasy. They projected a fanciful, mass-media world

Figure 4: Carlos's Future Visions Plan

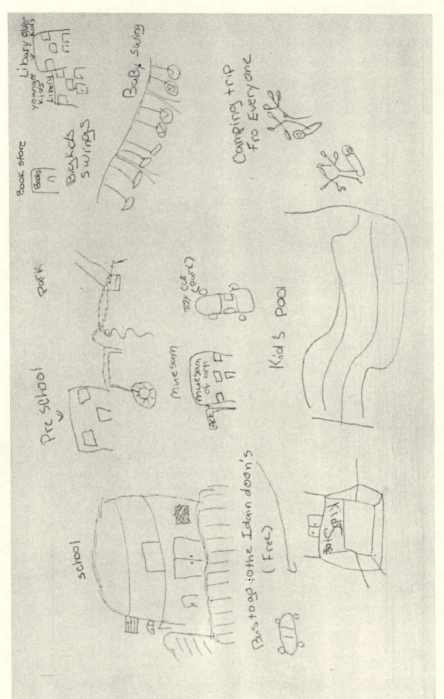

Figure 5: Tameka's Future Visions Plan

with mechanical devices that freed them to do things like shopping and going to restaurants—a world they assumed little personal responsibility for creating. Most of the children presented themselves and their neighborhood in an abstract, impersonal manner and with a great deal of gaiety, especially the boys, who mocked the girls while they were on camera. Most of their videotaped conversations consisted of talk shows in which four children sat self-assuredly in swivel-type chairs, twirling themselves left and right as they stole glances at the TV monitor to check their appearance.

Kimsung participated in one of the talk shows and, as had been true during earlier classroom activities, he was clearly the leader. You will remember that Kimsung was born in Thailand to parents who were missionaries and, like Justin, he had an absolute fascination with all sorts of high-technology gadgetry. As one of only about two dozen Asian students at Gardendale, Kimsung seemed compelled to distinguish himself intellectually and socially, the mocking humor that made him so popular clearly coming through in his journal photography. Among others, he included a photograph of a toilet labeled "My Favorite Place," one of about ten boys (who were making devil horns on one another's heads) labeled "A Few of My Pals," and another, labeled "My Hero," of himself seated in a triumphant position on a metal sculpture of a horse.

During the talk show, Kimsung discussed robots and mechanical devices with his friends, Charles, Jeremiah, and Michael. Michael, who had described San Lupe as a "peaceful, quiet village," ran toward the video camera to show his future visions plan; to the tranquil San Lupe, he had added a small shopping mall across the street from his house, another huge one two blocks away, and a Disney World at the end of his street. Then Charles showed his future visions plan, which contained a sailboatlike "hover car," driverless and moving down a highway that was devoid of all landscape. Jeremiah went third, holding in front of the camera a beautifully colored drawing, which showed his idea for making San Lupe's shops more playful (see Figure 6). Kimsung went last, proudly pointing out the features of a skillfully detailed drafting of a space-age city (see Figure 7). This was a videotaped conversation that occurred when Jane interrupted the merriment of the talk show to get more specific information on their future visions plans:

Jane   So, what *is* your future plan for this neighborhood?
Kimsung   We need a better movie theater—on hot days it stinks up. We should have more restaurants, get rid of Heritage House. We only have Red Zingers and Heritage House and Heritage House stinks.

Jeremiah	It's a ripoff there. We need better food. We need bigger stores where you can pick out whatever you want. Everything should be free.
Jane	So, your future plan is to get rid of Heritage House.
Charles	We don't want moldy cheese and we need robots so we don't have to do anything.
Jane	So, what would the robots do for you?
Jeremiah	They can do a lot of our work. Your bedroom would be all like all robots and stuff.
Jane	Sort of like on the *Jetsons*?
Kimsung	We should have cars that run on air pollution because we want the air to be cleaner. We should have moving sidewalks and cars that fly that are like hovercrafts. Telephone wires should be underground, and there should be a lot more grass and stuff.
Michael	I think we need less pollution. Since our state is the fifth most polluted in the country, it stands to reason that San Lupe is polluted even if you can't see it.
Kimsung	(Putting his hands on his hips to emphasize his point of view) It may be polluted, but as a suburb it's *not* very polluted because we have all these other trees. My dad says that the environment is pure here because we have many trees to protect us.

Which of These Dreams Will Come True?

The imagination can help create internal worlds that are very different from a person's real circumstances. It can enable a vision of the future and a sense that you can take action to achieve your vision, sometimes inspiring socially conscious insights, at other times sustaining self-centered narcissism. The following pair of essays, both written by boys who were unquestionably leaders among their peers, represent differing uses of imagination. The community-oriented Carlos created a scenario for escaping poverty through a combination of sports skills, intellectual ability, and activism—all things that he had demonstrated in his real life. This was Carlos's imaginary walk in which he envisions not only his own success but a more equitable society without homelessness and war:

One day, I was walking down the street and some of my friends joined me. Then a man walked up to me and gave me this award that said I was the best student at my school. Then this limousine pulled up and a man walked out. He was the manager for the Minnesota Twins. He said he wanted me to play for the Twins in place for Harmon Kilabrew at first base. I told him

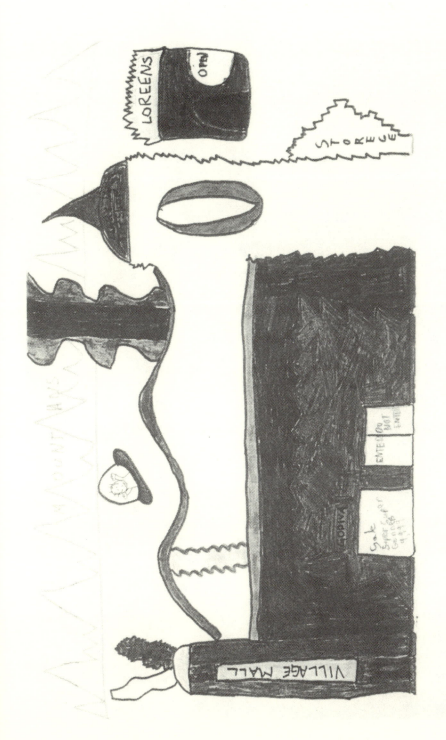

Figure 6: Jeremiah's Future Visions Plan

Figure 7: Kimsung's Future Visions Plan

that I would if he would let me finish college. In college, I hit 450. Then we walked to a news stand and bought a paper. It said the homeless problem has been solved. Inside, it said there was peace between all the countries. That was great to hear.

A letter written by Kimsung, Carlos's counterpart, suggested a different outlook in which he was at the center of things, an important person who would help to invent a problemless space-age future. Kimsung had only been in San Lupe three years and remembered another life ("Thailand is a very poor country, one of poorest country in the world. Taiwan is more civilized but crowded. I can't say I hate Thailand because I was born there. . . . I'm used to it"). Perhaps for this reason, he always seemed to be reaffirming his abilities to Mrs. Rayburne and Jane. This was the letter Kimsung wrote in applying for the architecture team:

> Sometimes I think about the future; will there be a population overflowing or is it going to be amazingly wonderful? Will people be able to live in Mars and reach the stars in a matter of seconds? Will there be robots that do your work for you and machines on our heads that give you smart waves. Come to think of that, I want to be a famous scientist, to help the world a little more.

Both boys imagined the possibility of being highly successful, but Kimsung seemed to lack an understanding of "the world" he proposed to help. Kimsung's vision is disengaged from any particular place or group of people, which may limit his capacity to connect with others. Emily, on the other hand, seemed to have gained an ability to extend herself, even as her family was working its way up the economic ladder. Emily was born on Detroit's East Side, where she lived for one year. Her family moved to Dearborn Heights shortly before her younger brother was born. They arrived in San Lupe just a year earlier, which was one of the reasons that Mrs. Hansen was making an extra effort to be involved in Gardendale. When describing herself, Emily wrote: "I try to be fair and nice to people. I hate it when other people make fun of others. . . . On weekends, I'm pretty lazy. I also babysit for money since I don't get an allowance." This was Emily's imaginary walk (see Figure 8), which she rewrote at the end of the year. In this version, she fancied that one of the Limone children had found a room of her own:

> Her walk was very good. She spent the night in the Limone Haven. It all started when she was wandering through the night and by some chance, when she got there it was day. A rainbow was over the sky. Everyone there was very nice. She stayed for two days. She slept in a big beautiful house. She walked through a garden and went through the town. The last night she stayed there, she woke up in her own room.

She had a wonderful time there. At first I didn't know why they called
it the Limone Haven, but now I know why. It's the best place to be.

OBSERVATIONS OF THE ENVIRONMENT AS INSPIRATION OR IMPAIRMENT

One of the strongest themes that came through in the children's
communications related to their contrasting use of their neighborhoods.
Oak Hills's physical and social devastation made childhood play and
exploration a very dangerous proposition. In another era, children
might have safely engaged in all sorts of adventures in the fields,
backyards, playgrounds, or community centers of a poor neighborhood. However, the adventures that were available to Noreen's class
included exploring abandoned buildings, peering into the interiors of
crack houses, disassembling rusty cars, or picking through garbage in
overgrown vacant lots. Most of the parents seemed to protect their
children from such assaults on their physical beings and esthetic sensibilities by limiting the area where children could go unsupervised and
by taking advantage of whatever free or low-cost activities they could
find, including volunteer work at Saint Andrew's Church. Thus
Noreen's students spent their time after school playing four square or
baseball (if they could afford the cost of being in Little League), visiting
with relatives, taking music lessons from neighbors, or going to
church—all these activities taking place within a limited geographic
area and requiring adult supervision.

The Gardendale children had free range in their community, and their
detailed maps verified their extensive knowledge of San Lupe and, in
particular, its uptown shopping area. Instead of needing to be protected
from dangerous places, the Gardendale students seemed to have complete freedom to bicycle all over the village and, except for Emily, who
received no allowance, also had the wherewithal to shop, eat in restaurants, and engage in an array of exotic recreational activities, including
unstructured adventures in the lagoon. This unfettered use of their local
neighborhood combined with travel (national and international) and
with their families' mobility to create a sense of freedom in stark
contrast with the Frederick Douglass children's sense of confinement.

A second theme in the children's communications reflected their
differing expressions of lived experience in their neighborhood. Many
of the Frederick Douglass children described the neighborhood as a
social place, imagining nature where there was very little and enlarging
on the nurturing activities that went on at Saint Andrew's Church.
Although quite a few of the Gardendale children used the extraordinary
environment of the lagoon as the focus for their writing, many of them

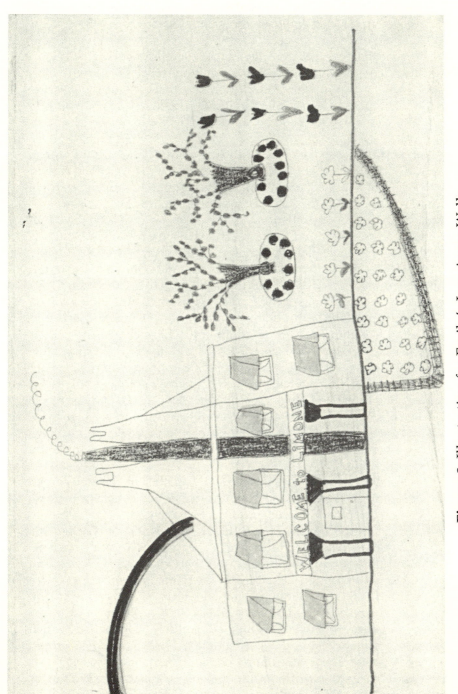

Figure 8: Illustration for Emily's Imaginary Walk

also concentrated on high-technology devices and possibilities for being acquisitive. Their emphasis on consumerism is especially odd not only because of the engaging quality of San Lupe's natural environment but because their emphasis on commercial establishments actually contradicts other research documenting the importance of nature to children. Thus, one group saw a neighborhood that an outside observer might deem unlivable as a community; the other saw a neighborhood that was distinctive for its open space and access to nature as a commodity.

The third theme spoke to how children related to significant others, especially adults, in their communications. You will recall that Chester, with his "nobody neighbors," talked about adults who were always drinking right next to the Police Department whereas Madison with his "star neighbors," wrote about his dad's office workers who gave him feedback on his film. Yet, a broader look at the Frederick Douglass children's communications indicated that they had a number of beneficial relationships with adults in their community. Quite a few children mentioned having relatives who lived in Oak Hills, others said they went to neighbors' houses for music lessons, and still others talked about being involved with adults at Saint Andrew's Church. This reality seems to have allowed them to add helpful adult characters to their stories. There were fewer mentions of adults in the Gardendale children's communications, probably because so many of their neighborhood wanderings were unsupervised, and their autobiographies did not describe extended family relationships. Thus, in comparison to the Gardendale children, the Frederick Douglass children seemed to be more connected to an extended family of adults, which would have been in keeping with the African adage: "It takes a whole community to raise one child."

The last theme, which was especially apparent in the videotaped conversations, was the Frederick Douglass children's realistic engagement with the practical problems they experienced in Oak Hills in comparison to the fantasy and futuristic visions of the Gardendale children that often had no grounding in a real place. Noreen's students became quite serious when asked about their vision of the future and seemed to have acquired something of the moral imperative of service that Coles (1993) talked about in that they proposed actions they themselves might take (or had already taken), in the present and in the future. Whereas the Frederick Douglass children were active participants in a specific place, the Gardendale children seemed to project more passive roles that were not particular to San Lupe or to *any* place. They had rich ideas, both drawn and spoken, for a space-age, hedonistic future, but they did not indicate what they would do to make their visions happen; it was only with Jane's probing that the group focused on specific, and highly self-indulgent, proposals for their own neighborhood. The question that this theme raises is whether Noreen's students would continue to imagine themselves as active participants in improving their community, given the enormity of problems they faced on a daily basis. Since the Gardendale children were buffered from a realistic understanding of others who are less fortunate, how would they be able to put the mechanical devices and consumerism that filled their journals into a more realistic perspective? More specifically, how could Carlos's vision of an equitable society not be extinguished by the conditions of poverty? How could Kimsung develop an awareness for problems that robots and smart waves may not be able to solve? How could Emily's capacity for caring and concern not be tarnished by the conditions of wealth?

THE REALITIES OF A CALCIFIED SOCIAL ORDER

The educational system, perhaps more than any other contemporary social institution, has become the laboratory in which competing solutions to the problems of personal liberation and social equality are tested and the arena in which social struggles are fought out. The school system is a monument to the capacity of the advanced corporate economy to accommodate and deflect thrusts away from its foundations. Yet at the same time, the educational system mirrors the growing contradictions of the larger society, most dramatically in the disappointing results of reform efforts. . . . Were egalitarian education reformers to win spectacular victories—the social relations of economic life remaining untouched—we can confidently predict that employers would quickly resort to other means of labeling and segmenting working people so as to fortify the structure of power and privilege within the capitalist enterprise [Bowles and Gintis, 1976, pp. 5, 14].

In his book *Savage Inequalities*, Jonathan Kozol (1991) took the reader across the nation to visit schools in inner cities and less affluent suburbs, documenting their low yearly allocations per pupil, enormous class sizes, inadequate libraries and teacher salaries, and lack of basic supplies and equipment (p. 180). The images he painted of school buildings and neighborhoods would make Frederick Douglass and Oak Hills appear palatial. These poorest of schools call attention not only to an extremely unjust distribution of resources that traps some children forever in a one-down position, but they also reveal a libelous lack of sanitation, ventilation, and fire safety in the buildings where poor children are compelled to spend their days.

Yet, my visits to Frederick Douglass were even more disturbing than Kozol's journeys because this school appeared to have the basic ingredients (even if not in abundance) that should have given its students a fair chance to realize the widely touted panacea of social progress through education. Because of the demonstration, the Markington Board of Public Schools had allocated a reasonable amount of money per student; class size was reduced; most teachers seemed to be under forty-five; the building was spotless (if aging); and children had basic supplies, books, and equipment. Though not underserving of her share of criticism, Mrs. Driskell was making a formidable effort to end her career as an educator with a big success, and she had provided development opportunities for teachers so they would have the skills to help her create one. The disciplinary code was demeaning, but all in all the exchanges between students, teachers, and parents were relatively gracious and professional. Despite human failings, the staff was diligent and most seemed to really care about their work. To be sure, Frederick Douglass was far from the worst inner-city school in the United States. Nor was growing up in Oak Hills as bad as it might have been. Even though children were limited in their explorations of the neighborhood owing to crime, and even though most lacked extracurricular enrichment opportunities, Oak Hills seemed to have a reasonably viable social life. Many residents worked at improving their own property; others volunteered time to do a variety of community-caretaking activities and provide a safety net for the neediest persons—and children participated in these volunteer activities.

Given the educational and social supports in their school and neighborhood, what were the chances that great numbers of the Frederick Douglass students would succeed within the terms of mainstream society? In light of the correlation between educational attainment and parental socioeconomic status (Bowles and Gintis, 1976), how many children would end up as middle-class professionals? Since the average wealth of white families is eight to ten times higher than that of black families (Goldsmith and Blakely, 1992), it certainly seems improbable that more than a few would be admitted to a public institution like the University of Michigan with its out-of-state tuition of about $15,000 per year.[5] Those who did gain admission would still have only a long shot at success since 70 percent of African Americans attending four-year colleges drop out as compared to 45 percent of whites, and 18 to 33 percent of those who drop out have a combined verbal and quantitative score on Scholastic Achievement Tests of around 1400 (Steele, 1992). Thus, probably an even smaller number of Frederick Douglass's graduates would earn their degrees, and fewer still would find high-level employment, especially since the number of Ph.d.'s earned by African

Americans in the last decade decreased—and took longer to earn as compared to whites (ibid.). Some would make it up the educational ladder only to find themselves in unemployment lines; others would opt out of the process altogether, turning to crime, violence, and ha- tred—especially the males, since inner-city black men experience more than two to three times the unemployment of white men with compa- rable education (Goldsmith and Blakely, 1992), and since there are almost as many black men incarcerated as there are in college.

Although there is a certain futility in acknowledging the improbabil- ity of widespread educational advancement for the Frederick Douglass children, there is an even greater frustration in thinking through a success. For example, imagine that a great majority of these students are able to rise above their birth status—to meet, and exceed, the goals of the demonstration. As students' test scores advance, their parents attend evening classes and soon gain the knowledge and personal connections to get their children into good middle schools where, though the competition is stiffer, most keep progressing. Some are even admitted into selective public high schools with track records for get- ting students into Ivy League colleges. Mentors are available to help their charges fill out applications, get scholarships and financial aid, and select an appropriate path of study. In the college dormitories that are so different from their lives in Oak Hills, students adapt to a more impersonal existence and are able to endure the undue scrutiny and discrimination they encounter as students of color.

Imagine that, of the 625 children enrolled at Frederick Douglass during a given year, 50 percent earn bachelor's degrees, a few from Ivy League colleges—a considerable accomplishment, since nationally only about seven out of ten eighteen-year-olds graduate from high school and fewer than three have the academic preparation to enter four-year liberal arts colleges (Cookson and Persell, 1985, p. 183). As other educators of impoverished children learn of Mrs. Driskell's success, they copy her strategy and soon 50 percent of the nation's thirteen million poor children are enrolled in college and excelling. Could Garrison Keillor's vision of Lake Wobegon come true? Given the history of economic and social life in this country, would it be possible for even half of all children to be well educated and well employed in high-level jobs? Or are Bowles and Gintis correct in predicting that a spectacular success in educational reform would result in other devices for maintaining a stratified social order? Given this improbability of educational and economic equality, what will be the social and environment costs of maintaining a stratified society as demographics change and increasing numbers of low-level jobs are eliminated or exported?

An imagined success at Frederick Douglass makes apparent the improbability of the children being able to significantly improve their ranking in the social order—an even more savage truth than all the blatant failures in Kozol's story. But to what degree are the Gardendale children being socialized into an equally calcified position? If one group is being kept near the bottom academically because of the economic interests of the dominant class, is the other group being kept near the top by those same interests?

Though Gardendale was not one of the very best private schools, its well-to-do parents saw to it that their children would have the best possible chance for a life of power and privilege. Their superior status would be ensured in part by the richness of their life experiences, in part by parental models of authority, in part by having situations in which to exercise choice—all deriving from their inherited socioeconomic status. Because of its location in one of the nation's wealthier suburbs, Gardendale had the resources to offer extremely favorable child-to-adult ratios, an array of before- and after-school activities, teachers who were continuously nurtured in their own development, and a well-equipped facility that accommodated a range of formal and informal learning activities.

Nor did Dr. Marcus need to endure the oversight of Dr. Johnstone to obtain these resources. In addition to having a higher tax base than Oak Hills, San Lupe's well-educated, well-connected parents wrote grant proposals and made substantial contributions, so that Gardendale had a more-than-generous budget for a public school. Additionally, parents held expectations for their children that were in sync with the aspirations of the school culture. The active oversight of the school and its educational staff by parents communicated to children that they were to take an assertive role with teachers—one that was much greater than would have been acceptable at Frederick Douglass. After school in their home and neighborhood environment, the Gardendale children encountered an array of additional enrichments.

Yet a closer look at the apparent success of the Gardendale children will reveal flaws. Unquestionably, these students would stand a much better chance of getting into good colleges and achieving high-level employment than academically comparable children in less affluent circumstances. For example, it seems reasonable to assume that most of Gardendale's 865 students would go on to attend selective public high schools, thereby having a pretty good chance of going to Ivy League colleges. A smaller number of children probably would be among the 10 percent of high school students who attend private schools, and the remaining few might be among the less than 1 percent of the total high school population admitted to an elite college preparatory school

(Cookson and Persell, 1985); several such students might even have parents who had attended such institutions. As this cohort proceeded through college, their differential ranks would stay fairly constant with the preparatory school students, especially those whose parents had elite educations, staying in the lead for filling the nation's top executive posts. For example, a 1984 study of senior corporate managers found that 10 percent of the members of the board of directors of large American business organizations were educated at just thirteen elite boarding schools, a striking fact since these schools account for less than 1 percent of the high school population. Thus, the Gardendale students who were educated at elite schools and colleges would most likely be represented far beyond their proportion of the population in business as well as banking, law, policymaking, the arts, and charitable activities:

> Ties in the financial and corporate world are not confined to economic institutions alone. They also connect to political individuals and institutions through political action committees, personal political contributions, service on government advisory boards, and influence over the appointment of cabinet members. The business elite also influences American government policy formulation through numerous advisory panels. These panel members advise government agencies on virtually all major questions of public policy [ibid., p. 200].

Although only a very few of the Gardendale children would be likely to make it into the very top echelon—a small minority of persons who have the social, economic, and political clout to ensure their profits and class privileges—many more would achieve high-level positions and continue to aspire to the top. The few persons who made it through the eye of the needle would guarantee that a stratified social order stays in place, using their power to get everyone else to act and think in ways that benefit their interests (Parenti, 1978, p. 5). Thus, while the Frederick Douglass children were unlikely to make it in the framework established by the dominant society, Gardendale children were busy learning to construct that framework, one that would make racism, sexism, and extremes in wealth continuing realities. I maintain that this stratification will become increasingly unsustainable in a global society.

In the conclusions, I explore alternatives to this calcified social order.

NOTES

1. The probes for writing the stories and making the drawings were as follows:

My Tourist Trail. "Suppose other children are going to visit your neighborhood. Please help them get around by drawing a tourist trail." You were to label important places, color in pleasant and unpleasant places, draw a solid line around the area you can go without an adult, and draw a dotted line to show where you go after school.

My Imaginary Walk. "Suppose you are taking an imaginary friend on a tour of your neighborhood. Please tell your friend what you see, feel, hear, and smell. Circle all the words on the opposite page that describe your neighborhood. Use these words (and any other ones you think up) to write a story about your imaginary walk."

My TV Program. "Let's say you are a TV producer. You are making a TV program about your neighborhood." You were to say where you were filming the program, who were the stars, what the program was about, who the audience was, and why you want to make a TV program about your neighborhood.

My Life Story. "Write a story about your life by answering these questions." The questions were related to age, birthplace, occupants of your home, tenure, description of your home, other places of residence, the best and worst places you have been, and what you do after school.

My Future Visions Plan. "Let's suppose that the mayor wants your neighborhood to be the best place in the whole world for children to live. Please draw a future visions plan for your neighborhood. These are the things the mayor wants you to consider." The list included keeping the nice parts of the neighborhood, changing or improving the bad parts, making exciting places for children to play and learn, and making anything else that children might want in a neighborhood.

My Story about Moving. "Suppose your mom or dad was thinking about moving to a different neighborhood." You were to say why they would want to move, where you would go, how you would feel about leaving your neighborhood and friends, how you would feel about making new friends, and what your new neighborhood would be like.

2. Keep in mind that these stories were created within the context of the Urban Network, which accounts for the unusual focus on such topics as recycling, saving the Earth, and architecture.

3. I believe this is a reference to an incident (that was highly publicized during the summer before this story was written) in which three heavy-set black teenagers were videotaped beating up several white women at a festival in Detroit.

4. This is a reference to the cost of joining the Little League team.

5. According to Goldsmith and Blakely (1992), the "median net worth in 1988 for white households was $43,260, eight to ten times as high as for African Americans ($4,160) or Hispanics ($5,524)" (pp. 28–29). And 70 percent of Frederick Douglass's students came from single-parent (female) households; in 1988 the median net worth of black female-headed households was just $757. Among other things, this lack of personal assets denied these households the unearned income that accrues to better-off (even middle-class) families in the form of interest, dividends, and rent.

Conclusions: Weaving a Tapestry of Resistance

When Moses led the Jews out of Egypt, he and his followers spent forty years in the desert. The modern Israelis have proven in a number of recent wars that the Sinai is easily crossed, and even for the primitive transport of Moses's time, forty years of travel seems outlandish. Why did Moses and his followers take so long to cross this modest desert? It seems that the personal and social transitions from the fleshpots of Egypt to freedom in the Promised Land required a change of perceptions, and the human mind is not easily transformed. It was essential to give up the slavelike ways that had been learned in Egypt. By the time the Jews reached their homeland, all but two persons who remembered Egypt had died off, so that the new people, readied in the desert for the Promised Land, completed the journey and entered upon their inheritance reborn [Duhl, 1990, p. 7].

If places are texts that instruct children about a way of life, what types of landscapes might enable them to take leave of their assigned ranks and roles in the hierarchies of the dominant culture? Lacking a period of isolation such as Moses had to relinquish the atomistic, authoritarian belief systems upon which most of our careers are built, how can educators adopt more inclusive, participatory instructional methods? Given the concentration of wealth and power in the hands of a few persons—given the extraordinary calcification of the social order— what processes might give us the inner strength and will to start a movement to reconceive Earthly relationships? These three questions outline one dimension of a model of learning in a sustainable society, encompassing physical contexts, governance structures, and learning processes. They form the warp of what I refer to as a *tapestry of resistance* to the status quo; they are the continuous threads that are the foundation of the mental shift I am about to describe. The other dimension relates to how revolutionary individuals choose to be in transforming those three aspects of mainstream education.

In the introduction, I discussed the urgent need for redefining traditional approaches to education due to the population explosion and its accompanying depletion of the landscape worldwide. As a number of persons in the environmental movement have noted, two Chinese characters translate into the word *crisis*, the first meaning "danger," the second meaning "opportunity." What many perceive as profound threats to the future of life on the planet also create unique occasions for personal and social growth. While it seems inconceivable that those few persons who exercise power over the Earth's resources (including the very conception of human potential) would voluntarily surrender such power, perhaps it is possible. Until now in modern Western society, members of the dominant culture have thought of themselves as autonomous beings, the best and the brightest of whom move into positions of power within the institutions that make up the larger society. As it becomes increasingly clear that no one exists in isolation—that our fates are linked through the ecosystem—the haves might be convinced to share their power and join with the have-nots in collective resistance to enslaving patriarchal contracts. Perhaps it *is* possible.

Within sustainable relationships, power would be experienced not as a negative force but as a positive one—sometimes referred to as *empowerment*—that results in feelings of mutual responsibility and personal control. Henry Giroux (1985) commented on Paulo Freire's notions of power as both a negative and positive force.

> For Freire, power works both on and through people. On the one hand, this means that domination is never so complete that power is experienced exclusively as a negative force. On the other hand, it means that power is at the basis of all forms of behavior in which people resist, struggle, and fight for their image of a better world [p. xix].

This view of power as a positive, empowering struggle for equity is generally invoked with respect to disadvantaged persons who are seeking to increase their fair share of resources. I have attempted to show that the struggle for a better world must also take place among privileged groups who are setting the norms for unsustainable lifestyles by imposing on impoverished persons "their way of being, talking, dancing, their tastes, even their way of eating" (Freire, 1985, p. 192). The concept of empowerment necessarily includes those affluent persons who must gain the courage to share their advantages.

But what would a tapestry of collective resistance look like? If education in a sustainable society is about inclusiveness, how can persons with diverse political views participate in differing, but complementary, ways. bell hooks (1994) recalled the intensity of her early education in a segregated southern school in which black "teachers were enacting a revolutionary pedagogy of resistance that was profoundly anticolonial" (p. 2) by teaching black children that they could be reborn as scholars and thinkers. She contrasted that experience with attending imprisoning integrated schools in which white teachers reinforced racial stereotypes—places in which apathy, boredom, and disinterest replaced the joyous struggle for personal and social growth that hooks had known in her all-black school. What kind of pedagogies would create places of resistance—Promised Lands—in which teachers and students of all socioeconomic backgrounds could struggle to be reborn as members of a heterogeneous and sustainable society? I use the plural deliberately to avoid the shortsightedness of proposing a single conceptual framework, and because I believe that there is a continuum of possibilities for engaging in resistance, depending on how individuals see themselves in relation to the mainstream. This continuum of possibilities forms the second dimension of the tapestry, or its woof—the varied threads that loop around the warp, bringing color, life, and multiple dimensions to it.

The most conventional threads in this tapestry of possibilities are persons such as Tom Mintz and Jane Andre, who work within traditional institutions while seeking to broaden the social justice agenda of those institutions. Such persons are valuable insiders because they often can win over others like Noreen Clark, who would like to be more progressive in their work but have not yet found the means to do so. Among the ranks of conventional change agents are those educators who seek to broaden students' understanding of social issues through community-service learning, a pedagogy described earlier that has a long-standing tradition in elementary, secondary, and higher education. More recent are those involved in diversifying curricula to include multicultural or feminist perspectives. In these instances, the larger institution does not change, but individual educators create alternative learning spaces for their students.

The most transformative threads in the tapestry are educators like Myles Horton, who believed that the school system had become too corrupted by its own power to ever promote real social change. As Horton did, such persons leave the mainstream and find other venues for engaging in out-of-school education, but this may result in a loss of one's status and recognition. Explaining the costs of his decision to operate a radical school for the poor called the Highlander Research and Education Center in Tennessee, Horton said (1990):

We knew that if we worked outside the system, we would not be recognized as educators, because an educator by definition was somebody inside the system. Nevertheless, we decided we'd work outside the system and be completely free to do what we thought was the right thing to do. . . . Whether we had any recognition or even if we had opposition, that wouldn't affect our position. . . . It wasn't surprising to us that we were not considered educators. We were condemned as agitators or propagandists, the most kindly condemnations, and mostly we were called communists or anarchists or whatever cuss words people could think up at the time [p. 200].

Another progressive educator, Paulo Freire, shared Horton's commitment to liberatory education for oppressed persons but chose to work within the system, thus falling somewhere in the center of this continuum of possibilities. Freire accepted that the school system was intractable but felt it was important to create change-making subcultures within mainstream institutions. Hooks (1990) and others have written about the duality of being inside an institution while struggling against its norms, referring to this position as one of creative marginality. Marginality is "a site one stays in, clings to even, because it nourishes one's capacity to resist. It offers to one the possibility of radical perspective from which to see and create, to imagine alternatives, new worlds" (p. 150). These three points along the continuum—which I refer to respectively as conventional, transformative, and alternative—seem equally valuable and necessary to widespread personal and social change. Figure 8 illustrates the tapestry, its warp formed by sustainable physical contexts, democratic governance structures, and empowering learning processes, which create the necessary foundation for a shift in thinking; its woof formed by the multidimensional threads of resistance.

In this last portion of the book, I begin by presenting a theoretical perspective on each aspect of the model's foundations—its warp—in sections titled "Creating Landscapes of Connectedness," "Community Caretaking as the Practice of Democracy," and "Learning through the Arts of Empowerment." To give this idealized model a real-world grounding, I illustrate its varied possibilities for resistance to the status quo—its woof—with concrete examples. These include a program that created an innovative environment within a traditional school ("Threads of a Conventional Woof"), another that changed traditional operational procedures ("Threads of a Alternative Woof"), and a third that created a community-based context of learning ("Threads of a Transformative Woof"). I end the book with some broader insights into educators' role in personal and social change.

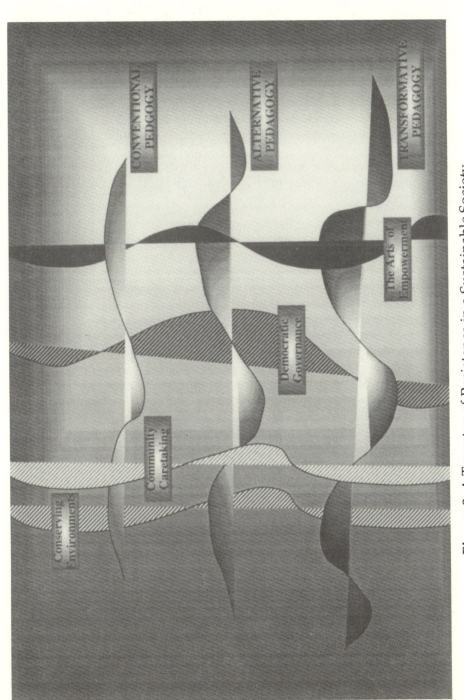

Figure 9: A Tapestry of Resistance in a Sustainable Society

CREATING LANDSCAPES OF CONNECTEDNESS

In the introduction, I stated that the same physical environment may have different meanings for different people; however, some meanings are widely shared within a given culture. For instance, studies have shown that most people in the United States prefer single-family homes in socioeconomically homogeneous neighborhoods. Another widely held view is that the cost, size, and location of a residence reflect the social status and even the moral character of its occupants. The notion that a person's worth derives not only from significant others and achievements but from the capacity to amass material goods was articulated over a hundred years ago by psychologist William James (1890) when he characterized self-identity as

> the sum total of all that he [sic] can call his, not only his body and his psychic processes, but his clothes and his house, his wife and children, his ancestors and his friends, his reputation and works, his lambs and horses, his yacht and bank account. All things give him the same emotions. If they wax and prosper, he feels "triumphant"; if they dwindle and die away he feels cast down—not necessarily in the same degree for each thing, but in much the same way for all .

Market interests have so magnified this early insight into the possessiveness of the patriarchal psyche that materialistic gain may be the most commonly shared value in today's pluralistic society, and this shared value is resulting in increasing devastation to the physical environment—the most visible of all status symbols. Since there is no limit to what constitutes a good life, housing standards and the process of "keeping up with the Joneses" have escalated over time, resulting in a continuing pattern of abandonment of older, developed areas in favor of virgin land. Thus, the same suburbs that enticed the 1960s middle class away from urban areas are viewed as too small and unfashionable by today's middle-class consumers, who are abandoning them in search of the larger, more luxurious homes of the 1990s. The continuing cycle of flight from older, more modest housing, which is driven by fear of "the other" and the presumption of buying and selling property to accumulate wealth, is rapidly reaching its limits. Recently government officials, planners and designers, and even the banking industry, have begun to recognize the social, environmental, and economic costs incurred through the dominant culture's pursuit of housing that is termed the "American Dream"—costs incurred as higher walls with more guards and gates are needed to protect property, as farmland and wildlife habitats are destroyed,[1] as people spend more time and money driving,[2] as new roads and sewers are built while old infrastructure is left underutilized,[3] as the differences between a life of affluence and one of poverty escalate. I hope that this book has also shed light on the developmental costs to both poor and affluent children in terms of their capacity to become caring, productive members of a multicultural society.

Is it possible to revise James's early notions of self-identity? Is it conceivable that adults would not feel compelled to express their worth by purchasing lavish residences and then adopting exclusionary zoning laws and deed restrictions to secure their investments? Is it possible for educators to conceive of a learning process that would not encourage children to compete with their peers for the biggest share of the pie? Could a new generation grow up with the inner strength to not take more of the Earth's resources than it needs—to give back as much as it takes? Several mental shifts have occurred during this century, suggesting that it also is possible to change how we view our use of the landscape. To name a few instances of recent mental shifts, smoking and consumption of red meat, once identified with ruggedness, are recognized health hazards; many old buildings that were considered eyesores are considered historically significant; and having a "designated driver"—a term popularized by a Harvard University professor who had the Hollywood connections for introducing such characters into television scripts—became a widely accepted practice at social events in a very short period of time. It *is* possible that possessiveness and competition for the biggest chunk of the Earth's physical resources can be erased, and educators can play a key role in helping young people imagine alternative landscapes of conservation and connectedness. As psychiatrist Leonard J. Duhl (1990) explained:

> The game rules of the dominant American culture define the goals of life as wealth, power, and success . . . contemporary society is so obviously and overwhelmingly materialistic that it is almost tedious to speak about it. But we must remember that this dominant and pervasive materialism is JUST ANOTHER MAP. As drab and commonsensical as it may appear, it is not, as so many tough-minded business people seem to believe, any more the "real world" than is the communion rail or the poem [p. 60].

One way to create new maps of human settlement is to replace myths about the benefits of current living patterns with factual information on the hidden costs of those patterns, and a variety of place-related classroom projects might help young people to generate such information. As mentioned in the Foreword, environmental education programs are fairly widespread and, in some areas, part of a state-mandated curriculum. However, these programs are typically reflective of the general public's environmental concerns, focusing on "very local, even personal,

'Green behavior'—such as recycling trash, using only certain products, and driving less. And then, there is a second, planetary level of concern, as in campaigns to protect endangered species, the tropical rain forests, or the ozone layer. The mediating relationships that link the individual household with the planetary ecosystem are left out" (Bellah et al., 1992, p. 14). By focusing on this missing link, namely, how families live together in communities, new maps of human settlement might emerge.

The possibilities for place-related projects in this area are almost limitless. To give a few examples, students might begin by scanning local newspapers or visiting the local planning department to identify some issue that interests them. Most communities nowadays are beset by a variety of dilemmas ranging from debates over subdivisions that significantly increase the population of rural areas to conflicts over the pros and cons of constructing gambling casinos in deteriorated cities. Such issues not only offer a means to develop critical awareness related to imbalances in power and resources, they create a context for taking action within the local community. Another possibility is to use students' residential histories as the basis for investigating how single-family detached houses, row houses, low-rise apartments, and multi-story apartment buildings are grouped to form different types of neighborhoods; looking at how infrastructure (transportation, schools, recreational spaces) changes when houses are spread out or grouped close together; and then exploring how various residential forms influence social relationships, living expenses, daily schedules, and nature.

Yet another possibility is to track the history of change in an older neighborhood in your area to better understand how personal life choices intersect with market interests to generate patterns of overdevelopment followed by decline and abandonment. These investigations might spark discussions about nonmaterialistic ways of life in which the decent properties of one era would not end up as the slums of another era. They can also be a point of departure for discussing how the hidden curriculum of separation is expressed through your school building's design and use. Showing slides of historical and current communities around the world might help students to visualize more conserving ideas about what makes places desirable, and hands-on design projects would involve them in imagining—and positioning themselves in—a truly *good society* in Dewey's sense of an association of individuals who contribute to the common good.

Such place-related projects are fascinating for young people because they provide a framework for thinking critically about their own visions of the future, and because they offer a concrete means to gain some sense of control over that future. The complexity of place-related study gives teachers an opportunity to subvert the meritocratic framework of schooling because it encompasses a range of interests and abilities, not just mental abilities, which might enhance children's sense of being unique parts of an indivisible whole. They can also help children to gain a sense of responsibility for a particular community and culture while increasing their knowledge about how that place fits into the larger ecosystem. However, none of these or any other place-related activities will result in a real mental shift if carried out within the traditions of objectivity and neutrality, because the uneven patterns of development that exist in this country are neither objective nor neutral. They are politically charged—driven by racism, classism, and economic power—and a reinvention of the landscape will require students and teachers to reflect on all their work through a lens of social and environmental justice.

COMMUNITY CARETAKING AS THE PRACTICE OF DEMOCRACY

> Education can never merely be for the sake of individual self-enhancement. It pulls us into the common world or it fails altogether. . . . We should recover a more classical notion that it is the whole way of life that educates. Our jobs, our consumer marketplaces, our laws and our government agencies, our cities and neighborhoods, our homes and churches, all educate us and create the context in which our schools operate, supporting them or undermining them as the case may be [Bellah et al., 1992, p. 176].

While schools are only part of anyone's total educational milieu, the events in this book suggest a disjuncture between the broad lessons—both positive and negative—that are contained in children's life experiences and their schoolwork. How might schools be more positively engaged in clarifying and building upon what students learn from their everyday engagement with the environment? How can school learning promote the sense of being part of a common world for which we are individually and collectively responsible? In an essay entitled "The School and Society," John Dewey (1964) explored how to connect life experiences and formal education so as to build students' capacities for responsible citizenship. Because industrialization had disrupted children's active participation in the life-sustaining activities that had taken place in the homes and neighborhoods of an earlier period, Dewey believed that schooling should encompass the "types of processes by which society keeps itself going, as agencies for bringing home to the child some of the primal necessities of community life" (p. 300). In Dewey's view, such active participation would allow students to develop personal capacities in relation to the common good of a community—a balance that requires continual calibration in a democracy.

There would seem to be an even greater need nowadays than the one Dewey observed for young people to participate in the life-sustaining activities of a local community due to the increasing complexity and globalization of society. Certainly, modern infrastructure, from running water to transportation or telecommunication, has become more unintelligible and seemingly less in anyone's control than it was in Dewey's day. At the same time, "the growing economic, energy, and environmental crises are now showing us [that] decisions taken at one point in time have the power to affect future generations in ways that are by and large irreversible. The consequences of what our parents and the older generation among us did . . . are being felt by the younger generation of today" (Kothari, 1990, p. 30). Young people need insights into the long-range consequences of their actions within an incomprehensible global system, yet opportunities for assuming responsibility within a local community are minimized by competitive, privatized lifestyles and authoritarian modes of governance.

More than ever, according to Aronowitz and Giroux (1993), we need a distinctly contemporary approach to education for democratic citizenship. In their view:

> Our problem is, who can think through what's going on in the world, the changes in our lives underway as a result of decisions made at the political level? More importantly, the changes in our ways of working and living, the relation of the United States to the rest of the world, especially those parts of it suffering chronic privation. Our problems are preeminently public ones, for the gulf between the private and the public is no longer so wide that one may pursue his [sic] destiny without regard to institutional and political choices (p. 62).

Given the increasing stresses on the ecosystem as more of the planet is designed and used (or misused) by human beings, I go further and propose that we need a distinctly cooperative approach to education in which students can learn to participate in the life-sustaining activities of their physical surroundings.

Earlier, I referred to community caretaking as the process that occurs when domestic skills are applied outside the home, and neighbors join forces to improve the living conditions in their community. When a group of people feel they belong together and have some sense of obligation for each other and for their surroundings, they develop what Lappé and Du Bois (1994) described as a *culture of shared responsibility*, which begins with the democratic governance of the group or organization. In a three-year study of how people engage in participatory democracy, Lappé and Du Bois identified a number of primary and secondary schools that had evolved a culture of mutual responsibility through cooperative, student-directed, community-based learning within small, democratically managed schools. In these schools, Lappé and Du Bois saw evidence of traditional, authoritarian structures being dismantled through self-determination on the part of individuals as well as shared decision-making and accountability among members of an entire school community including students, parents, teachers, and local residents (pp. 201–231). Beginning with their framework of participatory democracy, I would like to elaborate those efforts that would allow young people to reframe the processes that are required to sustain domestic life as processes of community-caretaking, which seems essential for nurturing the local sense of place that can connect individual families to the national and global arenas of power.

Consider how household management might be extended to the larger community within an educational context. Among other things, household management might include the nonmonetary exchange of goods and services, budgeting, allocating resources, resolving conflicts, assuring equity among family members, and passing family traditions from one generation to the next. When translated into public life, a range of projects open up like setting up a community greenhouse to provide residents with locally grown vegetables, providing a service to replace selectively seeded, chemically treated lawns with natural grasses, figuring out how to reduce the school's operational costs through energy-saving devices and programs, setting priorities for improving the school's property, or organizing storytelling events in which elders are invited to share their memories of the neighborhood. Older students might operate latchkey programs for younger ones, younger students might design programs to assist elders with housekeeping tasks, both resulting in intergenerational contexts in which to experience the waxing and waning of existence—of giving back what you have received. Instead of approaching learning as the accumulation of value-free knowledge about an objective world, young people would learn by practicing life-sustaining roles and by getting feedback from significant others about the consequences of their actions. Instead of learning through structures of dominance and dependence, they would learn through their willingness to take responsible action and through a sense of connection to others. It goes without saying that parents and guardians would not only have to accept such community-caretaking activities as viable means of learning, they would have to actively participate in shaping the process.

Such an educational approach encompasses community-service learning in that it encourages civic and social responsibility within a real-life context and creates opportunities for students to collaborate with local residents on social and environmental problems. It differs by focusing, not on isolated issues or projects, but on the continuous nurturance of a living organism—the community. To harvest the lessons of such learning experiences, systematic critical reflection would be needed to explore the degree to which isolated actions contribute to the ongoing support systems, networks, and alliances that are prerequisite to a sustainable society. Such involvements would seem especially important in communities like San Lupe where households as well as neighborhoods are cared for invisibly by anonymous persons; in communities like Oak Hills, bringing the community caretaking that occurs among neighbors into the classroom would validate students' real-life experiences and competencies. In both situations, community caretaking is an opportunity for youth to practice democracy through shared, self-reliant responsibility for each other and for their surroundings.

LEARNING THROUGH THE ARTS OF EMPOWERMENT

> The dominant culture can afford to cast power purely in terms of power-over, for it has at its disposal the backing of that power: the guns, the prisons, the laws, the economic wealth. . . . But the dispossessed, to survive, to have power at all, must seek another source. They know the power of the common bonds of culture, of song, of ritual, of drum and dance, of healing to sustain hope and strength to resist oppression [Starhawk, 1987, p. 18].

Throughout this book, I have pointed to the need for educators of both poor and privileged youth to resist imposing the values and norms of the dominant culture—to open up instead the sources of empowerment that come from a sense of connectedness with the world. What kind of learning processes would tap into the magic of power-from-within, which can rupture the fabric of old beliefs and allegiances? How could we use that magic to construct new personal and societal identities—new mental maps of sustainability? The Civil Rights movement, which was grounded in the common bonds of a dispossessed culture, provides an example. In this instance, a new vision of society was made tangible through a song, "We Shall Overcome," which was simple enough for anyone to sing yet powerful enough to capture the imagination of the nation. The act of singing helped to inspire young and old, poor and privileged, uneducated and educated to join together and run the gauntlet of mobs and police billy clubs to end apartheid in the South. In the labor movement fifty years earlier, in many social justice organizations, in the long history of tribal cultures, in many instances of social progress, people have dug into the rich well of cultural activity—storytelling, music-making, dancing, singing, cooking, carving, building—to imagine their relatedness.

The arts inculcate a sense of organization and discipline, which in turn contribute to feelings of inner power and control over one's life. Architectural space gives shape, order, and meaning to human activity. Music makes public and, therefore, universal a whole range of private emotions. Dance makes tangible the passage of time and the rhythm of life. The arts go beyond the practical—the knowable. They teach us humility by revealing the mysteries of being human. They transcend linguistic and cultural differences. They give expression to the individual, but they also nurture the collective imagination and spirit so that a community of people can comprehend its relatedness.

I am not referring to the virtuoso arts, which are meant to be passively consumed by patrons to museums, concert halls, or theaters. Rather, I am referring to the arts of tribal and folk cultures like the "Circle of Life" *cuadros* sewn by Peruvian women who have been forced from their homelands, the graffiti or noncommercialized rap singing by ghetto youth who have been disenfranchised from the mainstream, and the barn raisings and quilting bees of early American pioneers. In these instances, the process of creating something together generates power-with as well as power-from-within.

I had a firsthand experience of community-building through the arts in the 1970s when I worked with low-achieving minority children in a New York City school on large-scale design projects. Because the children did not live in the immediate affluent neighborhood, there were ongoing conflicts between the school and nearby residents, many of whom characterized the children as hoodlums. The teachers and principal were convinced of their creativity and hired me with the explicit charge of constructing a public stage upon which to display the children's capacities. At the same time, I was to make the children aware of their responsibility to respect the property rights of their well-to-do neighbors. I began by helping a core group of youngsters learn about and critique their physical surroundings. Later, this contingent became the ambassadors for organizing a larger group of students, teachers, and parents who designed a variety of imaginative three-dimensional structures for the school yard. Over a four-year-period, many of the formerly hostile local residents began to join in the construction, embellishing the dirty work of building with artful celebrations. In addition to bringing together large numbers of people who had been in open conflict with one another, our structures seemed to have an amazing immunity to the vandalism that defaced the rest of the school yard.

Unlike learning through an estranged view of a world in which mind, body, and spirit are separate, learning through the arts of empowerment provides access to a language of wholeness—poetry, metaphor, symbol, ritual, myth—"which speaks to the body and to all the senses in ways that can never be completely conveyed in words" (Starhawk, 1987, p. 15). The arts of tribal and folk cultures offer a sense of collective history and continuity, which in turn contribute to a personal sense of time, place, and self—to empowerment. *If* well-directed, artistic enterprises can be potent tools of social change. Weaving a tapestry of resistance to patriarchal ways of being requires the inspirational force of tribal and folk arts to give us the strength and the will to change ourselves and our world.

PEDAGOGIES OF RESISTANCE

In this section, I present three case studies, all located in New York City, illustrating varying patterns of resistance to education that reproduces the status quo. I chose this site because it is the educational milieu with which I am most familiar and because, despite its layers of behemoth bureaucracies, New York City is also in the vanguard of school change, especially with respect to art and environmental education. One reason for the city's high level of innovation might be the presence of a vibrant artists' community (in need of alternative employment) that has been supported in varied K–12 projects by federal and state agencies as well as by a plethora of private foundations and corporations since the early 1960s. Another reason might be the activism of institutions like the Cooper-Hewitt, National Design Museum, or Henry Street Settlement (among many others) who provide a vital link between schools and their surrounding communities. Yet another reason might be the inspiration that derives from being situated amid a complex real-life learning laboratory with an array of cultural, educational, and business enterprises as well as some of the nation's most egregious social and environmental problems. Or perhaps the state of education in New York City can be traced back to the Chinese characters for the word *crisis*—where there is disaster, there is also possibility.

Threads of a Conventional Woof: Public School 110

Adults don't usually let kids do anything. We showed that when you give kids a chance, they can do important things. We started taking classes, learning how to use T-squares, sketching our ideas, building scale models. We looked through magazines and visited other playgrounds for ideas.

Even though I won't be here to play in [the playground], my sister and my
cousins will. And then there's all the other kids.

Danielle Morales, Sixth Grade

The Young Architects Club at Public School 110 on the Lower East
Side of Manhattan is exemplary of the degree to which a conventional
approach to educational change can enliven the learning milieu of a
traditional school. Stewarded by enrichment resource teacher Janet
Sygar in collaboration with architectural consultant Joanne G. Yoshida,
Public School 110 was an active Urban Network participant during the
1989–1990 academic year.[4] However, place-related learning was not a
new idea at this school, which had an ongoing involvement with Henry
Street Settlement, a social service and arts agency that dates back to
1893. Susan Fleminger, director of the settlement's Visual Arts and
Arts-in-Education program, provided support for Yoshida and Sygar to
create a venue for involving three classes of sixth-grade students in
learning about the Lower East Side during their weekly art classes.
Amplifying work done earlier at Henry Street by a consortium of
activist art teachers and architects, Sygar and Yoshida used Urban
Network principles to involve students in studying their low-income,
ethnically diverse neighborhood while making badly needed improvements to the school's deteriorated property.

Crammed next to the noise and fumes of the Williamsburg Bridge,
the building was one of the dreariest places I had encountered in my
years of touring public schools. The main entry had been closed off,
replaced by a large windowless interior room where a guard oversaw
the comings and goings of the entire school. The playground was even
worse, with broken concrete pavement, cyclone fencing, and a total
absence of landscaping. During the first year of the Young Architects
Club, Sygar and Yoshida initiated a study of building entrances that
culminated with a core group of sixth-graders staying after school to
refurbish the windowless cavern that confronted building occupants
every morning, creating a lively space with a mural wrapping around
all four walls to form something of an interior neighborhood. In the next
three years, the Sygar–Yoshida team continued their work, slowly overseeing student enhancements of a good portion of the building's
ground floor. Expanding their expertise and winning support from
hundreds of local residents and volunteer professionals, the women led
a major redesign of the school's playground, turning it into a community resource during the fifth and sixth years of the program. In addition
to these design projects, three desktop publications of neighborhood
walking tours were created and made available to other schools in the
area. Throughout each step of these many-staged, year-long projects,

students actively charted the course of their work. Explained participant Jocelyne Serrano: "What I liked most about the playground was
that the ideas didn't come from an adult, it [sic] came from a children's
point of view."

The community playground won first prize in an Urban Network
competition that was judged anonymously by four University of Michigan graduate students who each represented a different academic
discipline.[5] What was especially impressive to the jury was the
children's insights into the purpose of their work—to leave a legacy for
the younger children as a way of saying thanks for their education. They
also noted that quite a few alumni of the Young Architects Club had
returned to the school after graduation to assist new classes of sixth-
grade students in continuing the legacy. In addition to being excellent
by design standards, this program provides a wonderful example of
power-with and power-from-within in that the two adults—without
the authority of important titles—were able to use their creativity and
daring to suggest a direction that, in turn, engaged the creativity and
daring of both children and adults. One sixth-grade girl explained the
cumulative effect of their community-caretaking efforts in this way:

> I think our success will lead to many others. From one class doing a project
> like this, many others are inspired to also do this kind of activity. They
> learn that trying and effort pays off. They then teach this to the next
> graduating class. Who in turn teach it to the next. . . . We aren't making our
> school a better place for us, but for the future students of the school. We
> weren't thinking only of ourselves, we were thinking of others.
>   Dania Cordova, Sixth Grade

But the Young Architects Club is not simply a touchy-feely, do-good
experience; in addition to learning basic principles of sustainability,
students gain valuable planning skills and knowledge about how people relate to their environment while developing insights into their own
learning process. Here is what one student wrote when asked to explain
why he thought the community playground had won a national award:

> I think the jurors picked our work because we really paid attention to what
> we were going to do, like we didn't want to put objects in the middle of
> the yard because all of the kids like to walk there and that we put benches
> in areas where the majority of the kids like to stay which is usually in the
> shade.
>   I think that if other kids participate in activities this big that they will
> learn that sometimes you have to work together. I also think that they will
> learn that architecture isn't as easy as drawing on a piece of paper what
> you want the thing to look like. You have to take things into consideration.
> You have to pay attention to the sizes of things, the environment around

the thing being built. Such as, if you want to put plants you have to put it [*sic*] where it gets light. And also you have to take care in the way the people walk. The kids in the school run out of the doors at the end of the day so we didn't want to make the play structures get in the way of the students.

Timothy Caraballo, Sixth Grade

One possible explanation for the success of the Sygar-Yoshida team is that they were working within the context of an art class in a city that places a relatively high value on utilizing the arts in education. Operating outside the scrutiny of grades and standardized test scores, they were able to engage students in a liberatory educational experience while at the same time transforming the oppressive physical milieu of the school and the students' relationship to it. Although this case study is limited by not having an institutional framework to ensure its continuance, the Young Architects Club illustrates the importance of activities that allow youth and adults of all ages to experience such things as memory, persistence, giving back what you have taken, and the continuity of place. Even if the program ends or their projects are destroyed by a change in school leadership (as my 1970s efforts were), the acts of appropriating space that these children and their neighbors have experienced will live on in their memories.

Threads of an Alternative Woof: City-as-School

City-as-School High School, the first and largest of New York City's alternative secondary institutions, has been operating in the creative margins of the NYC Board of Education since the early 1970s. Beginning as a small school, it now has a faculty of ninety and a student body of 950 located in four of the city's five boroughs and a number of replications throughout the country. Within this nationally acclaimed model of experiential learning is an innovative horticulture program called Project Grow—an alternative within an alternative—which was spearheaded by social worker Mary Ellen Lewis with assistance from bilingual guidance counselor Gail Rothenberg and several other staff persons.

Under the leadership of principal Robert Lubetsky, City-as-School serves intellectually gifted students as well as those with nontraditional abilities, both of whom are likely to drop out of school due to their disaffection with typical classroom instruction. Its course of study includes internships in countless areas from carpentry to law and publishing, a learning plan that is carried out during each internship under the combined supervision of a faculty advisor and an outside resource person, a required weekly seminar, and elective as well as remedial classes. One key to the school's success (78 percent of students graduate, many of whom continue on to college or advanced technical training) is its program of individual counseling. During registration for each of the year's four cycles, faculty advisors assist students to choose community internships, select in-house or free college courses, and develop daily schedules. Throughout the cycle, student progress is monitored through phone calls, visits to internship sites, and evaluation of assignments.

Another key to the school's success is the flexibility that teachers have for shaping their own professional careers, and Lewis has taken full advantage of this enterprising milieu. She arrived at City-as-School seventeen years ago when she was hired as a social studies teacher. Subsequently, when the school began to strengthen its guidance services to meet students' growing needs, Lewis took a leave of absence to earn a graduate degree in social work and eventually became the school's full-time school social worker. In 1989, as she was considering how to create better connections between students' coursework and their internships, Lewis had an opportunity to join a foreign-study, community-development project that included work with Mother Theresa. Seizing the moment, she and a group of students set out for India, where they had a truly unique experiential education. Lewis was most impressed by the transformation her students experienced serving as stewards in community environmental projects, living close to nature, and also meeting Mother Theresa. The students' (and her own) excitement about these efforts was unmistakable; Lewis left India with the determination to continue this type of work at City-as-School.

Back home, Lewis took courses in horticultural therapy and teamed up with Rothenberg, who works with English-as-a-second-language (ESL) students, to lay the groundwork for Project Grow. They began by developing an integrated curriculum that brought Rothenberg's ESL students together with English-speaking students for science and language arts classes centered around various indoor horticulture projects. A small cadre of faculty underwent team-building and planning exercises under the tutelage of the NYC Outward Bound program. The group secured funding from the NYC Board of Education by integrating special populations in a mainstream project, and Project Grow began in full force with an enrollment of thirty-five students.

In 1992, having gained experience in integrating hands-on activities with coursework, the in-school experiential component was expanded into the community as a *group* internship (unlike the individual ones students usually experienced). The class accepted an assignment at the Hong Ning Housing project, which needed assistance in designing and constructing a garden at a building on the Lower East Side that houses elders. Thus, Project Grow evolved as the first comprehensive (and somewhat controversial) curriculum at City-as-School that not only connects schoolwork with fieldwork around a discrete disciplinary focus—horticulture—but that put students into a participatory team relationship. A program of study was designed that interfaced one day of fieldwork with four days of classes in science, math, social studies, and ESL, each class providing the academic background for students' hands-on experiences.

As Lewis explained:

> Unlike the individualized internships in the school, this was a package deal so the focus in all the classes was the [community gardening] project. In science, students would look at the angle of the sun, how much water certain plants needed. In history, we looked at the Lower East Side . . . at immigration. The math class worked on computers to process measurements, project time lines, and figure out the division of labor and costs. Fortunately, we got a lot of support from Outward Bound. All of us had to create a curriculum to go along with this project—integrating group work, process, and journal writing along with everything else. The project gave us an opportunity to work side-by-side in the field with the students. It was very democratic; even though we were still the teachers, the students had a big say in the planning, and we did the dirty work along with them. We would say, "What do we need to get done? How should we go about it?" Students were always invited to weekly planning meetings and came when their schedules allowed.

The social worker and the director at Hong Ning served as an interface between the class and the tenants, but so did Chinese-speaking students (who made up about 20 percent of the class) and a Chinese paraprofessional. A garden, which was created to be responsive to residents' cultural and recreational needs, included an area for Tai Chi; it now offers the students and the tenants an ongoing laboratory for community-caretaking (maintaining a garden in New York City requires constant vigilance). In return for their assistance, residents provided the students with instruction in brush painting and Tai Chi but, more importantly, with implicit lessons in multicultural understanding.

In addition to the Hong Ning garden, Project Grow has a number of other ongoing projects on its agenda, including landscaping the unyielding brick paving that leads into the 100-year-old, five-story school building. The students reconceived this area as a "landscaped park" with wall-to-wall, environmentally themed murals and groupings of planter boxes that form seating areas. With support from the NYC Sanitation Department, a compost-heated greenhouse was added to the installation, so that school lunches, waste from local restaurants, and stable manure from the NYC Police Department can be recycled as compost, which in turn heats the plant-producing greenhouse and provides finished compost for local community gardens. Since this latter project involves three-dimensional design, architect Dan Nuñez volunteered his services, providing in-house design instruction and motivating students to apply the math that is required to turn two-dimensional drawings into habitable space.

Lewis and Rothenberg acknowledge that Project Grow is not without its problems. In their view, the school's mode of operation constitutes both an asset and a liability. Since teachers are accustomed to developing individual internships in the local community, a cooperative endeavor like Project Grow is at odds with the prevailing institutional culture, especially since so much extra time and effort required to coordinate a large, participatory team effort. Although faculty realize that students would benefit from more structured learning experiences, conflicts arise between Project Grow's needs and teachers' regular duties, for example, when the staff take time off to visit other internships. As Lewis explained: "We have a lot of flexibility as educators in the school, but that doesn't exempt us from our prescribed professional responsibilities. We try to accomplish traditional academic and counseling goals through nontraditional means, but this kind of combined teaching and counseling takes a lot of extra time."

Yet, they are convinced that Project Grow offers a tremendous communal learning experience within City-as-School's atmosphere of innovation. The biggest impact, they say, is the encouragement students get through their connections with the business and with nonprofit communities—encouragement that empowers them to dream and then make their dreams come true. The result is that young people see that they can visibly change their environment.

Threads of a Transformative Woof: The Children's Art Carnival

The major obligation that adults have to our children today is to try and find a way to instill in them a sense of stability, and the knowledge that someone really cares what happens to them with regard to their own individual personalities. Our children need to know—know that they are and will continue to be and become that which is unique and different from any other self. To become individuals who happen to things and not individuals to whom things are always happening. . . . In this age of ultrasophistication with our vast mechanical knowledge—knowledge of everything but ourselves—it is time we allow our children to become what is best in themselves, to become balanced human beings. To begin, we must have some idea of what it means to be creative, for only through the act of creativity can we begin to truly know and become ourselves. . . . Through the use of the mind and the use of the hands, we are able to make our thoughts become things [Blayton-Taylor, 1978, pages unnumbered].

The importance of having a supportive physical environment in which to learn how to turn one's visions into reality is not something I learned in architecture school. Rather, it was Betty Blayton-Taylor, director of the Children's Art Carnival, who provided my first lesson in the relevance of the physical environment to children's development. Her quarter-of-a-century effort to bring beauty and discipline to the lives of inner-city youth is exemplary of a transformative approach to education. The Art Carnival is an especially instructive case study because, although operating outside the formal educational system, its programs are highly interactive with that system, improving youth's potential for success within mainstream institutions but also infusing those institutions with new ideas.

I met Blayton-Taylor while completing my architectural internship when she contacted me for advice on converting a four-story brownstone in NYC's Harlem, which had been a single-family residence, into a community art school. Knowing how difficult it would be to upgrade a residential property to an institutional use, I firmly recommended that she look for a different building. Perhaps, she might find more suitable space in one of the area's many underutilized school buildings or abandoned factories, I suggested. Impatient with my inability to recognize the obvious, Blayton-Taylor just as firmly declared that the brownstone *did* suit her needs precisely because it *was* a home—a place where she could create the nurturing environment that her students lacked in institutional-looking school buildings. And, it was my problem to figure out the technical details. Over the years, as I observed small groups of children sewing a banner in the sunlit space created by a bay window or watched teenagers crowded together to produce a film in what had been a bathroom, I was won over to Blayton-Taylor's point of view about the architectural needs of an extended family, whose creativity is inspired by feelings of being "at home."

The Art Carnival was founded as a community-outreach program of the Museum of Modern Art in 1969, a period when the arts were first recognized as catalysts for inner-city development. Blayton-Taylor's initial ideas about building self-esteem by being artistically expressive about one's life history and surroundings crystallized with the assistance of psychologist Gilbert Voyat, a protégé of Piaget. Voyat and his doctoral students at the City College of New York Psychological Center worked with the artists and designers who made up the Art Carnival's staff to develop motivational teaching techniques and measure the effect of those techniques on the children's progress. In the intervening years, the staff have used their disciplines (painting, photography, ceramics, printmaking, video, drama, three-dimensional construction, to name a few) as vehicles for teaching reading, writing, and social studies to between 6,000 and 15,000 young persons every year.

Some of the Art Carnival's programs occur during the school day as youth, ages four to twenty-one, are bused to its facilities from Manhattan, the Bronx, and Queens; others take place after school or on Saturdays. Participants—who come from private, public, and parochial schools—comprise entire classes of first- through sixth-grade students, high school interns, apprenticeship trainees, disabled students, and even preschoolers. During the summer, programs are offered that include art activities in local parks (which usually draw a crowd of onlookers), day camps, and summer youth employment and apprenticeship opportunities. The staff also make site visits to schools throughout the city, introducing classroom teachers to the Art Carnival's method of using the arts as a vehicle for teaching the core curriculum. Because of its success—youths reading below grade level demonstrate a two-year improvement in reading skills after an eighteen-week exposure to the Art Carnival[6]—the organization has received numerous awards including national recognition and dissemination of its career training approach.

Even though the emphasis at the Art Carnival is on "the effect that the creative process has on the child, not the object that is produced" (Blayton-Taylor, 1978), the products themselves are unquestionably extraordinary. Multimedia work created by Art Carnival students is frequently exhibited throughout the city, and many permanent installations can be found in New York City's schools as well as in corporate buildings and public spaces. In addition to allowing youth to make their imprint upon the world—to appropriate it by overlaying their visual imagery—these professional-quality products provide an important source of economic support. For instance, the Art Carnival was once contracted by the NYC Parks Department to paint designs on the walls of its homely bathhouses, and another not-for-profit entity, Harlem Textile Works, was formed as a spin-off to the Art Carnival after Third Avenue fabric companies became regular clients for its textile patterns.

A theme that runs through all of this creative invention is an idea that was captured early on with the slogan "doo-it," which conveyed the notion that, in a family, each person ought to actively take responsibility for contributing something ("Who gonna do it?" the artists would ask. "I'm gonna do it," students would respond); and that older persons are obligated to make the contributions of younger persons a reality. Using this imagery of hands-on action, the Art Carnival has created countless representations of doo-it cities where doo-it families live with their productive doo-it children, the ideas of younger children being perfected by older ones and sometimes turned into professional products by teenage apprentices and professional artists and designers. Harlem Textile Works is just such an effort in which children's sketches are developed as repeating patterns, then silkscreened onto fabric by teenage apprentices with input from professional textile designers—a revenue-generating effort that has allowed the organization to survive escalating cutbacks in funding to arts organizations.

In the early 1980s, after having some success not only in marketing the Art Carnival products but in creating an entrepreneurial atmosphere that spawned many alternative careers for its students, Blayton-Taylor had an architectural concept that would have allowed her to exploit more fully the school's link with the business community. She proposed to renovate three vacant apartment buildings to form one entity. The corner building would house the Art Carnival while the other two would provide mixed-use rental space for shops, offices, cottage industries, and housing. Although the vertical distinctions between the buildings would remain, Blayton-Taylor envisioned horizontal connections in the programming of space so that, for instance, the office space of the Art Carnival would be on the same floor as the rental office space. In this way resources would be shared between the for-profit organizations and the Art Carnival, and youth would have greater opportunities for learning in Bellah et al.'s sense of being educated by their total environment since each floor would represent a different slice of life. Not only would the building's rent roles stave off Reagan-era cutbacks, the traffic that tenants would attract would increase the Art Carnival's business. Blayton-Taylor's selling point for this three-million-dollar scheme was that a large one-time contribution would make the Art Carnival more self-reliant—a point that netted an immediate infusion of public funding, including a one-dollar pricetag on the three city-owned buildings. Unfortunately, the Art Carnival's most ingenious survival idea never came to fruition because the required private match for the public funds that had been allocated was never forthcoming. Possibly, the idea of self-reliance was simply too transformative.

These three case studies illustrate how young people can achieve more productive relationships with their environment as long as imaginative teachers and organizations are willing to invest extraordinary efforts to reinvent mainstream educational methods. The persons just described see their work not as a nine-to-five job but as an avocation—a calling that links a them to a larger community. A blessing in the Episcopal Book of Common Prayer reads: "So guide us in the work we do, that we may do it not for the self alone, but for the common good." These educators are carrying out their work for the common good while helping young people to learn that same lesson. They also demonstrate their willingness to take the risk of not being neutral in a have-a-nice-day society that requires teachers to avoid exposing children to potentially controversial issues. Finally, these case studies show the difference between the authoritarian power that is bestowed on individuals by powerful institutions and the personal authority that accrues to those who have excellent ideas with which to inspire strength and authority in others.

EDUCATION AS THE PRACTICE OF WEAVING

Weaving—the metaphor for the educational approach presented in this book—"makes use of many different threads to create something larger, stronger, more useful, more durable, and more beautiful than any individual string" (Tainter, 1990, p. 2). Through weaving, educators can create a tapestry of human connectedness, where more and less gifted, young and old, poor and privileged can use the inspiration of cultural activity to bridge their differences; where children and adults feel empowered by a process of defining a strong, collective purpose; where a community of people take responsibility for guiding change and for bettering the human condition in a way that respects the sacredness of nature. Teaching as the practice of weaving means that educators would venture beyond nurturing intellectual life to assume a broader socializing function—it means that they would trade in their stance of objectivity and openly assume responsibility for shaping the nation's consciousness. By accepting the position of being unbiased, apolitical technocrats, educators are disempowered from intervening in those ideas that give meaning and purpose to a society, relegated instead to providing the state with a literate population that speaks a common language and shares a middle-class ethic of delayed gratification. It is precisely this role that would seem to contribute to teachers' low status in this hierarchical society—they are technocrats who serve a political system, not philosophers or humanists who shape that system.

Yet, those who develop literacy are major contributors to the moral foundation of a society because language is a filter of what we know and do (with direct experience and belief systems being the other filters). Environmental lessons are being taught every day through countless words and actions, so the issue is how to make these lessons socially responsible. It is how to educate citizens who can actively engage in an ongoing process of articulating the common concerns of this diverse planet—of elaborating a philosophy-in-action that can transform how we see ourselves. Active participation at both the personal and societal levels is especially important at this moment in history because open dialogue is necessary for deriving collective responses to current environmental challenges. In the words of Frances Moore Lappé (1989):

> A democratic society is more than a collection of people developing their individual talents and shouldering responsibility. It is also the dynamic of the common life itself, in which citizenship means joining in public dialogue to uncover and give shape to our common values and to decide how to act upon them. Citizenship . . . promotes a public arena of deliberation over common concerns, an interchange that is itself morally transformative, inseparable from our individual moral development [p. 63].

To assure the survival of life on Earth in the twenty-first century, substantive discussions are needed in every arena—in classrooms as well as on the streets of neighborhoods, in the workplace as well as around kitchen tables, in the media as well as in local organizations, in religious as well as political arenas, in art galleries as well as gift shops. Since educators knowingly or unknowingly transmit the values that will shape future ecosystems, it seems entirely appropriate for them to assume a leadership role in articulating more inclusive, equitable values and norms. It also seems appropriate to use another factor in the development of children's outlook on the world—their reading of the physical environment—as a point of intervention, and to draw on their artistic abilities to project new mental maps of society. The question is not *whether* educators should expand their institutional obligations to encompass a social justice agenda; rather it is *how to begin* an integrated agenda to personal and social growth within a context of environmental sustainability. I hope this book has offered several possibilities.

One final caveat. Whatever your own choice might be for contributing to the tapestry of resistance that is evolving in the educational community, it is important to find like-minded persons who can provide a safe space within which to articulate new alternatives. As Starhawk explained (1987):

> To resist effectively, we must create, for resistance is not a mere withdrawal of energy, but a posing of a reality that challenges power-over. . . . We need help in this work. In community, we can support each other through lean times and difficult transitions. We can create islands . . . where we can be nourished and healed. And, we can experiment with ways of interacting and organizing on a small scale that can eventually be adapted to larger systems [pp. 314, 337].

In community, we can dare to dream of an Earth that is governed by cooperation and responsibility—an Earth in which more and less gifted, young and old, poor and privileged, join hands to seek the common good—an Earth that engages persons in using their minds and their hands to shape destiny. If we do not assume the risks of dreaming such dreams of a sustainable way of life, they surely will not come to pass.

NOTES

1. Rural farmland was lost at the rate of ten acres per hour over the last decade, which equals an area the size of Rhode Island.

2. Currently about 18 percent of a household budget is spent to maintain the multiple family cars that are needed in sprawling suburban developments.

3. For example, some of Detroit's major arteries carry as low as 30 percent of their intended capacity while suburb-to-suburb travel on two-lane roads is causing traffic congestion and hazardous driving in other parts of the region.

4. Data from Public School 110 were not included with the seventeen schools that were used for the main body of this book. Because the program was so much more distinctive than the rest, I made the decision to view it as an isolated case study.

5. To avoid my influence, the jury was convened independently by a fifth student. They represented the disciplines of architecture, education, geography, and planning.

6. The Chapter 1 program that generated these data is no longer in operation at the Art Carnival because of funding cutbacks at the NYC Board of Education.

Bibliography

Aronowitz, S., and Giroux, H.A. (1993). *Education Still Under Siege*. 2nd ed. Westport, CT: Bergin and Garvey.

Banning, J.H. (1990). The relationship between the physical environment and learning. Unpublished paper presented at *"Children, Learning, and School Design: A National Invitation Conference for Architects and Educators"* at Northwestern University.

Bell, D. (1992). *Faces at the Bottom of the Well: The Permanence of Racism*. New York: Basic Books, Inc.

Bellah, R.N., Madsen, R., Sullivan , W.M., Swidler, A., and Tipton, S.M. (1992). *The Good Society*. New York: Vintage Books.

———. (1985). *Habits of the Heart: Individualism and Commitment in American Life*. New York: Harper and Row.

Berg, M., and Medrich, E.A (1980, September). Children in four neighborhoods: The physical environment and its effect on play and play patterns. *Environment and Behavior* 12(3).

Blayton-Taylor, B. (1978). *Making Thoughts Become: A Handbook for Teachers and Adults*. New York: The Children's Art Carnival.

Block, P. (1987). *The Empowered Manager: Positive Political Skills at Work*. San Francisco: Jossey-Bass Publishers.

Board of Education of the City of New York (1979). *Architecture, A Design for Education* (Curriculum No. 00-0500-40). New York: Author.

Bowers, C.A. (1993). *Critical Essays on Education, Modernity, and the Recovery of the Ecological Imperative*. New York: Teachers College Press.

Bowles, S. and Gintis, H. (1976). *Schooling in Capitalist America: Educational Reform and the Contradictions of Economic Life*. New York: Basic Books.

Bryant, B. (1993). Detroit summer: A model for service-learning. In Howard, ed., *Praxis I: A Faculty Casebook on Community-Service Learning* pp. 67–73. Ann Arbor, MI: University of Michigan OCSL Press.

224 Bibliography

Carnoy, M., and Levin, H.M. (1985). *Schooling and Work in the Democratic State*. Stanford, CA: Stanford University Press.

Coles, R. (1993). *The Call of Service: A Witness to Idealism*. Boston: Houghton Mifflin.

———. (1986). *The Moral Life of Children*. Boston: Houghton Mifflin.

———. (1977). *Privileged Ones: The Well-off and the Rich in America*, Vol. 5 of *Children of Crisis*. Boston: Little, Brown and Company.

Cookson, P.W., and Persell, C.H. (1985). *Preparing for Power: America's Elite Boarding Schools*. New York: Basic Books, Inc.

Crowfoot, J.E. (November 1994). The challenges of sustainability: Changing relationships and organizations. Unpublished paper presented at "Power and Sustainablity: Rethinking Relationships" of the American Collegiate Schools of Architecture Administrators Conference.

Darden, J.T., Hill, R.C., Thomas, J., and Thomas, R. (1987). *Detroit: Race and Uneven Development*. Philadelphia: Temple University Press.

Dewey, J. (1964). The school and society. In *John Dewey on Education: Selected Writings*, pp. 289–310. Edited and with an introduction by Archambault. Chicago: The University of Chicago Press.

Dreeben, R. (1968). *On What Is Learned in School*. Reading, MA: Addison-Wesley.

Duhl, L.J. (1990). *The Social Entrepreneurship of Change*. New York: Pace University Press.

Dutton, T. (1991). The hidden curriculum and the design studio: Toward a critical studio pedagogy. In Dutton, ed., *Voices in Architectural Education: Cultural Politics and Pedagogy*, pp. 165–194. Westport, CT: Bergin and Garvey.

Ehrenreich, B. (1989). *Fear of Falling: The Inner Life of the Middle Class*. New York: Pantheon.

Engel, J.R. (1990). Introduction: The ethics of sustainable development. In Engel and Engel, eds., *Ethics of Environment and Development: Global Challenge, International Response*, pp. 87–96. Tucson: University of Arizona Press.

Feldman, R.M., and Stall, S. (1994). The politics of space appropriation: A case study of women's struggles for homeplace in Chicago public housing. In Altman and Churchman, eds., *Women and the Environment*, pp. 167–200. New York: Plenum Press.

Freire, P. (1985). *The Politics of Education: Culture, Power, and Liberation*. Westport, CT: Bergin and Garvey.

Giroux, H.A. (1985). Introduction. In Freire, *The Politics of Education: Culture, Power, and Liberation*, pp. xi–xxv. Westport, CT: Bergin and Garvey.

———. (1984). Marxism and schooling: The limits of radical discourse. *Educational Theory* 34 (2): 113–35.

———. (1983). *Theory and Resistance in Education: A Pedagogy for the Opposition*. Westport, CT: Bergin and Garvey.

Giroux, H.A., and Purpel, D., eds. (1980). *The Hidden Curriculum and Moral Education*. Berkeley, CA: McCutchan Publishing.

Goldsmith, W.W., and Blakely, E.J. (1992). *Separate Societies: Poverty and Inequality in U.S. Cities*. Philadelphia: Temple University Press.

Goodlad, J.I., and Anderson, R.H. (1987). *The Nongraded Elementary School: Revised Edition*. New York: Teachers College Press.

Graham, P. (1992). *SOS: Sustain Our Schools*. New York: Hill and Wang.

hooks, b. (1994). *Teaching to Transgress: Education as the Practice of Freedom*. New York: Routledge.

———. (1990). *Yearning: Race, Gender, and Cultural Politics*. Boston: South End Press.

———. (1984). *Feminist Theory: From Margin to Center*. Boston: South End Press.

Horton, M., and Freire, P. (1990). *We Make the Road by Walking: Conversations on Education and Social Change*. Bell, Gaventa, and Peters, eds. Philadelphia: Temple University Press.

Huckle, J. (1983). Environmental Education. In Huckle, ed. *Geographical Education: Reflection and Action*, pp. 99–111. Oxford, UK: Oxford University Press.

Hummons. D.M. (1990). *Commonplaces: Community Ideology and Identity in American Culture*. Albany: State University of New York Press.

Irvine, J.J. (1990). *Black Students and School Failure: Policies, Practices, and Prescriptions*. Westport, CT: Greenwood Press.

James, W. (1890). *Principles of Psychology*. New York: Holt. Cited by S. Coopersmith in *The Antecedents of Self-esteem* (San Francisco: W.H. Freeman and Company, 1967).

Jung, C.J. (1961). *Memories, Dreams, Reflections*. New York: Pantheon Books.

Katz, M.B. (1975). *Class, Bureaucracy, and Schools: The Illusion of Educational Change in America*, expanded edition. New York: Praeger Publishers.

Kemmis, D. (1993). The last best place: How hardship and limits build community. In Walker, ed., *Changing Community*, pp. 277–287. Saint Paul, MN: Graywolf Press.

Kothari, R. (1990). Environment, technology, and ethics. In Engel and Engel, eds., *Ethics of Environment and Development: Global Challenge, International Response*, pp. 27–35. Tucson: The University of Arizona Press.

Kozol, J. (1991). *Savage Inequalities: Children in America's Schools*. New York: Crown Publishers.

Kurth-Schai, R. (1988). The roles of youth in society: A reconceptualization. *Educational Forum*, 52(2): pp. 113–132.

Lappé, F.M., and Du Bois, P.M. (1994). *The Quickening of America: Rebuilding Our Nation, Remaking Our Lives*. San Francisco: Jossey-Bass, Inc.

———. (1989). *Rediscovering America's Values*. New York: Ballantine Books.

Leavitt, J., and Saegert, S. (1990*). From Abandonment to Hope: Community-households in Harlem*. New York: Columbia University Press.

Lynch, K. (1979). The spatial world of the child. In Michelson, Levine, and Michelson, eds., *The Child in the City: Today and Tomorrow*, pp. 102–127. Toronto: University of Toronto Press.

Maguire, P. (1987). *Doing Participatory Research: A Feminist Approach*. Amherst: University of Massachusetts School of Education.

McLaren, P. (1993). *Schooling as a Ritual Performance*, 2nd ed. New York: Routledge.

Meier, K.J., Stewart, Jr., J. and England, R.E. (1989). *Race, Class, and Education: The Politics of Second-Generation Discrimination*. Madison: University of Wisconsin Press.

Merry, S.E. (1987). Crowding, conflict, and neighborhood regulation. In Altman and Wandersman, eds., *Neighborhood and Community Environments*, pp. 37–68. New York: Plenum Press.

Meyerson, D., and Scully, M. (1993). Tempered radicalism and the politics of ambivalence: Personal alignment and radical change within traditional organizations. Unpublished manuscript.

Moore, R., and Young, D. (1978). Childhood outdoors: Toward a social ecology of the landscape. In Altman and Wohlwill, eds., *Children and the Environment*, pp. 83–130. New York: Plenum Press.

Nicholls, J.G. (1989). *The Competitive Ethos and Democratic Education*. Cambridge, MA: Harvard University Press.

Orwell, G. (1958). *The Road to Wigan Pier*. First published (Gollancz), 1937. Uniform Edition. London: Secker and Warburg.

Palen, J.J. (1995). *The Suburbs*. New York: McGraw-Hill.

Parenti, M. (1978). *Power and the Powerless*. New York: St. Martin's Press.

Parsons, T. (1959). The school class as a social system: Some of its functions in American society, *Harvard Educational Review*, 29(4): 297–318.

Polakow, V., & Sherif, L. (1987). An ethnographic portrait of young children's culture of place, *Elements*, XIX, No. 1, Fall.

Relph, E. (1976). *Place and Placelessness*. London: Pion Limited.

Rivlin, L. (1987). The neighborhood, personal identity, and group affiliations. In Altman and Wandersman, eds., *Neighborhood and Community Environment*, pp. 1–34. New York: Plenum Press.

Rivlin, L., and Wolfe, M. (1985). *Institutional Settings in Children's Lives*. New York: John Wiley & Sons.

Rosenberg, M. (1979). *Conceiving the Self*. New York: Basic Books.

Seamon, D. (1980). Afterword: Community, place, and environment. In Buttimer and Seamon, eds., *The Human Experience of Space and Place*, pp. 188–196. New York: St. Martin's Press.

Sennett, R. (1978). *The Fall of Public Man*. New York: Vintage Books.

Starhawk (1987). *Truth or Dare: Encounters with Power, Authority, and Mystery*. San Francisco: Harper and Row.

Steele, C.M. (April 1992). Race and the schooling of black Americans. *The Atlantic Monthly*, pp. 68-78.

Sterling, S.R. (1990). Towards an ecological worldview. In Engel and Engel, eds., *Ethics of Environment and Development: Global Challenge, International Response*, pp. 87–96. Tucson: University of Arizona Press.

Sutton, S.E. (1992). Enabling children to map out a more equitable society. In *Children's Environments*, 9(1): 37–48.

———. (1991). Finding our voice in a dominant key. In Travis, ed., *African-American Architects in Current Practice*, pp. 12–14. New York: Princeton Architectural Press.

———. (1989). *The Urban Network: An Urban Design Program for Elementary Schools—Instructional Portfolio*. Ann Arbor: University of Michigan College of Architecture and Urban Planning.

———. (1985). *Learning through the Built Environment: An Ecological Approach to Child Development*. New York: Irvington Publishers.

Sutton, S.E., Crowfoot, J.E., Chesler, M., Lewis, E., and Weingarten, H. (1995). The connectedness of ivory towers and inner cities: Conversations about us and them. In *PCMA Working Paper Series #46*. Ann Arbor: The UM Program on Conflict Management Alternatives.

Tainter, S. (January-February 1990). Weaving the Urban Network. In *The University of Michigan's Research News*, pp. 2–7. Ann Arbor: The University of Michigan.

Thomas, P. (March, 1991). The Urban Network. In *Planning*, Vol. 57, No. 3, p. 13.

Tuan, Y.F. (1989). *Morality and Imagination: Paradoxes of Progress*. Madison: University of Wisconsin Press.

Wachtel, P.L. (1989). *The Poverty of Affluence: A Psychological Portrait of the American Way of Life*. Philadelphia: New Society Publishers.

Willis, P. (1977). *Learning to Labor: How Working-class Kids Get Working-class Jobs*. New York: Columbia University Press.

Wohlwill, J.F., and Heft, H. (1987). Chapter 9: The physical environment and the development of the child. In Stokols and Altman, eds., *Handbook of Environmental Psychology*, Vol. 1, pp. 281–328. New York: John Wiley & Sons.

Wynne, E.A. (1977). *Growing Up Suburban*. Austin: University of Texas Press.

Index

Main entries in *italics* are fictional names of "composite" persons, programs, and institutions (see Preface for discussion of author's methodology).

Abandonment, and middle-class norms, 13–14, 202

Achievement, and socioeconomic status, 72, 85 n.8. *See also* Educational attainment

Activism, children's: barriers to, 146, 165–66, 191; unrealized potential for, 151; and the environment, 155

Activism, grassroots: and place, 5

Adults: children's views of, 173–76, 190; children's relationships with, 190. *See also* Parents

Advocacy, learning about, 123, 210–13

After-school activities, 118–119, 167, 176, 177, 178, 188

Anderson, Robert H., 61 n.5

Andre, Jane: and first semester activities, 77–80, 110–11, 112–13; background on, 70, 87, 104–6; and initiating the Urban Network, 106–8; and community-service learning, 123–24; and the enhancement project, 125, 135–36, 137–40, 140–43, 147–48; and the journal project, 136–37

Annual Spring Festival (Gardendale), description of, 146–48

Architects Club, Young: and Public School 110, 210–13

Architecture: aging, 45, 57, 64; learning about, 109–11, 122, 135, 136, 146

Aronowitz, Stanley, 206

Art activities: and community-building, 208–10, 217; and differences in experimentation, 78–79, 95–97, 180; economic support for, 218–19; and liberatory experiences, 213

Art Carnival, Children's (New York City), 216–19

Aspiring Professionals Program, 107–8, 135, 136, 146, 147–48

Authority. *See* Power

Banning, James H., 6

Bassett, Anne, 49, 89, 149

Behavior, disruptive: and Frederick Douglass, 56, 96–97; and Gardendale, 112–13; sanctioning of, at Gardendale, 99–100, 112–14

Behavior management, and Frederick Douglass, 54–56, 59–91, 95–100, 119, 158

Bellah, Robert N., 18, 159, 204, 205, 219

Berg, Mary, 39

Blakely, Edward J., 27 n.3, 61 n.3, 192, 193, 196 n.5
Blayton-Taylor, Betty, 216–19
Block, Peter, 7, 20, 162
Bowers, C.A., 1, 12–13, 26 n.1
Bowles, Samuel, 26 n.1, 60, 61 n.4, 84 n.4, 191, 192, 193
Building descriptions: and Frederick Douglass, 54–56, 91, 158; and Gardendale, 63–64, 110, 138–39, 158–59; and Limone Elementary, 142; and School of Planning, 131–32, 133, 134
Buildings, school: design of, and learning, 54

Carnoy, Martin, 11, 103
Celebration: enhancement project, at Gardendale, 146–48; enhancement project, at Frederick Douglass, 149–50
Change agents, conventional: role of, in social change, 199
Charity, meaning of, 143–45, 164
Citizenship, practicing, 221, 205–6
City-as-School (New York City), 213–16
Clark, Noreen: classroom of, 58; and initiating the Urban Network, 93, 94; "Good and Bad" lesson, 95–98; and the enhancement project, 126–31, 148; teaching style of, 129–30, 149, 158
Classroom management. *See* Behavior management; Rules
Classroom descriptions: and Frederick Douglass, 56, 58–59, 158; and Gardendale, 73, 74–76, 109, 158–59; and Limone, 142
Coles, Robert, xviii, 41, 65, 66, 72, 143, 164, 169, 190
Community: and individual restraint, 119; loss of, 16–17, 116–18; significance of, 81–84, 156, 205; and sustainability, 204; systems of, governance, 14–16; types of, 118
Community-building: and the Urban Network, 25; unrealized potential for, 157–59
Community-caretaking, 7, 155, 205–8. *See also* Sociability; Governance, neighborhood

Community-service learning, 92, 122, 152 n.2, 164, 199, 207–8
Compliance: and Frederick Douglass teachers, 51–54, 93, 161; preparing children for, 58–61, 93–100, 148–50
Confinement. *See* Freedom, lack of
Conflict resolution, and Gardendale, 73–74
Conservation, learning about, 215–16
Consumerism: children's views of, 178–79, 183–84, 190; and competitiveness, 203; role of television in, 18
Cookson, Caroline Hodges, 71, 74, 84 n.3, 85 n.8, 114, 193, 195
Cooperation: institutional barriers to, 216; learning about, 212
Cooper-Hewitt, National Design Museum, 210
Creativity: and empowerment, 23–24; inspiring, through the environment, 217; stifling of, at Frederick Douglass, 95–98, 150, 161
Crowfoot, James E., 12
Cultural awareness: bridging differences through, 220; learning about, 215

Danger, children's views of, 171–73, 175–76
Darden, Joe, 13–14
Democracy, participatory, 206–8
Desktop publication, learning about, 210
Dewey, John, 204, 205–6
Discipline: and Frederick Douglass, 55, 56, 59–60, 97, 158, 192; sorting of students through, 59, 61–62 n.6
Disciplinary code. *See* Rules: and Frederick Douglass
Disjunctures, school and neighborhood, 99, 104, 205
Dreeben, Robert, 99
Driskell, Delores: and the banner, 91, 126, 149–50; building tour by, 55–57; and enhancement project, 126–28, 131, 149–50; and discipline, 59; and initiating the Urban Network, 89, 90–93, 140; leadership style, 51, 53, 161, 162; role of, in demonstration, 46–47, 192

Du Bois, Paul Martin, 206–7
Duhl, Leonard, 197, 203

Economic inequities, children's awareness of, 169–70
Education: and population growth, 8, 10;
and social stratification, 10, 17–18, 192–
95; total environment as, 205, 219; un-
sustainability of, 76, 84 n.5
Education, environmental: benefits of, xv–
xvi, 92; barriers to, 25; content of, 68,
203–4
Education, liberatory: formal and informal, 199–200; and art, 213
Education, multicultural: and Frederick
Douglass, 49, 160–61; role of, in social
change, 199
Educational attainment, and socioeconomic status, 27 n.5, 61, 84 n.4, 192–95.
See also Achievement
Educational change: alternative approach
to, 213–16; conventional approach to,
210–13; transformative approach to,
216–19
Educational program: and Frederick
Douglass, 47–53; and Gardendale, 66–
70
Educational system, transformation of,
12, 22, 197–98, 210, 219–22
Ehrenreich, Barbara, 13, 20
Empowerment: and social change, 23–
24, 198, 216; need for, and empathy,
150–52
Engel, J. Ronald, 6
Enhancement project: description of, 122–
23; and experiences of homelessness,
137–40; and Happy Toy, 128–34, 148–
50; and the journal project, 125–26, 136–
37, 166, 195–96 n.1; and Limone, 137,
140–48; planning, at Frederick Douglass, 125, 126–28; planning, at Gardendale, 135–36; and socially critical
inquiry, 152
Environment: children's differing views
of, 158, 187, 188; and Frederick Douglass, 57; freedom to transform, 113,
213, 218; and grassroots activism, 5;
importance of, xiv–xv, 3, 37, 39, 40–
41, 217–19; race and class aspects of, 2,
40–41, 113–14, 167, 168–69; role of, in
psychology, 4, 39, 40, 155; role of, in
self-concept, 81, 100, 115–16, 119, 169–
71; and sense of community, 116–18;
symbolic meaning of, xiii–xiv, 4, 5–6,
116, 120 n.3, 202
Environment, children's: teachers' response to, 41–42, 127, 133
Environment, descriptions of: Limone,
141–43; Oak Hills, 37–38, 45–46; San
Lupe, 38–39, 63, 64, 66, 67, 68, 78
Environmental crisis, and education, xvii,
8–10, 11, 12–13, 198
Environmental design: community-building through, 24; excitement of, 214;
learning about, 95–98, 101, 121, 138–40,
145–46
Environmental observations: children's
differing, 155–56, 159; definition of, 6;
Frederick Douglass children's, 42, 100,
101, 126, 132; Gardendale children's,
42–43, 79–80, 136–37, 140, 144–146;
learning through, xiii–xiv, 2, 13, 16, 83,
155–56
Environmental quality, children's views
of, 168, 169, 170–71, 179
Episcopal Book of Common Prayer, 219–
220
Expectations: high, for Gardendale students, 71, 76, 77, 79, 163–64, 166, 183;
low, for Frederick Douglass students,
91, 102–4, 125, 132–33, 160–61

Failure, attitudes toward, 150, 157, 163–64
Farm workers, migrant: lifestyle of, 141–43
Feldman, Roberta, 5
Field trips, 131–34, 140–43
Forster, Gail, 52–53, 59, 131–34
Frederick Douglass Elementary School: and
the demonstration, 47–53; initiating
the Urban Network at, 88–93, 124–25;
social milieu of, 48–50, 51–54, 158, 192;
and socioeconomic data, 45–46; unreal-
ized potential for community-build-
ing, 157–58
Frederick Douglass parents. *See Parents,
Frederick Douglass*

Frederick Douglass students. *See Students, Frederick Douglass*

Frederick Douglass teachers. *See Teachers, Frederick Douglass*

Freedom, and Gardendale students, 112–13, 116, 183–84, 188

Freedom, lack of: and Frederick Douglass students, 97, 98, 131–32, 115–16, 171, 175, 176, 180, 188

Freire, Paulo, 198, 200

Future, the: children's views of, 179–88, 190; and children's views of success, 184–87

Gardendale Institute of Science and Technology: initiating the Urban Network at, 72, 106–8, 124, 135–36; and the science and technology curriculum, 66–70; social milieu of, 69–70, 74, 158–59, 194; and socioeconomic data, 64–65; unrealized potential for community-building, 158–59

Gardendale parents. *See Parents, Gardendale*

Gardendale students. *See Students, Gardendale*

Gardendale teachers. *See Teachers, Gardendale*

Gintis, Herbert, 26 n.1, 60, 61 n.4, 84 n.4, 191, 192, 193

Giroux, Henry, 2, 26 n.1, 198, 206

Goldsmith, William W., 27 n.3, 61 n.3, 192, 193, 196 n.5

Goodlad, John I., 61 n.5

Governance, neighborhood: role of, in learning, 14–16, 118–19, 157–59. *See also* Community-caretaking; Sociability

Graham, Patricia, 49–50

Greene, Diane, 127, 131, 133–34, 171, 173

Hansen, Helen, 138–40, 142

Happy Toy, 129–30, 133–34, 148–50

Heft, Harry, 4

Hegel, Georg Wilhelm Friedrich, 117

Helpfulness, children's views of, 176, 177–178, 188, 190

Henry Street Settlement, 210

Hidden curriculum: conveyed through space, 2, 157–60; and loss of community, 16–18, 118–19, 156, 158–60; socialization through, 1–2, 26 n.1

Highlander Research and Education Center (Tennessee), 199

High technology, children's views of, 79–80, 180–84, 187, 190–91

Homelessness, and the Urban Network, 124, 131, 137–40, 153 n.3

hooks, bell, 107–8, 151–52, 199, 200

Horton, Myles, 199–200

Human worth, conceptions of, 20, 102–3, 202–3

Hummons, David, 41, 63, 80

Imagined circumstances, reality in comparison to, 184–88

Improving school property, learning about, 210–13

Institutional change, and the Children's Art Carnival, 217

Intellectual abilities: emphasis on, 18, 19–20; and broader social skills, 205, 220

Interdependence, sense of: role of education in, 43, 206

Irvine, Jacqueline Jordan, 46, 59

James, William, 202, 203

Jefferson, Thomas, 117

"Joe, Mister," 54, 56, 57

Johnson, Frank: role of, at Frederick Douglass, 49, 52, 53, 60, 96; and the Urban Network, 89

Johnstone, Harold: leadership style of, 47, 48, 51, 53, 59; and the Urban Network, 89, 92, 128, 131

Journal project: description of, 166, 195–96; and Frederick Douglass, 125–26; and Gardendale, 135, 136–37

Jung, Carl, 115–16, 120 n.3

Katz, Michael, 54

Keemis, Daniel, 117, 119

Kothari, Rajni, 206

Kozol, Jonathan, 191

Kurth-Schai, Ruthanne, 23

Lappé, Frances Moore, 206–7, 221

Leadership: preparing children for, 110–11, 112–13, 133–34; children's views of, 184–87

Learning, and social responsibility, 207–8, 212–13

Learning, experiential: history of, 2

Learning, place-related: benefits of, 3, 204; examples of, 204, 210–16; and multicultural understanding, 215; social change through, 202–5; unrealized potential for, 151

Leavitt, Jacqueline, 7, 15

Levin, Henry M., 11, 103

Lewis, Mary Ellen, 213–14, 216

Lifestyles: and migrant farm workers, 141–43; privatized, and social responsibility, 15–16, 17, 206; reinforcement of consumptive, 12, 198; social costs of consumptive, 11, 202–3, 222

Limone: children's reactions to, 137, 142, 143, 144–45; field trip to, 140–43; redesign of, 145, 147

Lubetsky, Robert, 213

Lunch: and Frederick Douglass, 57, 91, 149; and Gardendale, 111–12, 143

Lynch, Kevin, 40

Maguire, Patricia, 21–22

Male students, deference to, at Gardendale, 109–11, 112–14, 162–63

Marcus, Marion B.: and Annual Spring Festival, 147–48; leadership style of, 68, 70, 194, 158; overview of Gardendale by, 71–72; and the Urban Network, 106–7

McLaren, Peter, 98–99, 114, 161, 162

MED. See Multicultural Education Development program.

Medrich, Elliot A., 39

Mental shift, social change through, 198, 200, 203, 205

Merry, Sally Engle, 14, 15

Meier, Kenneth J., 61, n. 1, 61–62 n.6

Meyerson, Deborah, 120 n.1

Mintz, Tom: background on, 87, 88–90; and community-service learning, 123–24; and the enhancement project, 125, 126–31, 148–50; and initiating the Urban Network, 90–93

Mobility: differing degrees of, 171–72; Gardendale children's, 159, 173, 188, 190;

Money, children's differing views of, 179

Moore, Barbara: background on, 75; and deference to male students, 112–13, 162; and the enhancement project, 135; and the Urban Network, 77–80, 108;

Moore, Robin, 85 n.7

Mothers. *See* Parents

Multicultural education: and Frederick Douglass, 49, 160–61; role of in social change, 199

Multicultural Education Development program (MED); role at Frederick Douglass, 49, 88–89

Multicultural understanding, and place-related learning, 215

Nature, children's views of, 79, 85 n.7, 169, 177, 179, 190

Neighborhood. *See* Community; Environment

New York City, and educational reform, 210

Nicholls, John G., 20

Norms: social costs of, 11, 12, 21; transformation of, 198, 200, 203, 205. *See also* Values

Nurturance: children views of, 176, 177–78, 188, 190; community of, 208, 217

Oak Hills: children's views of, 167, 176,188, 192; description of, 37–39, 45–46, 119; social milieu of, 157, 188, 192

Objectivity, role of, in education, 19–20, 205, 220

Orwell, George, 102

Outsider-within: Jane Andre as, 107–8, 144, 146; role of, in social change, 200

Palen, J. John, 63

Parenti, Michael, 3, 21, 53, 195

Parents, Frederick Douglass: and enhancement project, 127, 131, 133–34; role of,

49–50, 55, 60, 161; socioeconomic status of, 46. *See also* Adults

Parents, Gardendale: and enhancement project, 138–39, 142; role of, 69, 74, 110, 118, 147, 162, 194; socioeconomic status of, 65. *See also* Adults

Parsons, Talcott, 99, 100

Participation: children's views of, 190; and community-caretaking, 205–6; inclusive forms of, 199

Participation, children's: adult manipulation of, 150, 164–65; adult role in, 123, 135, 150–51; honoring, 130, 212; and the journal project, 166

Participation, farm workers': unrealized potential for, 151

Patriarchal contract: being socialized into, 7, 20, 157; breaking the, 22–25, 198; and Frederick Douglass, 61, 103; and Gardendale, 74

Patriarchy, evidence of: and Frederick Douglass, 47, 48, 51, 53, 59; and Gardendale, 68, 109–11, 112–14, 162–63

Persell, Peter W., Jr., 71, 74, 84 n.3, 85 n.8, 114, 193, 195

Photography, learning about, 135, 136, 141

Place. *See* Community; Environment

Planning, School of: field trip to, 131–34

Polakow, Valerie, 115

Positivism: and education, 19, 22, 156; and knowledge, 21–22

Poverty: children's views of, 65–66, 124, 141; effect of, on childrearing, 49–50; and privilege, xviii, 106; relationship to race, class, and gender, 61 n.3; stereotypic conceptions of, 103–4; and sustainability, 83–84

Power: and empowerment, 23, 198, 208–210; forms of, 18–19

Power, hierarchical: differing uses of, 150–51; dismantling of, 198, 207; personal authority in lieu of, 212–20; reinforcing status quo through, 19–20, 156–57, 195

Presentation, learning about, 134, 136, 147

Privilege: and children, 66, 81 ; children's fear of losing, 170–71; courage to share,

198; differing effects of, and oppression, 50; and sustainability, 80, 83–84

Professionalism: and City-as-Schools, 214; and Gardendale, 68–69, 109, 135–36, 150–51, 163

Professionals, definition of reality by, 102–4, 160

Project Grow, and City-as-School, 213–16

Psychology, and the role of place, 4, 39, 40, 155

Public School 110 (New York City), 210–13

Purpel, David, 26 n.1

Quick-to-See, Mary: background on, 49, 51–52, 59; and the Urban Network, 89, 93, 94, 100–101

Rayburne, Betty, 69, 108, 135

Recess, at Frederick Douglass, 95–96

Regon, Bob: building tour by, 72–76; and the enhancement project, 135–36, 141–42; role of, at Gardendale, 67, 69; and the Urban Network, 70–71, 106–7

Relph, Edward G., 40

Resistance: interdependence as motive for, 198; and the need for community, 221–22; reproduction and, in schooling, 103, 161–63; tapestry of, 197, 199, 200, 221

Responsibility, sense of, 206–7, 218–19

Rivlin, Leanne, 1, 8, 53

Rosenberg, Morris, 23, 43 n.1, 173

Rothenberg, Gail, 213–14, 216

Rules: and Frederick Douglass, 55, 56, 59–60, 158; and Gardendale, 71–72

Saegert, Susan, 7, 15

Saint Andrew's Church, 38; soup kitchen, 127–30, 133–34, 149–50

San Lupe: children's views of, 169–71, 179, 183–84; description of, 38–39, 65, 66, 67, 78, 118; and lifestyle enclaves, 158–59

School system, intractability of, 47, 103, 191, 199–200

Science and Technology Consortium (STC):
role of at Gardendale, 67–68; and the
Urban Network, 88, 136
Science laboratory, children's participa-
tion in, 109–11, 147, 165
Science, learning about, 136, 141
Scully, Maureen, 120 n.2
Seamon, David, 118
Segregated schools: effect of desegregat-
ing, 46; persistence of, 46, 61 n.1, 64,
109
Segregation, spatial: effect of, on learning,
16–18, 155; and suburbia, 13–14, 63, 84 n.1
Self-concept: and creative processes, 216,
218; role of environment in, 37–43, 80–
81, 115–16, 119, 100, 167, 171–73; role of
significant others in, 81, 173–76
Self-consciousness, differing degrees of,
180, 183
Sennett, Richard, 24, 117–18
Settlement patterns: causes of, 13–14; hidden costs of, 202–3, 222 nn.1–3; role of,
in learning, 16–18, 203–5
Sherif, Lobna, 115
Significant others. *See* Adults; Parents
"Sisters, the," 128–29, 131, 150, 177
Sociability: building on, in Oak Hills, 157–
58; children's views of, 167, 176, 188,
192. *See also* Community-caretaking;
Governance, neighborhood
Social change: approaches to, 4, 198, 199–
200, 203, 205; and the arts, 208–10;
children's views of, 177–78, 184–88;
and consumptive lifestyles, 11, 202–3,
222; and norms, 11, 12, 21; and settlement patterns, 203; and social stratification, 195; and the status quo, 11–12,
193; teachers' role as philosophers-in-
action, 220–21
Socialization: processes of, 1, 20, 40; and
the status quo, 114, 160–64
Socially critical inquiry, 22, 152, 204
Social milieu: and Frederick Douglass, 48–
50, 51–54, 158, 192; and Gardendale, 69–
70, 74, 158–59, 194
Social stratification, costs of maintaining,
195
Stall, Susan, 5

Starhawk, 18, 208, 210, 221
Status quo: costs of maintaining, 11–12,
193; reinforcing, through environment,
1–3, 155; reinforcing, through schooling, 98, 99, 103, 114, 119; resistance to,
151–52, 210–20; rigidity of, 191–95; socialization into, 114, 160–64
STC. See Science and Technology Consortium.
Sterling, Steven R., 19
Students, Frederick Douglass: disruptive behavior of, 96–97; engaged behavior of,
100–2, 128–29, 133–34; environmental
observations of, 42, 100, 101, 126, 132;
improbability of success for, 192–94;
lack of freedom of, 115–16, 161, 171,
175, 176, 180, 188; perceptions of, as deficient, 91, 102–4, 125, 132–33, 160–61;
self-concept, 37, 39, 41–42, 81
Students, Gardendale: disruptive behavior
of, 112–14, 137, 159; engaged behavior
of, 109–11, 138–40, 144–46; environmental observations, 42–43, 79–80, 136–37,
140, 145–46; freedom of, 112–13, 116,
183–84, 188; perceptions of, as capable,
146–48, 150–51, 162–64, 194; probability of success for, 194–95; and self-concept, 39, 41, 42–43, 80
Suburban development, policies support-
ing, 13, 26–27 nn.2,3
Suburbia, conceptions of, 63, 168
Success: children's views of, 184–87; improbability of, at Frederick Douglass,
192–94; mandate for, at Gardendale, 71,
76, 77, 79, 163–64, 166, 183; probability
of, at Gardendale, 194–95
Sustainability: and community, 204, 221–
22; definition of, 6; and destructive behaviors, 7; learning principles of, 152,
198, 199, 204, 212; and social class, 80,
83–84
Sutton, Sharon E., xvi, xxv n.2, 22, 25, 50,
120 n.1, 152 n.1, 163
Sygar, Janet, 211–13

Tainter, Suzanne, 220
Tall Pines, and Gardendale, 67, 68
Teachers: differing roles of, in the Urban
Network, 87–88; and Frederick Doug-

lass, 48, 51–54, 98; and Gardendale, 68–69, 76; and racial stereotypes, 199; and resistance, 199, 220–22; and reinforcement of status quo, 16–18, 156, 157–60; role of, in promoting a good society, 204–5, 219–20; and use of the Urban Network curriculum, 121–23, 124
Teaching style: and Frederick Douglass, 94–98, 129–30; and Gardendale, 108, 112, 118; as weaving 220–22
Television, effect of, on consumerism, 18
Tempered radical, role of Jane Andre as, 120 n.2
Tuan, Yi-Fu, 24

Urban disinvestment, 13, 14–15
Urban Network: benefits of, 92, 122; description of, xv, xxv n.1, 27 n.6, 121–23; differing implementations of, 87–88; evaluation of, xvii, xx, 164–66; initiating, at Frederick Douglass, 88–93, 124–25; initiating, at Gardendale, 72, 106–8, 124, 135–36; instructional approach, xvi, 23–25; Jane Andre's introduction to, 105–6; and Public School 110, 210–13; Tom Mintz's introduction to, 89, 90
Urban Network lessons: assessment of field trip, 140; building homeless shelter, 137–40; designing Happy Toy, 133–34; drawing to scale, 109–11; first semester, 152 n.1; "The Good and the Bad", 95–98; "Neighborhood Journal", 125–26, 135, 136–37, 166, 195, 196 n.1; The "Party", 112–13; play activities in Oak Hills, 130; redesign of Limone, 145–46; "Sharing Space", 101

Urban Network skills: architectural awareness, 135, 136, 146; architectural design, 109–11, 122, 210–13; advocacy, 123, 210–13; conservation, 215–16; cooperation, 212; cultural awareness, 215; desktop publishing, 210; environmental design, 95–98, 101, 122–23, 138–40, 145–46; improving school property, 210–13; leadership, 109–11, 133–34; photography, 135, 136, 141; presentation, 134, 136, 147; science, 136, 141; urban planning assessment, 95–98, 140; writing, 125–26, 135, 140, 146
Urban planning assessment, learning about, 95–98, 140
Urban planning students, and Frederick Douglass, 126, 128–30, 132–33, 148

Vallejo, Patricia, 48, 91–93, 100–1
Values: and consumerism, 202–3; transformation of, 152, 197, 208, 221. See also Norms
Voyat, Gilbert, 217

Writing, learning about, 125–26, 135, 140, 146
Wachtel, Paul L., 17, 76, 84 n.5
Willis, Paul, 114
Wohlwill, Joachim F., 4
Wolfe, Maxine, 1, 8, 53
Wynne, Edward A., 85 n.6

Young Architects Club. See Architects Club, Young
Young, Donald, 85 n.7
Yoshida, Joanne G., 211–13